Western Approaches to Eastern Philosophy

TROY WILSON ORGAN

WESTERN APPROACHES TO EASTERN PHILOSOPHY

OHIO UNIVERSITY PRESS Athens, Ohio

ISBN 0-8214-0194-7
Library of Congress Catalog Number LC-75-14554

Printed in the United States of America by Oberlin Printing, Inc.

Contents

Western Approaches to Eastern Philosophy

—1—

AN APOLOGY FOR EASTERN STUDIES

Before I completed my doctoral studies I had the uneasy feeling that something was missing in Western philosophy. According to my formal education the world is a hemisphere ending in the east at Babylon, in the West at San Francisco, and in the north and south at the frigid poles. My studies from the first grade through the doctorate included nothing of Oriental geography, history, literature, art, or philosophy. An innovative grade school teacher introduced me to Canadian history, and in high school I had a course entitled "World History" which was largely European history with some background on the Babylonians, Assyrians, and Egyptians. At church I learned of the existence of Chinese, Indians, and Japanese, peoples sadly lacking the twin blessings of Christianity and civilization. This prompted me to read biographies of Christian missionaries to these "benighted peoples." I found the lives of Carey in India, Judson in Burma, and Morrison in China so thrilling that for a time I dreamed of becoming a missionary in order that I too might bring hope and salvation to those in foreign lands living in "darkness and sin." But in college my study of the classics wooed me into scholarship, and I chose philosophy in preference to the mission field. In my first teaching position I was assigned a class in comparative religion, a subject in which I was almost totally untrained. J. B. Pratt's *A Pilgrimage to Buddhism* was the first book to convince me that Eastern thought is more than an anomaly. Attendance at the second East-West Philosophers' Conference at the University of Hawaii in 1949 was the turning point in my intellectual development. From that time on in my teaching and research I kept one foot in the East. Whatever the topic under consideration, I brought in perspectives Hindu, Buddhist, Confucian, and Taoist. But, despite four extensive study trips to India and a quarter-century of study of Indian philosophy and religion, I remain a Western man. No one is more pathetic than the Western person trying to ape Eastern ways. Perhaps some day the East and the West will be fully integrated, although I have serious doubts about the desirability of complete East-West unity. Dialogue is more exciting and more fruitful than assimilation. It is my privilege and joy to have been a part of the post-World War II discovery of the East. If our original motivation for study of the East was intellectual curiosity, our motivation now is survival. We are beginning to realize that the planet which is our home cannot continue to support life if the waste, exploitation, and destruction associated with Western civilization continue. Progress as we have understood it in the West needs careful examination. This was what I tried to say in the following portion from the commencement address at Ohio University in June, 1974, which was my farewell to teaching and, in part, an *apologia pro vita sua.*

We in the Western world have had sufficient warnings of disaster, but, like the ancient Israelities, we'd rather abuse our prophets than listen to them. There was Henry Adams, who wrote in 1904 that the world is coming to an early terminus. There are four ages of human history, he said, and they stand in the relation of square root to each other. The first was the Age of Religious Thought. It lasted ninety thousand years, coming to an end in 1600. Following this was the Mechanical Age, a period of three hundred years, which ended in 1900. Next was the Electrical Age, which according to Adams would last eighteen years; and the final age was the Ethereal Age which would last only four years. Adams could see no future beyond 1922.

The next social prophet of the Western world was Oswald Spengler, a German teacher of mathematics, who published after World War I a book entitled *The Decline of the West*. He said civilizations go through four stages which he called "the four seasons" or "the four periods of human development." We are in the winter season, or the period of old age and death, said Spengler. It is marked by the rise of large cities, dictatorship of money, slavery to machines, intellectual skepticism, and war. Spengler said the decline of the West is inevitable. But we did not choose to listen to him. We preferred Herbert Spencer who said, "The ultimate development of the ideal man is logically certain," and J. B. Bury who praised the West for making indefinite progress an axiom. We did not agree with E. R. Dodds that history "has . . . a short way with optimists." And we laughed at W. R. Inge, the "Gloomy Dean" of St. Paul's Cathedral, who is reputed to have said that he was not a pessimist because things always turn out worse than he anticipated.

Another of our twentieth-century prophets was Pitirim Sorokin, a Russian immigrant who rose to become Chairman of the Department of Sociology at Harvard University. In his four volume *Social and Cultural Dynamics* he argued that we in the West are passing from the sensate type of culture in which reality and value are measured in terms of sensory experiences into an ideational type of culture in which religious and ascetic values will be emphasized. But in the passage our whole sensate culture will collapse. The transition cannot be prevented; we can only retard it or make it less violent. He wrote in 1957, "It is high time to realize that this is not one of the ordinary crises which happen almost every decade, but one of the greatest transitions in human history." We must prepare ourselves, says Sorokin, for a complete change of contemporary mentality and a fundamental transformation of our system of values.

Two other Western interpreters of history have perhaps been more appealing. One of these is Arnold Toynbee. He says that Western society is losing its vitality and creative power because of our militarism, our idolatry of institutions, and our worship of the machine. He thinks that a profound moral and spiritual transformation may arrest the decline, and he has discussed the possibility of a universal religion. The other is Albert Schweitzer. He roots our Western illness in our lack of regard for reasoning, in our decay in moral convictions, our narrow specializations, and in our prejudices of race and nation. He offers a healing through an all-encompassing ethical attitude he calls "reverence for life."

Other twentieth-century philosophers of history could be cited, but Adams, Spengler, Sorokin, Toynbee, and Schweitzer suffice. They agree that Western civilization is in no ordinary crisis. Adams and Spengler advise resignation; Sorokin thinks we can delay the collapse; Toynbee and Schweitzer hold out faint hopes for a remedy. When we read these five authors today we feel a certain sense of quaintness. From our current point of view all of them seem to contain a Wilkins Micawber syndrome. Even in their pessimism they seem to be "waiting for something to turn up." But the notion that the Western world can heal itself, that we can find within our own traditions the resources we need, may be part of our problem. The expectation that with a few more laws, a new arrangement of administrative plumbing, a few more workshops, more task forces, more committees, and more ombudsmen we can lick our problems and go merrily on our progressive paths is, I suggest, part of our problem. We've got to go deeper and wider for insights. There is no cure in cosmetics. There is no easy way out, no panacea. For example, the Watergate mentality—the view that one must win at any cost, and that a good end justifies any means—is more deeply rooted in our tradition than we may wish to admit. When Vince Lombardi made his famous remark about winning in professional football, he was reflecting a well-established Western moral principle. The Green Bay Packers, the Committee to Re-elect the President, and the Christian Crusaders all agreed that winning is the only thing.

The impasse which our modern prophets have predicted and which we have reached is worsened by our supposition that a solution lies within our Western tradition. The time of "unthinkable thoughts" is now. We must question the assumptions of our culture. Is the value-free pursuit of truth any longer a virtue? Has the law of non-contradiction any priority? Should human life always be preserved? When can civil laws be rightly broken? What claims can a nation justly make upon us? What relevance have religious traditions? One example from religion may suggest what I mean. Rabbi Richard L. Rubenstein of Florida State University has recently written, "I am willing to believe in God the Holy Nothingness Who is our source and our final destiny, but never again in a God of history. . . . Few ideas in Jewish religious thought have been more decisively mistaken, in spite of their deep psychological roots, than the terrible belief that God acts meaningfully in history."[1] The time has come for Jews and Christians to assess their belief in Providence, for philosophers to question the dedication to truth, for scientists to ponder over the value of methodological objectivity, for lawyers to examine the importance of law, and for all of us to rethink and to realign our moral values. The crisis we face in the West has been brought about under the aegis of our Western assumptions. I suggest we need to look beyond the West for therapy. I shall only hint at a possibility by appealing to three Eastern conceptions: Cyclical Time, Rhythm, Polarity.

The language and images we use for time reveal our Western assumptions. We speak of time as an arrow which shoots into the unknown. Time moves. It carries all its sons away. It is the ravager which uses us and discards us. Time lays us low, cuts us down, destroys. At the end of each year we picture time as an old man with a scythe. The old man is pushed aside by a baby who is the new year with all its promises of good things to come. But in the Orient there are different conceptions of time. In Buddhism time is a still pool of water into which events are cast. In Hinduism time is not taken very seriously. Cosmical time in Hinduism is conceived in such large numbers as to be psychologically meaningless. Calendar time was borrowed by the Indians from the Chaldeans, and the signs of the Zodiac were borrowed from the Greeks. While a wristwatch is a status symbol in India, one soon learns that it does not insure punctuality. A business meeting scheduled for ten o'clock will probably get under way a few minutes before eleven o'clock. Some who wear wristwatches do not bother to wind them. But more significant than the general indifference to time is the belief in Hinduism that time moves in circles rather than in a straight line. Time, whether conceived in terms of epochs, or years, or days, is believed to have two wings known as "day" and "night," and they are separated by two intermediate periods known as "dawn" and "twilight." In addition, time is primarily a psychological measurement. Objective time is relatively unimportant. How long a period of time feels is more important than how long it is. Time depends upon the state of development of the individual. The more advanced a person is in his total human development the less is his awareness of time. Theoretically, the perfected person has no consciousness of time.

This view of time practically eliminates our conception of progress. Rhythm displaces progress. For example, Darwin's theory of evolution tends to become in the West a theory of progress. To evolve is to get better, to move forward, to advance, to develop. But in Indian studies evolution is balanced with involution. A movement from the one to the many is balanced by a movement from the many to the one. If night follows day, so does day become night. Death follows life, and life follows death. Rebirth is the redeath of death. The absoluteness and the finality of time becomes harmony and rhythm. Old age is not the prelude to annihilation but the fulfillment of an incarnation and the door to further growth.

Finally, there is polarity. We in the West are constantly aware of the clash of opposites: male and female, youth and age, freedom and law, science and religion, right and wrong, man and God. Not so in the East. They see juxtaposition and identity of polarities. The Western conflict of generations is the Eastern harmony of differences—young people enjoy their youth and look forward to becoming adults like their parents. A home without three generations is less than a home. Grandchild and grandparent belong. Each station in life has its duties and its privileges. When each does what his role requires, the home, the school, the city, and the nation come to be; or conversely, one fulfills one's role as wife, husband, student, teacher, citizen, ruler in the doing of what the station requires. One becomes one's self, not in destroying another or in defeating another, but in the strange pattern of differing enough to complement the other. As the Chinese might say, the Tao becomes Tao in the Yining of the Yang and in the Yang-ing of the Yin. We must achieve unity in plurality, likeness in polarity, and eternity in time.

NOTES

1. Richard L. Rubenstein, "Cox's Vision of the Secular City" in *The Secular City Debate*. Edited by Daniel Callahan. New York: The Macmillan Co., 1966, p. 142.

—2—

TWO PROBLEMS IN THE STUDY OF EASTERN PHILOSOPHY

Although we in the West have known for centuries of the existence of philosophies and philosophers in Oriental lands, we have only recently been willing to accept them as worthy of study. How many textbooks entitled *A History of Philosophy* are in fact histories of *Western* philosophy. The earliest reference of a Western philosopher to Indian philosophy is that of Megasthenes, the ambassador of Seleucus Nicator at the court of Chandragupta Maurya, who reported in the third century B.C. that he had visited "gymnosophists" (literally "naked wise men") in India. He wrôte, "They live in a simple style, and lie on beds of rushes or skins. They abstain from animal food and sexual pleasures, and spend their time in listening to serious discourse and in imparting their knowledge to such as will listen to them." The philosophies of India were studied at the ancient university in Alexandria, Egypt. The Gnostics were particularly impressed by Indian thought. Clement of Alexandria, a Christian Gnostic of the second century, suggested that Greek philosophy was an importation from India and speculated that Pythagoras visited India, studied under Brahmin sages, and became the Buddha. Marco Polo's report of his travels to China in the fourteenth century aroused the imagination of the medieval world, but no serious study of Eastern thought resulted from his travels. Jesuit missionaries at the end of the sixteenth century came into contact with Chinese thought. The Chinese chronologies were disquieting. According to B. A. G. Fuller the Jesuits "were puzzled to find that the history of China was not amenable to the chronology revealed in the Bible and recorded events occurring if not before the creation of the world at least before the Flood, which, according to the word of God, Noah and his family were the only human beings to survive. How the Chinese could have gone on making history under water was something of a problem for the theologians."[1] During the next two centuries—the period commonly called the European Enlightenment—a few Western men began the serious study of Eastern thought. Arthur Schopenhauer glorified Indian philosophy, finding the *Upaniṣads* far superior to Western philosophy. He said that this collection of ancient Hindu writings "has been the solace of my life, and will be the solace of my death." It is important to keep in mind that the *Upaniṣads* which so favorably impressed Schopenhauer were Latin translations made by Anquetil-Duperron in 1801-1802 of seventeenth-century Persian translations of the original Sanskrit.

The first Americans to study Indian thought were the transcendentalists. Ralph Waldo Emerson was introduced to Indian philosophy by his aunt, Mary Moody Emerson, who in 1820 asked him to read Ram Mohun Roy's views on religion. Benjamin Franklin and Cadwallader Colden were aware of Hindu thought, but they found little of worth in it. Thoreau spent the summer of 1841 reading Indian philosophy. He found it exhilarating: "I cannot read a sentence in the book of the Hindoos without being elevated as upon the tableland of the Ghauts."[2]

An occasional lecture on Indian philosophy was offered at the summer sessions of the Concord School of Philosophy in Amos Bronson Alcott's orchard. George Santayana was one of the few American philosophers of the first half of the twentieth century who had an appreciation of Indian philosophy. He remarked once during World War II, "I am reading the *Upaniṣads*, St. Augustine's *Confessions*, and Spinoza's *Politics* to take the bad taste out of my mouth."

Since World War II many Western philosophers have begun making somewhat guilt-ridden studies of the philosophical traditions originating in the East. The prefaces to three editions of a well-known textbook in philosophy nicely illustrate the changing points of view. Ledger Wood wrote as follows in the 1914 edition of his *A*

History of Philosophy, "A universal history of philosophy would include the philosophy of all peoples. Not all peoples, however, have produced real systems of thought. . . . Many do not rise beyond the mythological stage. Even the theories of Oriental peoples . . . consist, in the main, of mythological and ethical doctrines, and are not thorough-going systems of thought." Second and third editions of this textbook were brought out with the assistance of Frank Thilly. In the second edition (1951) the last lines of the above quotation were modified to read "are not complete systems of thought," and in the third edition (1958) were modified still more to read "are rarely complete systems of thought." It is interesting to conjecture an appropriate modification for the fourth edition of the textbook.

The first comparative studies of Eastern and Western philosophy consisted of efforts to name broad differences, e.g., mystical *vs.* empirical, religious *vs.* scientific, world-denying *vs.* world-affirming. There were also efforts to find key concepts to unlock the mysteries of Oriental thought. Filmer Northrop's "concepts of intuition" and "concepts of postulation" in his *The Meeting of East and West* was an early and challenging effort in this direction. One of the defects in these studies was the assumption that Eastern thought is of one piece. Not until we disabuse ourselves of the notion of Western pluralistic thought and Eastern monolithic thought can we begin serious dialogue with Eastern philosophers.

My suggestion to the person who wishes to study Eastern philosophies is that he place squarely before himself two problems. These I call the problem of identification and the problem of accent.

The Problem of Identification

The Western student may seek among Eastern cultures for a counterpart to the Western philosophical tradition and identify this as "philosophy" without consideration of the possibility of there being in the East something vastly different which is their "philosophy." The following five factors are the important ones to have in mind in the identification of an Eastern philosophy.

1. The cultural differences of Asian countries. We used to think we could identify a West and an East in the area of philosophy, e.g., the West is scientific, empirical, rational, pragmatic, this-worldly,

etc., and the East is poetic, intuitive, mystical, dreamy, otherworldly, etc. We know now that this is a gross simplification, but we have not yet realized that we cannot pigeonhole specific Eastern philosophies. The claim is still being made that each Eastern country or culture has its own philosophical characteristics, e.g., India is sometimes said to be spiritualistic, idealistic, theoretical, and traditional but not historical, whereas China is materialistic, realistic, practical, and both traditional and historical. Hajime Nakamura in his fine book, *Ways of Thinking of Eastern Peoples*, is guilty of painting with too wide a brush the ways of thinking of India, China, Tibet, and Japan. Philosophies in India, for example, range from materialism to idealism, from pluralism to monism, and from hedonism to asceticism.

2. The close relation of religion and philosophy. Eastern philosophies are ways of life as well as ways of thought. They are life styles, and they are also forms of speculation. The same writings may be basic to both the religious and the philosophical aspects of the culture, e.g., the *Upaniṣads* are interpreted religiously in the *Bhagavad Gītā* and philosophically in the *Brahma Sūtras* of Bādarāyaṇa. In China there is both religious Taoism and philosophical Taoism.

3. The relation of science and religion. The scientific and industrial revolutions of the West had little impact on the East until the twentieth century. Hence it is not surprising to find some Eastern philosophers who are unaware of the sciences as alternatives to metaphysical speculation, and some who are openly anti-scientific. Thus some of the methodologies and epistemologies of Eastern philosophies seem strange, naive, and in some cases primitive to scientifically-oriented Western minds.

4. The problem of who is the better interpreter of Eastern philosophy. There is a danger in assuming that since a Western-trained mind cannot understand Eastern thought on its own terms, an Eastern philosopher is better qualified to present Eastern philosophy to the West. This was the assumption made by the authorities at Oxford University in hiring Radhakrishnan to teach Indian philosophy from 1936 to 1952. This assumption has many flaws. One is that a man who knows an Eastern philosophy may not know enough about Western philosophy to present it so a Westerner can

understand it. Another is that many Eastern philosophers are in fact Western by training. The color of skin, texture of hair, slant of eye, and quality of earwax do not identify the character of the mind. Also there is a notion that knowledge of the original language makes one qualified as interpreter, and ignorance of the original language disqualifies one as interpreter. This does not follow. Max Müller was a fine Sanskrit scholar, but his writings on Indian philosophy are not reliable; on the other hand, G. R. Malkani is a reliable authority on Indian philosophy, but he knows very little Sanskrit. A Western philosopher may not be as picturesque as a Ramakrishna monk, but he is more likely to be impartial in his presentation of classical Indian philosophies.

5. The matter of distinguishing speculation and philosophy. Much which laymen might call "philosophy" is not what is denoted by the term as used by academic philosophers, and similarly in the East there are vast bodies of writings which are called philosophies by the Easterner but not so by the Westerner. The *Upaniṣads* are a case in point. There is no question about the fact that they present monistic, dualistic, idealistic, naturalistic, etc., points of view, but are they "philosophies"? The Indian scholar is likely to say "Yes." But the Western scholar will raise doubts on the grounds that without argument for position there is no philosophy. This is a delicate and controversial issue, but it is one which needs to be raised constantly in the study of Eastern thought.

The Problem of Accent

Huston Smith in an article entitled "Accents of the World's Philosophies"[3] offers an interesting guideline for understanding the philosophies of the East and the West. He takes a cue from Bertrand Russell's *New Hopes for a Changing World* in which Russell states that man is perennially engaged in three basic conflicts: (1) against nature, (2) against other men, and (3) against himself. On the basis of this distinction Smith argues for a difference of "accent" in the typical philosophizing in the West, in China, and in India. The Western philosopher is a natural philosopher. He is chiefly concerned with problems of the external world. He is realistic in his ontology, hylomorphic in his anthropology, and sense-involved in his epistemology. The Chinese philosopher is a social philosopher. His overriding concern is helping people live together in harmony and good order. Nature is something to be appreciated, intuited, and communed with. But nature is not set over against human beings. The Indian philosopher is a psychological philosopher. His problem has to do with man, and above all with the philosopher as a self. The minds and the senses are turned inward. Ananda K. Coomaraswamy claims that for every psychological term in English there are four in Greek and forty in Sanskrit. Smith argues that an adequate philosophy must strike all three accents as a chord.

There are probably other differences of emphasis which might be subsumed under the heading of accents. One of these is that of analysis or existentialism. A striking example is the appearance of logic in Greece and India. In Greece Aristotle formulated the syllogism as a way to explain and examine valid reasoning. At approximately the same time Gotama in India created similar syllogistic forms; but, as he stated at the opening of his *Nyāya Sūtra*, the purpose of the study was to aid human beings in the attainment of "supreme felicity." I do not wish to affirm that the West is analytical and the East is existential, but I do claim that the general tone of Western philosophy is primarily analytical and secondarily existential, whereas Eastern philosophy is primarily existential and secondarily analytical. Historians of Western philosophy frequently call attention to the fact that both Plato and Aristotle said philosophy begins in wonder, but they do not often enough note that Aristotle said that his ethical and political studies are designed to make men good, and that Plato dropped his teaching in the Academy when he had an opportunity to put his theories into practice at Syracuse. Nonetheless, the mainstream of Western philosophy has been accented by the nonutilitarian pursuit of clarity and truth. Philosophers like David Hume, Charles Peirce, G. E. Moore, Ludwig Wittgenstein, and Nelson Goodman are in the main stream of Western philosophy, and intellectuals like Frederick Nietzsche, Soren Kierkegaard, Jean-Paul Sartre, and Martin Buber are not in the main stream. The conflicts between analytic philosophers and existentialists (sometimes called philosophers of man) since World War II is one of the scandals of twentieth-century Western philosophy. The student of comparative philosophies should at the outset of his studies be alerted to the possibility of a different aspect with respect to analysis in Eastern philosophy. The logic of an Indian or Chinese philosopher can be as rigorous as A. J. Ayer or Rudolph Carnap, but the intent of the rigor may have existential overtones foreign to the Western positivist.

The importance of noting these two problems—the problem of identification and of accent—is to remind the student of the danger of expecting Eastern peoples to react like Western peoples. This was one of the tragedies in the United States' involvement in Vietnam. An editorial in *Life* for July 2, 1972, stated, "In any future conflict, an American government will surely show a far greater awareness that non-Western nations can react in unusual ways to diplomatic and military pressures." Although I cannot be as optimistic about future American governments as is the author of this editorial, I do believe that East-West understandings can be improved through the intellectual grasp of differences in philosophies. The implementing of these intellectual considerations into social behavior is a still bigger problem.

NOTES

1. B. A. G. Fuller, *A History of Philosophy*, Vol. II. New York: Henry Holt and Co., 1938, p. 179.
2. Bradford Torrey (editor), *The Writings of Henry David Thoreau*, Vol. I. Boston and New York: Houghton Mifflin Co., 1906, p. 266.
3. Huston Smith, "Accents of the World's Philosophers," *Philosophy East and West*, Vol. VII, Nos. 1 and 2 (April, July, 1957), p. 7-19.

—3—

THE NATURE OF INDIAN PHILOSOPHY

Philosophy is usually said to have arisen in the West when a few Ionic Greeks sought to account for the facts of our experienced world without appeal to the Olympian mythology. However, if argument for position is an essential ingredient of philosophy—as I believe it is—then the first Western philosopher was not Thales, as is commonly stated, but probably Zeno, who supported the speculations of his teacher Parmenides by arguing that the opponents of Parmenides landed themselves in logical paradoxes. If "philosophy" is used in the narrow sense as argument for position, the earliest philosophical writing in India does not appear until the third century A.D.; this is the *Sāṁkhya Kārikā* of Īśvarakṣṛṇa. However, if "philosophy" is used in the broad sense, that is, as speculation, then philosophy may be said to have "originated" in India with the earliest *mantras* of the *Ṛg Veda*, which means at least as early as the middle of the second millennium B.C. Surendranath Dasgupta writes, "The beginnings of the evolution of philosophical thought, though they can be traced in the later Vedic hymns, are neither connected nor systematic."[1] Again he writes of the *Vedas* that "there is not much philosophy in them in our sense of the term."[2] He also says of the *Upaniṣads* that they are "utterances of truths intuitively perceived or felt as unquestionably real and indubitable, and carrying great force, vigour, and persuasiveness with them"[3] But note—they are "intuitively perceived or felt." An example of the nonsense one often finds about the origin of Indian philosophy is this opening sentence of chapter 2 of John M. Koller's *Oriental Philosophies*:

"Indian philosophy began before recorded history. The first bits of speculation which could be called philosophical date back over five thousand years, to about 4000 B.C."[4] If one recognizes "the first bits of speculation" as philosophy, then perhaps philosophy begins with the first *homo sapiens.*

The Greek word of which "philosophy" is the transliteration means the love of wisdom. No Sanskrit word has exactly this connotation. There are, however, a good many Sanskrit terms which designate the activity of philosophizing. The most important are the following:

1. *dṛṣṭi.* This comes from the root *dṛś*, "to see." It connotes beholding, looking at, regarding, and having an opinion.
2. *darśana.* This term also means a seeing, but it has two meanings: an active and a passive. The active meaning is that of inwardly beholding or becoming one with an object of awareness. Possible translations would be seeing, looking at, beholding, meeting with, visiting, inspecting, investigating, and understanding. The passive meaning is the object of seeing, looking at, etc. The active refers to having a point of view, and the passive refers to the point of view one has. The term *darśana* in the passive sense is the term customarily used for the great systems or schools of Indian philosophy. This is very significant. The system which an Indian philosopher defends is a point of view, not the absolute truth. The implication is that there are other defensible points of view. This is the foundation of the tolerance often mentioned as a characteristic of the Indian mind. This characteristic may be overstressed by Indophiles, but it is generally the case in Indian philosophizing that each philosopher recognizes the defensibleness of other *darśanas.*
3. *tattva-jñāna.* The word *jñāna* stands for true or superior knowledge. It is close to the Greek *sophia.* The word *tattva* is from *tat* (that) so it means thatness, very essence, true nature, and essential reality. In the Sāmkhya system *tat* identifies the twenty-five fundamental realities; and in the Vedāntic *tat tvam asi* (That thou art), *tat* means Absolute Reality and *tvam* means phenomenal reality. So *tattva-jñāna* means the true knowing of the essence of things. *Tattva-jñāna* is closer to *philousia* (love of substance) than to *philosophia* (love of wisdom).
4. *viveka-jñāna. Viveka* means discrimination, distinction, investigation, discussion, discernment, and judgment. Therefore, *viveka-jnāna*, when used for philosophy, means discriminative knowledge.
5. *ānvīksakī.* Literally this term means second thought, but when used in philosophical discourse it means to think about thinking. Westerners would call this metaphilosophizing, but Indians use the term specifically for logic.
6. *adhyātma-vidyā. Vidyā* is a rather unexciting term for learning or science. *Adhyātma-vidyā* refers to learning about the inner nature of

things rather than looking at externalities. *Ātma-vidyā* (self knowledge) is used for philosophy when what is intended is the metaphysics of the self. Indian philosophy is an ātmanology.

7. *prajñā*. This is another term for wisdom, knowledge, information, discrimination, understanding, etc. It stresses the showing of things directly without distortion.
8. *bodhā*. This term originally designated the blooming of flowers, but it came to mean the "opening up" which followed from successful meditation. Psychologically it means to be fully conscious, to be awake existentially. It is used philosophically for the expanding understanding accompanying the self-awakened experience.
9. *sādhana*. *Darśana* and *sādhana* are the two most striking Sanskrit terms for philosophy. The former is essentialistic; the latter is existentialistic. No English word does justice to *sādhana*. It stands for the total comprehensive discipline designed to accomplish the full development of man. Terms such as guiding, directing to a goal, procuring, securing, subduing, vanquishing, gaining power over, acquiring, and attaining only hint at the richness of *sādhana*. In Hinduism it is a psychological-philosophical-religious term which indicates the process of becoming fully human.
10. *anu-īksakī*. This is a rather loose term meaning the survey of all things.
11. *mata*. The term *mata* means opinion or view. It can be used for "doctrine," but it does not have the richness of *darśana*.

Hindu Orientation

Indian philosophy is more than a counterpart of Western philosophy which happened to originate and flourish in the subcontinent of Asia known as India. Indeed to try to fit Indian philosophy into the molds appropriate to Western philosophy is to misunderstand it. Philosophy is the finest and most important product of the old civilization of India, for it was the unity in the apparent diversities of music, sculpture, painting, architecture, literature, dance, science, ethics, and religion.

It is an indigenous product of the Indian people. If one insists on a Western counterpart, perhaps the best is to say that Indian philosophy is to Hinduism as Scholastic philosophy is to Christianity. Indian philosophy may therefore be described as the intellectual aspect of Hinduism. But we must be careful. Hinduism is not a religion in the sense in which Christianity is a religion. To pull philosophy out of Hinduism is to destroy Hinduism.

Hinduism is inseparable from both philosophy and the communal life of the people. Another way of stating this is to say that a study of Indian philosophy cannot avoid being a study of the Hindu religion, and conversely a study of Hindu religion cannot avoid being a study of Indian philosophy. In other words, Indian philosophy did not have to develop a system known as "Existentialism," because it has always been existential. Philosophy in India is religious in the widest sense. As Sarvepalli Radhakrishnan has said, "Every doctrine is turned into a passionate conviction, stirring the heart of man and quickening his breath."[5] The English philosopher C. E. M. Joad wrote in 1940, "I doubt whether any single person has found life easier to live, problems easier to solve, or the universe easier to understand as a result of studying the works of those twentieth-century philosophers who have occupied themselves with the problem of philosophical analysis."[6] This could never be said of Indian philosophy. Indian philosophy is pragmatic in the broadest sense of that much-abused term. All the systems—even the logical systems—set as end the diagnosis and therapy of the human condition. The Indian intellectual accuses Western philosophy of being too intellectualistic, too largely a matter for academicians; he charges Western religions of being too creedal, too dogmatic, too insistent on fixed beliefs, and too removed from the questing spirit. Hinduism is both a religious philosophy and a philosophical religion. Eliot Deutsch writes, "This intimacy between religion and philosophy in Advaita Vedānta, as in much of the Indian tradition, has been pointed out frequently. It bears constant repetition, however, for there are still a few philosophers who, in their desire to find a dominant naturalistic tradition in India, are determined to neglect (or even to deny) this relationship."[7] Deutsch does not say so, but he may have had in mind Bimal K. Matilal, editor of a new publication called *Journal of Indian Philosophy*, who announced that in his magazine, "The field of our contributions will be bound by the limits of rational inquiry; we will avoid questions that lie in the fields of theology and mystical experience." "Philosophy" as he understands it moves "without recourse to religious or ontological commitment." There is no doubt that Indian thought may be so examined, but does this get to the heart of what we know as Indian philosophy? Another way to put this is to state that whereas a Western philosopher is criticized with regard to the consistency of his ideas, the Indian philosopher is criticized with regard to the consistency of his ideas and his life. David Hume and Siddhartha Gautama arrived at approximately the same conclusions about the nature of the self. But after reaching this conclusion Hume lived as he did before, i.e., his life style continued as though he believed in the reality of a substantial ego. But Gautama's life style changed radically after he came to this conclusion. Hume's conclusion started a round of arguments which we still continue in the West; Gautama's conclusion began a life style which has shaped East Asia for 2,500 years. Hume taught how to think about personal identity in the absence of belief in a substantial ego; Gautama taught how to live a selfless life.

The charge is often heard that classical Indian philosophers were more concerned about human needs than were the Greeks. This depends upon which needs one has in mind. The Greek philosophers were city men, living within the city in order to exert political action. Plato and Aristotle could not conceive of man living apart from the polis. Even a misanthrope like Diogenes of Sinope remained within the city to rail against man. Heraclitus was a rare dropout. But the Indian philosophers were men of the forest. They withdrew in order to meditate, and often when they established a school, it was a forest *āśrama* where study would be engaged in without the distractions of home and community. They were concerned about the soteriological aspects of human life. "In India, truth is not precious in itself; it becomes precious by virtue of its soteriological function."[8]

Mokṣa Orientation

According to Plato and Aristotle philosophy begins in wonder. Not so in India. Orthodox Indian philosophy begins with an awareness of suffering and with a desire to do something about it. According to an Indian philosopher, "A philosophy, which is merely an enquiry into the ultimate nature of the spatio-temporal world or the nature of consciousness as such and is thus merely a philosophy of being, is a truncated thing."[9] Indian philosophy is a means, not an end in itself. Philosophical truth is prized not because it is true but because it leads to liberation. Philosophy in India is existential-soteriological. As the *Śvetāśvatara Upaniṣad* says, "That Eternal should be known as present in the self. Truly there is nothing higher than that to be known."[10] Man's life, according to the Indian philosopher, is filled with frustration, transiency, and sorrow. The Buddha's emphasis on misery was a Hindu emphasis. Nothing can give lasting happiness to man in this life. Each Indian philosophy is an effort to deal practically with *duḥkha*. Surendranath Dasgupta writes, "In fact it seems to me that a sincere religious craving after some ideal blessedness and quiet of self-realization is indeed the fundamental fact from which not only her philosophy but many of the complex phenomena of the civilization of India can be logically deduced."[11] If this suggests a pessimistic beginning of philosophy, do not forget that the goal is to attain lasting bliss (*ānanda*). Dasgupta continues, "The sorrow around us has no fear for us if we remember that we are naturally sorrowless and blessed in ourselves. The pessimistic view loses all terror as it closes in absolute optimistic confidence in one's own self and the ultimate destiny and goal of emancipation."[12] Indian philosophies are intellectual, moral, aesthetic, social, and religious devices to relieve man of sorrow and to achieve perfect joy. Because of the religious nature of Hindu philosophy and of the philosophical nature of Hindu religion we might avoid confusion by referring to Hinduism as neither philosophy nor religion but *sādhana*, a comprehensive discipline for the full development of the potentialities of man. The religious nature of Indian philosophy is illustrated in four criteria Śaṅkara established for any student who wished to study with him:

1. He must be able to distinguish the abiding from the fleeting.
2. He must have a degree of detachment from this world (and any other world), knowing that all worlds are transitory.
3. He must have already cultivated such virtues as poise, truthfulness, etc.
4. He must have a strong desire for liberation from the wheel of life.

The *mokṣa* aspect of Hindu philosophy results in action to relieve man of his suffering. The relief has taken two forms: the path of active life (*pravṛtti mārga*) and the path of renunciation (*nivṛtti mārga*). These two paths have continued throughout the history of Indian philosophy. But the interesting fact is that in India the two paths have not remained antithetical. Rather they tend to be incorporated into human life as stages of the ideal life history.

Ātman Orientation

Indian philosophy is directed inwardly rather than outwardly. It seeks to understand and to develop the self rather than to know and to manipulate the external world. The third eye of Śiva is more important than the two eyes which look outward. Intuition is stressed as a way of knowing; in fact, it is usually the ultimate point of view. Logic and reason are used in Indian philosophy to convince others of the intellectual respectability of one's point of view, but they must be superceded finally by a personal conviction of the rightness of the position. Philosophy as a logical system must always step aside for philosophy as a way of life. The inward viewpoint of Indian philosophy must not lead us to believe that the Indians were not—and are not—interested in the external world. They were and are; but the interest often takes a different slant from what we are familiar with in the West. What we might call "philosophy" and "physics" tend to get confused in India. Betty Heimann brings this out well when she says that in India theology is second physics, ontology is extended physics, and eschatology is renewed physics.[13]

Darśana Orientation

Each system of philosophy in India is called a *darśana*, a point of view. As long as one stays within the boundary of the six fundamental orthodox (*āstika*) systems, each system is recognized as a legitimate system. The systems do not seek to destroy one another—as a rule! But this lauded principle of tolerance must not be overstressed. There have been—and there are—genuine differences among the *āstika* philosophers; and the conflicts among *āstika* and *nāstika* philosophers have been as vicious as any of the conflicts in the West. In fact the systems both *āstika* and *nāstika* developed through the dialectical process of conflict with each other.

Indian philosophy is not tied to personalities. Little is known about the lives of the classical philosophers. Even Śaṅkara cannot be established as a historical person. The *āstika* philosophers say that this feature of Indian philosophy is evidence that the philosopher is a discoverer, not a formulator, of truth. The very words used to designate the systems are terms which describe the system rather than terms which identify the founder. The West has its Platonism, Aristotelianism, Kantianism, etc., but in India there is no "Patañjali-ism" or "Śaṅkara-ism."

We must not fail to notice the implications of using the word *darśana* for a system of philosophy in India. Whereas we in the West think of a system of philosophy as a full, complete, and exclusive organization of thought, an organization which rejects other organizations, India thinks of a system of thought as a point of view which recognizes the legitimacy and worth of other points of view. Rather than seeing things as black or white, good or evil, true or false, the Indian tends to take an inclusive attitude toward positions and systems. Rather than accepting an Aristotelian two-valued logic, the Indian thinks in terms of many degrees and aspects of truth. Differences of points of view do exist, and truth and value shift as one takes a different point of view. Much nonsense has been spoken about the tolerance of Indians. Often this is affirmed by Westerners who are taken in by clever Indians who discover that flattery of the sahib is a very effective way to manipulate Westerners. Indians often reveal an amazing instinctive psychology of human relations. Still, at the level of thought it is a fair generalization that in Indian philosophy an effort is made to reconcile differences within a larger whole rather than to push differences into sharp conflict.

Conservative Orientation

Indian philosophy seeks to preserve the insights of the past. Progress is not conceived as destroying the old in order to make way for the new. Truth is eternal. Hence, a truth once held continues to be held insofar as this is possible. A Western philosopher arguing with an Indian may find himself in the strange position of being disproven by a quotation from an *Upaniṣad.* S. K. Mitra once said that in India "contemporary" means within the last two thousand years. "Conformism is a fundamental characteristic of the Indian mind and there seems to have been no wish to deviate from tradition."[14] Richard Lannoy says that the Indian traditionalist "has no faith in his power to change history because for him there is no history."[15]

We in the West think in distinct independent steps. These steps are organized logically and/or chronologically. We are interested in the end, the results. We drop the means when the end is reached. If A leads to B, then we drop A upon reaching B; and if B then leads to C, we drop B upon reaching C. This is linear thinking. In India thought proceeds by radiations from a productive center. That which is regarded in the West as a means is in Indian thought treated as a value in itself which must not be lost in the movement of thought. Indian thought is non-linear, clustery, and configurative.

Conservatism in Indian thought does not mean holding to the old without change. It is a conservatism of moving out without losing the reality and value of the original. This can be illustrated also from the zero in mathematics—which, by the way, was an Indian invention. While in Western mathematics zero means nought and in Buddhism *śūnya* means an empty circle, the Indian zero (*bindu*) is a solid dot symbolizing a fertile seed. Zero is the productive point of potentiality. Zero is the matrix of negative and positive. Zero in Indian thought keeps wandering from the formality of mathematics into the enigma of a reality positioned between life and death. One *guru* in India, when asked to sign autograph books, made only a dot in the center of the page with the remark, "In the *bindu* all is contained."[16]

Development in Western thought usually involves destruction of the old to make room for the new, but development in Indian thought consists in retaining the insights of previous thought and building upon these insights. An ancient sage expresses his views. His followers define and systematize the views by putting them into collections known as *sūtras* or *kārikās*. Later followers write commentaries on the *sūtras* or *kārikās*, and still others write commentaries on the commentaries. Dialogue takes place with little regard to the historical date of the ideas expressed, but with great concern for the preservation of the traditional values and truths. This has been possible because of a stability unknown in the West since the Renaissance. The tolerance characteristic of Indian thinking makes it possible for Indian philosophy to avoid a shattering revolution when thrust into violent and conflicting relations with the philosophies of the West. Modern India's most unsettling experience is the attempt to become an independent, self-supporting nation among the modern nations of the world. Although Prime Minister Nehru never stressed his non-alignment policy as rooted in Indian philosophy, one can recognize unwillingness to take sides in the cold war as a fitting manifestation of the philosophical tradition of India.

Conservatism is also noticed in the Indian attitude toward change. Richard Lannoy writes, "Change does not increase the good; there is no such thing here as progress; value lies in sameness, in the repeated pattern of the known, not in novelty. What is good in life is exact identity with all past experience, and all mythical experience. . . . In the West we see our history climactically; we plan our future experiences climactically, leading up to future satisfaction or meaning, and to fulfilment through pursuing a career. In India, action is a series of anti-climactic masquerades."[17] For example, Ānandamayi, a woman mystic of Bengal born in 1896, says no crises, no changes, have ever occurred in her life: "I am always the same." This non-climactic on-going-ness is seen in the monotony of Indian food habits, in tending of cattle, in cinema plots, and even in the anti-climactic sexual activity recommended in Tantra. The universe in its activity is a perpetual-motion machine. In fact, Āryabhaṭa, one of India's great mathematicians, wrote in A.D. 499 how to make a perpetual-motion machine: "One could cause a sphere of light wood, equally rounded, and of weight on all sides, to move in regular time by means of quicksilver, oil, and water." Bhāskara in 1150 gave even more explicit plans for a perpetual-motion machine with hollow rims filled with quicksilver. Endless cyclical change—*kalpas* and *mahākalpas*—is the order of things. The village Indian today lives a life of monotonous routine which would drive most Westerners insane. But in Hinduism the man liberated from time—which means psychologically the man free from any compulsion to program his activities to the accomplishment of goals—is the highest human ideal, the *jīvanmukta*.

Another aspect of the conservative orientation of Indian philosophy is noted in that, while the Western intellectual moves from a known A to an unknown B, the Indian counterpart moves from an unknowable, pre-empirical and pre-rational indistinct A through empirical phenomena to an indistinct post-empirical and post-rational B which is essentially the same as the pre-empirical and pre-rational A. Intellectual research in Indian philosophy is not the creation of new knowledge but the explication of wisdom already possessed. Thus *Swāmi* Dayānanda Saraswati, the founder of the Ārya Samāj, contended that the *Vedas* contained all the knowledge men had or would ever have. He located the latest discoveries of chemistry and physics and all the latest technological advances in the *Vedas*—and even hinted of scientific knowledge in the *Vedas* which future research and experiments would discover. Dayānanda was stating what had been believed opaquely for generations by intelligent Hindus.

Not all Indians take such a charitable attitude toward Indian thinking, e.g., Nirad C. Chaudhuri writes, "There is no such thing as thinking properly so called among the Hindus for it is a faculty of the mind developed only in Greece, and exercised only by the heirs of the Greeks. A very large part of what is called Hindu thinking is woolly speculation or just mush."[18]

The conservative orientation expresses itself in synthesizing items into wholes. The Indian philosopher "is more interested in the synthetic group of the underlying principles of all knowledge than in the analytic method of discovering distinctions,"[19] writes a modern Hindu. But this, as we noted above, is a primary emphasis, not a sole emphasis. S. Radhakrishnan argues that what is needed is a synthesis of all philosophies: "The need of philosophy today is for a world perspective which will include the philosophical insights of all the world's great traditions."[20]

We must admit that Indian thinking sometimes seems to the Western philosophy too unrealistic, too fuzzy. Matters are not helped by the observation that "Hindu philosophy is too human to be logical."[21] The difference of style of thinking is rooted in different assumptions. In the West the law of non-contradiction is assumed, but Indians characteristically ask if the law of "either-or" ought not to be discarded for the law of "this-as-well-as-that." For them the thesis and the antithesis are necessary correlatives.

Indian Philosophy and Indian Culture

There is a tendency among Western philosophers who discover Indian philosophy to think of India as a nation of philosophers. The average Indian is thought to be a philosopher, and philosophy is assumed to be the very heart and core of Indian life. This is not true. It is one of the many stereotypes that Westerners have, and one which some Indian intellectuals have encouraged in the West. Philosophy was not regarded in traditional India as a proper study for the average person. It was carefully nurtured as a special study for special people. Dasgupta says, "Any one in olden times who took to the study of any system of philosophy, had to do so with a teacher, who explained those terms to him. The teacher himself had got it from his teacher, and he from his. There was no tendency to popularize philosophy, for the idea then prevalent was that only the chosen few who had otherwise shown their fitness, deserved to become students of philosophy, under the direction of a teacher. Only those who had the grit and high moral strength to devote their whole life to the true understanding of philosophy and the rebuilding of life in accordance with the high truths of philosophy were allowed to study it."[22] In India today a distinction is drawn between the philosophy taught in the universities and the classical tradition of study with a *guru*. Life in the half-million villages of India is caught up in the daily rounds of work, the seasonal activities of planting and harvesting, gossip and tale-bearing among families, attention to the village gods, and a few *melas* (fairs) each year. The immediate problems of food, clothing, shelter, and health supplant reflection upon philosophical problems. The average Indian is more interested in his next meal than in his next life. Philosophy belongs in India, but it would be dishonest to claim it as the chief concern of Indians.

One of the reasons why Western people study Indian philosophy has been and is because they believe there is something remedial in the Hindu style of life and thought. This may be true—indeed I believe it is true, but perhaps the most foolish thing a Western person can do is to try to adopt Hindu ways. Carl Jung warned against the effort. He said once that *yoga* is fine, but for the Western person it must be a Western *yoga*. Louis Renou has put this warning in stronger fashion. He writes that of "the different theosophical sects, the anthroposophists, traditionalists, and Western schools of yoga they can be described more justly if one simply mentions and then ignores them. . . . All that these people succeed for the most part in getting out of Hinduism is an artificial vocabulary and arbitrary interpretations chosen haphazardly from the total field. . . . Let us always remember that India is an Eldorado for charlatans. If Hinduism ever has a future as an integral part of a broad, generally acceptable spiritual movement beyond the borders of the country that gave it birth, this future will be created only by direct reflection from genuinely Indian forms of thought and spirit conceived and expressed by Indians."[23]

Indian philosophers have never claimed they were engaged in a value-free pursuit of learning. They begin with the sufferings of the human condition and seek to find a remedy. The Buddha, who was probably the greatest of all Indian philosophers, diagnosed the human condition as *duḥkha* (impermanence and suffering). He analyzed the cause as *upādāna* (cleaving), and he offered as therapy the Eight-fold Middle Way. To understand Indian philosophy we must put the question of the way of the human condition to ourselves. We have as yet an imperfect understanding of Indian life and thought. When we have a complete picture of Indian culture, speculates Peter Munz, "it is likely that it will cause a revolution in our thought and outlook which will dwarf the revolution wrought by the discovery of Greece some four or five hundred years ago."[24]

NOTES

1. Surendranath Dasgupta, *A History of Indian Philosophy*, Vol. I. Cambridge: Cambridge University Press, 1957, p. ix.
2. *Ibid.*, p. 6.
3. *Ibid.*, p. 7.
4. John M. Koller, *Oriental Philosophies*. New York: Charles Scribner's Sons, 1970, p. 15.
5. Sarvepalli Radhakrishnan, *Indian Philosophy*, Vol. I. Revised edition. New York: The Macmillan Co., 1929, p. 27.
6. C. E. M. Joad, "Appeal to Philosophers," *Proceedings of the Aristotelian Society*, Vol. 40 (1940), p. 34.
7. Eliot Deutsch, *Advaita Vedānta: A Philosophical Reconstruction*. Honolulu: East-West Center Press, 1969, p. 4.
8. Mircea Eliade, *Yoga: Immortality and Freedom*. New York: Pantheon Books, 1958, p. 4.
9. L. C. Gupta in a paper entitled "Philosophy and Life" read at the 1953 Indian Philosophical Congress.
10. *Śvetāśvatara Upaniṣad* 1. 12. Robert Ernest Hume translation.
11. Dasgupta, *op. cit.*, pp. 76-77.

12. *Ibid.*, p. 77.
13. Betty Heinmann, *Indian and Western Philosophy*. London: George Allen and Unwin, 1937, p. 46.
14. Michael Edwardes, *Everyday Life in Early India*. New York: G. P. Putnam's Sons, 1969, p. 1.
15. Richard Lannoy, *The Speaking Tree*. London: Oxford University Press, 1971, p. 339.
16. *Ibid.*, p. 351.
17. *Ibid.*, pp. 289-290.
18. Nirad C. Chaudhuri, *The Continent of Circe*. London: Chatto and Windus, 1965, p. 151.
19. P. N. Srinivasachari, *The Philosophy of Bhedābheda*. Second edition revised. Adyar, Madras: Adyar Library, 1950, p. 97.
20. Sarvepalli Radhakrishnan and Charles A. Moore (editors), *A Source Book in Indian Philosophy*. Princeton: Princeton University Press, 1957, p. xxix.
21. William George Archer, *India and the Future*. London: Hutchinson and Co., 1917, p. 23.
22. Surendranath Dasgupta, *op. cit.*, p. 2.
23. Louis Renou, *The Nature of Hinduism*. New York: Walker and Co., 1962, pp. 143-144.
24. Peter Munz, "India and the West: A Synthesis," *Philosophy East and West*, Vol. V, No. 4 (January, 1956), p. 322.

—4—

*THE QUEST FOR SELF-KNOWLEDGE IN THE WEST**

Many Indian philosophers are convinced that we in the West are preoccupied with material things and appallingly neglectful of the self. This is certainly the opinion of two well-known Indian intellectuals, Sarvepalli Radhakrishnan and Aurobindo Ghosh. Radhakrishnan writes, "There is a tendency [in the West] to overlook the spiritual and exalt the intellectual. It can be traced chiefly to the influence of the Greeks, who determined the bent of the Western mind towards science and the pursuit of truth for its own sake."[1] Radhakrishnan believes that the spirituality which the West lacks may be supplied by the East: "When Greco-Roman civilization was triumphant, it failed to supply its conquered peoples with a religion, and instead, was itself conquered by a religion supplied by them. May it not be that today the peoples of Asia may supply a spiritual orientation to the new world based on science and technology? By its material and political devices, the West is able to provide a secure framework of order within which different civilizations could mingle, and fruitful intercourse between them can take place by which the spiritual poverty of the world can be overcome. Without a spiritual recovery, the scientific achievements threaten to destroy us."[2] Aurobindo's charge against the West is that its mental attitude is analytic and external rather than synthetic and internal: "In the West where the

* Adapted from an article which first appeared in *Darshana*, Vol. II, No. 1, (January, 1962), pp. 80-87.

syncretic tendency of the consciousness was replaced by the analytic and separative, the spiritual urge and the intellectual reason parted company almost at the outset. Philosophy took from the first a turn towards a purely intellectual and ratiocinative explanation of things."[3] "The tendency of the normal Western mind is to live from below upward and from out inward. . . . The average European draws his guiding views not from the philosophic, but from the positive and the practical reason. . . . The West has *acquired* the religious mind rather than possessed it by nature and it has always worn its acquisition with a certain looseness. . . . The emphasis of the Western mind is on life, the outer life above all, the things that are grasped, visible, tangible. The inner life is taken only as an intelligent reflection of the outer world, with the reason for a firm putter of things into shape, an intelligent critic, builder, refiner of the external materials offered by Nature."[4] Although serious-minded Westerners will probably admit that parts of these criticisms are justified, they may wish to point out that it is an oversimplification to describe the West as materialistic and the East as spiritualistic, or Western philosophy as outlook and Indian philosophy as insight. Radhakrishnan himself has recognized this fallacy: "There is not much truth in the pseudo-science of national or continental psychology which affirms that all Easterns are this and all Westerns are that. The history of any people is slightly more complicated than these sweeping statements would suggest."[5]

Although the self as spiritual object and knowing subject has not been treated as extensively and comprehensively in Western philosophy as it has been in India, it has not been ignored. The historical divisions of Western philosophy were opened in each case by a fresh concern about establishing the existence and knowledge of the self. The Socratic "Know thyself" launched the creative period of Platonism, Aristotelianism, Stoicism, and Epicureanism. The medieval period opened with St. Augustine who cried, "*Quaestio mihi factus sum.*" (I have become a question for myself.) Descartes' *Cogito ergo sum* (I think therefore I am) began the modern period, a period which came to an end between the two World Wars. The period in which Western philosophy now finds itself has no suitable name. "Post-modern" may be the best, as it commits us to so little. It is a period of revising the old problems of philosophy, or rethinking the old methods. One group seem so concerned about maintaining the old methods that they relinquish the old problems; the other are so concerned about the problems that they relinquish the methods. The former, which can be designated as logical analysts, logical positivists, scientific empiricists, or language analysts, seek to clarify the meaning of language which can be used in science, ethics, religion, and art; the latter, which can be called existentialists or philosophers of man, hold that the real is the concrete and the existential, and repudiate attempts to grasp reality by linguistic and mental categories. Under the analysis of the first group the self becomes meaningless, since "Primitive experience, mere existence of ordered data, does not presuppose a 'subject,' or 'ego,' or 'Me,' or 'mind.' "[6] The self in existentialism becomes an object transcendent to consciousness: "We should like to show here that the ego is neither formally nor materially in consciousness; it is outside, in the world. It is a being of the world, like the ego of another."[7] In these four periods of Western philosophy there is a movement from self-confidence to self-negation. Socrates, not doubting the reality of the self, advised man to examine himself. Augustine was distressed by the conflicts he found in the self. Descartes felt obligated to demonstrate rationally that the self was a reality. Schlick negated the self, and Sartre finds no self as subject and locates the self as object in the external world.

Although other philosophical topics such as the world of matter, man in society, the structure of knowledge, and the meaning of values have frequently been given priority in Western philosophy, the self has not been ignored. Plato sought knowledge of the self because he regarded self-knowledge as a study of intrinsic value and also as a means for understanding the state. Aristotle's *De Anima* compares favorably with the treatment of the self in some of the systems of Indian philosophy. He appreciated the place of self-knowledge in man's understanding of the nature of things: "The knowledge of the soul admittedly contributes greatly to the advance of truth in general, and, above all, to our understanding of Nature, for the soul is in some sense the principle of animal life."[8] He also realized the problem of establishing reliable knowledge about the self: "To attain any assured knowledge about the soul is one of the most difficult things in the world."[9] Epictetus gave a typical Greek observation about the soul, i.e., the soul is the mind: "Of our faculties in general you will find that none can take cognizance of itself . . . except that faculty [the soul] which takes cognizance of itself and of things else. What is this? The reasoning faculty: for alone this of the faculties we have received is created to comprehend even its own nature."[10] Plotinus asked, "Concerning what would it be worth to speak and think, rather than about the soul? Let us therefore obey the command of the Deity who commands us to know ourselves."[11] For Plotinus the soul when it comes to itself alone becomes identified with the Absolute: "When the soul descends, she will by her nature never reach complete nothingness. She will fall into evil and, in this sense, into nothingness, but not into complete nothingness. In a similar way, when the soul reverses her direction, she does not arrive at something different, but at herself. But as she is in herself alone and not even in the world of Being, she is in the existence beyond. We too transcend Being by virtue of the soul with which we are united. . . . Such is the life of the gods and of divine and blessed men, detachment from all things here below, scorn of all earthly pleasures, and flight of the alone to the alone."[12] In Boethius' charming and tragic autobiographical story Philosophia reminds Boethius, "You have forgotten who you are." Abelard wrote a book entitled *Scito te ipsum* (Know yourself). Eckhart advised, "No one has known God who has not known himself." Kant in the preface to the first edition of the *Critique of Pure Reason* said of the book, "It is a call to reason to understand anew the most difficult of all its tasks, namely, that of self-knowledge."[13] Hume attacked the notion of the self: "There are some philosophers who imagine we are every moment intimately conscious of what we call our self. . . . For my part, when I enter most intimately into what I call myself, I always stumble on some particular perception or other, of heat or cold, light or shade, love or hatred, pain or pleasure. I never catch myself at any time without a perception, and never can observe anything but the perception. . . . I may venture to affirm of the rest of mankind, that they are nothing but a bundle or collection of different perceptions, which succeed each other with an inconceivable rapidity, and are in a perpetual flux and movement."[14] In the appendix to the *Treatise* Hume became skeptical of his own skepticism about the self: "Upon a more strict review of the section concerning personal identity, I find myself involved in such a labyrinth that, I must confess, I neither know how to correct my former opinions, nor how to render them consistent. . . . I must plead the privilege of a sceptic, and confess that this difficulty is too hard for my understanding." Bradley refuted the Humean view that "the self is no more than 'collective,' than a collection of sensations, and ideas, and emotions, and volitions swept together with one another and after one another by 'the laws of association' " and added, "The only thing which after all is hard to see is this, that we ourselves who apprehend the illusion [i.e., the illusion that there is something in the self that underlies the collection] are ourselves the illusion, which is apprehended by us."[15] For Emerson "The consciousness in each man is a sliding scale, which identifies him now with the First Cause, and now with the flesh of his body."[16] William James held that the constituents of the self may be divided into four selves: material self, social self, spiritual self, and pure ego.[17] F. R. Tennant believed, "No one has really dispensed with the subject of consciousness, whatever terms he may have used to hush up its existence."[18] George Arthur Wilson gave the self a central position in all metaphysics: "The great lesson that the history of philosophy teaches all the emphasis of repetition is the fragmentary character of all world views that ignore the central position of the self."[19]

These references, chosen at random and listed in chronological order, show that the self has not been ignored as a topic for philosophical study in the West. But in spite of this evidence it must be admitted that for the last five hundred years Western man has found the external world more interesting than the internal world.

After the Greeks there have been four forces determining Western man to look outward rather than inward. One was the discovery of a vast and relatively unpopulated continent which could be explored, exploited, and colonized. Another was the Renaissance, the revival of classical learning, which opened the minds of Europeans to another view of life on earth than the view of the medieval church which pointed attention to the afterlife. A third force was the industrial revolution which promised great improvement in food, clothing, shelter, transportation, and communication. The fourth consisted of the social, political, and religious reforms and revolutions which revealed the possibility of change.

The result of these forces was that Westerners embarked upon a period of active involvement with the riches of this life rather than hopes of riches in the next and with the world outside the self rather than the world within the self. Solitary occupations such as exploring, hunting, trapping, and gold prospecting fostered self-reliance, independence, and fearlessness, but it is only in the roughest sense that men of the American frontier such as Daniel Boone, Johnny Appleseed, and Jim Bridger can be described as self-knowers. Western men and women were too busy clearing the land, planting and harvesting, buying and selling, to examine the self. They were largely concerned with pushing back physical frontiers. Americans in particular were cutting the forests, damming the rivers, mining the mountains, and bringing oil and gas from the bowels of the earth. They climbed the highest mountains, sank to the deepest depths of the oceans, explored tropical jungles, and moved under the ice of the Arctic regions. In 1958 an American author suggested that the only frontier left for Americans was the self: "Today Americans have no outer or geographic frontier left to conquer. This pushes us, instead, to increasingly inward conquests. . . . Therefore, let us stop being defensive, stop being apologetic about affirming the dignity and importance of the so-called impractical; namely, the humanistic and the spiritual studies."[20] But he overlooked the fact that Americans had already discovered a new physical frontier—the frontier of space. Planetary exploration, exploitation, and colonization can postpone self-knowledge and self-cultivation for several generations!

Western man's activity is an opiate which deadens his self-awareness, and the man who enjoys solitude hides that fact as though it were a secret sin. The Greek word for solitude (*idios*) has become a term of reproach. Yet the Westerner still longs for solitude. His country estates, lakeside cottages, week-end farms, hunting lodges, fishing camps, and suburban homes are retreats from the city and the factory; but they are also places for securing strength to return to the organization where telephones, committee meetings, and conferences dull those fleeting feelings for ultimate values which may have appeared during the vacation. The individual caught in this whirl of activity calls it "a rat race" or "a treadmill." He may claim that he wants to get out of it, but most organization men fear to make the break. They feel at times as though they are fleeing from something—but they seldom suspect that it is the self that they fear. A recent study of American life reported that "a continuing tension between the needs of the organization and the integrity of the person . . . may well be one of the most fateful struggles of our future."[21] One hopeful sign is that a period of solitude can drive even an American male back to the self. A recent news story about five young men who live for one year at a time without relief at the United States Coast Guard Cape Spencer Lighthouse off the Alaskan coast reports an observation of one of the men: "With so much time to think, you begin to wonder who you are."

Another reason why Western man lags in his understanding of himself is because he has constructed an ideal for trustworthy knowledge which can be achieved in the physical sciences but which cannot be achieved in the knowledge of himself as knower. Reliable knowledge, he has determined, must be intersubjectively testable, quantitatively measurable, and linguistically expressable. Unfortunately, the "knowledge of ourselves will never attain the elegant simplicity, the abstractness, and the beauty of physics. The factors that have retarded its development are not likely to vanish. We must realize that the science of man is the most difficult of all sciences."[22] Aristotle, in his great practical wisdom, observed that "it is the mark of an educated man to look for precision in each class of things just so far as the nature of the subject admits."[23] But scientists and philosophers in the West tend to set up a paradigmatic ideal for knowledge and then attempt to force the subject matter to fit the epistemological model.

Western man is paying a heavy price for his concentration on the external world, and he is becoming aware of that price. Not all is well with him nor with his civilization. Because he has been unable to solve international problems peacefully, he has developed genocidal war weapons. He is horrified by the monster he has made. Leonardo da Vinci refused to make public his plans for a submarine, because, as he said, man was too devilish to be entrusted with such an invention. Likewise Leo Szilard, the physicist who instigated the making of the first atomic bomb, wrote to the President of the United States urging him not to use it. After the dropping of the bomb the scientists who worked on the development of the release of atomic energy formed a federation to promote international control of atomic energy. The situation is now so serious that some have entertained the notion of scrapping all scientific advances of the last three hundred and fifty years: "If the dismantling of every factory, if the extirpation of every item of scientific knowledge that has been accumulated since 1600, were the price of mankind's continuance, we must be ready to pay that terrible price."[24]

The personal price that Western man pays for his concentration on externalities is anxiety. Man has gained mastery of almost everything except himself. Lacking the power to direct himself, he becomes an "outer-directed" person. He guides himself like a blind man by touching things and people, rather than by moving purposively toward established goals. His anxiety reveals itself in emptiness, shallowness, loneliness, and fear. He sees himself as Willy Loman, the father in Arthur Miller's "Death of a Salesman," about whom his son says, "He had the wrong dreams. . . . He never knew who he was." According to Rollo May, "One of the few blessings of living in an age of anxiety is that we are forced to become aware of ourselves. When our society, in its time of upheaval in standards and values, can give us no clear idea of 'what we are and what we ought to be,' as Matthew Arnold puts it, we are thrown back on the search for ourselves."[25]

The self does have a way of intruding into our lives. According to an old Indian fable ten men once forded a swift and dangerous river. Upon reaching the shore they counted to see if all had arrived safely. But each man could count but nine. A passerby, hearing their wailing over the loss of a comrade, counted the men and discovered there were ten. He then asked each man to count, and when the counter counted only nine, the stranger touched him on the chest and said, "You are the tenth." A similar conclusion was reached by the English astronomer A. S. Eddington: "We have found a strange footprint on the shores of the unknown. We have devised profound theories, one after another, to account for its origin. At last we have succeeded in reconstructing the creature that made the footprint. And Lo! It is our own."[26]

NOTES

1. Sarvepalli Radhakrishnan, *Eastern Religions and Western Thought*. London: Oxford University Press, 1939, p. 38.
2. Sarvepalli Radhakrishnan, "The Ancient Asian View of Man" in *Man's Right to Knowledge*. New York: Columbia University Press, 1954, pp. 14-15.
3. Aurobindo, *The Life Divine*. New York: The Greystone Press, 1949, p. 782.
4. Aurobindo, *The Foundations of Indian Culture*. New York: The Greystone Press, 1953, pp. 23, 65, 81, 94.
5. Sarvepalli Radhakrishnan, *East and West*. New York: Harper and Brothers, 1956, p. 13.
6. Moritz Schlick, "Meaning and Verification." *The Philosophical Review*, Vol. 45 (1936), p. 369.
7. Jean-Paul Sartre, *The Transcendence of the Ego: An Ēxistential Theory of Consciousness*. Translated by Forrest Williams and Robert Kirkpatrick. New York: The Noonday Press, 1957, p. 31.
8. *De Anima* 402 a 4-6. J. A. Smith translation.
9. *De Anima* 402 a 10. J. A. Smith translation.
10. *Discourses* I. 1. P. E. Matheson translation.
11. *Enneads* IV. 3. 1. K. S. Guthrie translation.
12. *Enneads* VI. 9. 11. Joseph Katz translation.
13. *Critique of Pure Reason* A. xi. Norman Kemp Smith translation.
14. *A Treatise of Human Nature* I. 4. 6.
15. Francis Herbert Bradley, *Ethical Studies*. Oxford: The Clarendon Press, 1927, pp. 36, 37, 39.
16. Essay on "Experience." *The Complete Writings of Ralph Waldo Emerson*. New York: William H. Wise and Co., 1929, p. 260.
17. *The Principles of Psychology*, Vol. I, ch. 10.
18. F. R. Tennant, *Philosophical Theology*, Vol. I. Cambridge: The University Press, 1935, p. 18.
19. George Arthur Wilson, *The Self and Its World*. New York: The Macmillan Co., 1926, p. 275.
20. Peter Viereck, "The Unadjusted Man." *Saturday Review of Literature*, November 1, 1958, p. 13.
21. Fourth Report of the Special Studies Project of the Rockefeller Brothers' Fund, 1958.
22. Alexis Carrel, *Man, The Unknown*. Middlesex and New York: Penguin Books, 1935, p. 23.
23. *Ethica Nicomachea* 1094 b 24. W. D. Ross translation.
24. Lewis Mumford, *Values for Survival*. New York: Harcourt, Brace and Co., 1946, p. 80.
25. Rollo May, *Man's Search for Himself*. New York: W. W. Norton and Co., 1953, p. 7.
26. A. S. Eddington, *Space, Time and Gravitation*. Cambridge: The University Press, 1920, p. 201.

—5—

*THE SELF AS DISCOVERY AND CREATION IN WESTERN AND INDIAN PHILOSOPHY**

Two inscriptions were engraved on the façade of the temple of Apollo at Delphi: "Know thyself" and "Nothing in excess." These admonitions were not unrelated. Man was advised to know himself, yet in his knowing he was to avoid extremes. One extreme was the attempt to go beyond his finitude, to act as though he were a god. *Hybris*—the term used to designate this extreme—meant an outrage against the nature of things. Originally it denoted the offspring of the union of a wild boar and a domestic sow. The other extreme was the attempt to act as though the individual were not a member of society. The Greeks held that man is a city animal. He who lived outside the polis was called a private being. *Idios* was the name of such a being. At Delphi the Greeks were reminded of their natural and social contingencies: Know yourself, but in your knowing do not become a hybrid or an idiot!

Self-knowing is one of man's most pervasive behavioral characteristics. The humanities may be defined as the ways of self-knowledge. Ernst Cassirer in *An Essay on Man* identifies religion, history, and philosophy as three forms of self-knowing: "In all the higher forms of religious life the maxim 'Know thyself' is regarded

* This essay appears in *East-West Studies on the Problem of the Self*. Edited by P. T. Raju and Alburey Castell. The Hague: Martinus Nijhoff, 1968, pp. 163-176. The volume consists of papers presented at the Conference on Comparative Philosophy and Culture held at the College of Wooster, Wooster, Ohio, April 22-24, 1965. Reprinted by kind permission of Martinus Nijhoff.

as an ultimate moral and religious law. . . . History . . . is a form of self-knowledge. . . . Self-knowledge is the highest aim of philosophical inquiry."[1] Charles I. Glicksberg thinks that all literature is self-knowing: "The struggle of man to define himself, to know himself, is the story of literature virtually from the beginning of civilization."[2] Self-knowledge has been prominent in the thinking of philosophers in both hemispheres: "He who knows others is learned; he who knows himself is wise."[3] "What is the use of knowing everything except the Self? What else is there to know for anyone when Self, itself, is known."[4] "I sought for myself."[5] "Go not outside thyself, but return within thyself; for truth resides in the inmost part of man."[6] "One must know one's self before knowing anything else."[7] "To project feelings into outer objects is the first way of symbolizing, and thus of conceiving those feelings. This activity belongs to about the earliest period of childhood that memory can recover. The conception of 'self,' which is usually thought to mark this beginning of actual memory, may possibly depend on this process of symbolically epitomizing our feelings."[8] "Who in the world am I? Ah, that's the great puzzle!"[9] (Alice—one of the best of philosophers.)

While self-knowing has been a motivation of thought in both the East and the West, it must be admitted that for the last five hundred years Western man has found the external world more appealing than the inner world. There have been many reasons for this propensity of thought in the West: the discovery of America, the revival of classical learning, the industrial revolution, and the political reformations are some of the determiners of Western man's direction of thought. The twentieth century has been described as a time when man never knew more about the world and less about himself. In India, on the other hand, there has been since the earliest days of the Indus Valley culture a concentrated study of the inner nature of man. The goal of Indian philosophy is still defined metaphysically as self-knowledge (*ātmavidyā*) and religiously as liberation (*mokṣa*). Self-cognition is to be attained through discursive reasoning (*pramāṇa*); self-realization is to be attained through meditation (*sādhana*). Some day we in the West will recognize "the fragmentary character of world views that ignore the central position of the self."[10]

The quest for self-knowledge has many shades of meaning. For

Socrates it is the examination of ethical assumptions; for Augustine it is the avenue for attaining saving knowledge of the Christian God; for Śaṅkara a realization of identity of finite self and the cosmic principle; for Descartes the first step to intellectual certainty; and for some modern existentialists a prelude to suicide. There are also differences as to the ease or difficulty of self-knowledge. Rāmana Maharshi said, "Self-knowledge is an easy thing, the easiest thing there is."[11] But according to Kant metaphysics "is a call to reason to undertake anew the most difficult of all its tasks, namely, that of self-knowledge."[12] Modern man is often driven to despair because he is afraid that the self does not exist at all or that the self is a Capekan machine, a Skinneran robot, a Kafkan cockroach, an Ionescoan rhinoceros, or a Sartrean "useless passion."

However self-knowledge may be defined—as quest for identity, for axiological assumptions, for substratum, for essence, for specific differentia, or for salvation—the quest itself is the distinguishing characteristic of man. Man is the being who is aware of himself. The lower animals exist, and man exists—but man *knows* that he exists. An animal is; man is and knows *that* he is. Some hold that God knows both *that* he is and *what* he is. But man also seeks to know *what* he is. He would be as God. God is Being whose essence is existence. Man is the being whose essence is the *quest* for existence as a being-whose-essence-is-existence. Man is the contingent being that attempts to remove contingency from its being. This human propensity was a scandal to the Hebrews. The myth of the Tower of Babel is an expression of their horror at man's efforts to rival God. Sartre calls it the desire of the for-itself to become in-itself-for-itself. He writes, "Every human is a passion in which it projects losing itself so as to establish being and by the same stroke to constitute the In-itself which escapes contingency by being its own foundation the *Ens causa sui* which religions call God."[13] If the attempt to make himself God is not a successful venture—and there are empirical evidences as well as rational reasons for concluding that it is not, man has open to him another absolute. He cannot become the Ground of Being, but he can become a non-being. The Stoics used to derive comfort from the fact that a man can take his own life—or, as they said, the human being can leave by the back door. Today several nations have in storage the instruments of genocide. The day is not far distant when every major nation will possess the means for the total destruction of the human race. At last man faces squarely the problem of the value of his own existence. This is what Bonhoeffer called "the passionate subjectivity of modern man." Is the human race worth preserving? Would the world be a better place without man? Can man justify his own existence? The back door exit is now possible for all life on this planet, and maybe this exit will soon be possible for any life that happens to be on other planets in our solar system. Against such possibilities the questions "Who am I?" and "What is man?" take on new significance.

Thus far in this paper we have been observing that self-knowing is a universal activity of man, that it is the activity which makes man human, and that it is the activity in which man projects himself toward divinity. Now we shall examine some of the philosophical problems inherent in self-knowing. If we were to name the Western philosopher who most vigorously and consistently directed himself to self-knowledge, that philosopher would be Augustine: "God and the soul, that is what I desire to know. . . . Nothing more? . . . Nothing whatever."[14] At first he thought he might find the knowledge he desired in the external world, but he came to see that what he sought was within. As a result of his search he warned Christians against vain curiosity about the external world and advised them to look within for reality. When he turned within, he first established his own existence by arguing "*Si fallor sum*" (I exist because only an existing being can be deceived).[15] Then by appeal to the certainty of his own existence Augustine established the contemplative way of wisdom (*sapientia*) whose objects are the intelligible ideas received from the "Teacher Within" and the secondary or practical way of knowledge (*scientia*) of the temporal affairs of early life. Thus Augustine hoped to vanquish the Pyrrhonic skepticism which had taken over the Platonic Academy and the Ciceronian skepticism which had conquered his own mind at one time. And what was the result of the efforts of this man who was called "the master of the inner life"? We can appreciate his inner struggle and the honesty of his reporting of that struggle, but it is not a pleasant sight to watch him shift from *Intellige ut credas* (You must understand in order to believe)[16] to *Crede ut intelligas* (You must believe in order to understand)[17] as one or the other suited his purposes. Probably his most honest confession was *Quaestio mihi factus sum.* (I have become a question for myself.)[18]

It is interesting to note that although Augustine attempted to affirm the reality of a substantial self and Hume attempted to deny the reality of a substantial self both ended on a skeptical note. Hume in his *Treatise* attacked the notion of an existent self with characteristic enthusiasm: "There are some philosophers who imagine we are every moment intimately conscious of what we call our *self* . . . For my part, when I enter more intimately into what I call *myself*, I always stumble on some particular perception or other . . . I never catch *myself* at anytime without a perception, and never observe anything but the perception. . . . I may venture to affirm of the rest of mankind, that they are nothing but a bundle or collection of different perceptions, which succeed each other with an inconceivable rapidity."[19] Hume, as some historians of philosophy have suggested, may have noticed the number of times the word "I" appeared in his essay refuting the existence of the self; for he wrote later in the Appendix to the *Treatise*, "But upon a more strict review of the section concerning *personal identity*, I find myself involved in such a labyrinth that, I must confess, I neither know how to correct my former opinions, nor how to render them consistent. . . . I must plead the privilege of a sceptic, and confess that this difficulty is too hard for my understanding."[20]

At this point we should appeal to the poets, playwrights, and novelists. They enter where philosophers fear to tread, for they celebrate rather than argue. One of the best presentations of the status to which Western man is reduced by his failure to know himself is found in Ionesco's play "The Bald Soprano." Two couples—the Smiths and the Martins—sit in a room engaging in small talk which does not communicate. A weird clock on the wall which strikes at any time does not communicate either. At one point in the play the four characters angrily shout meaningless insults at each other: "Cockatoos, cockatoos, cockatoos . . . Such caca, such caca, such caca . . . Such cascades of cacas, such cascades of cacas, such cascades of cacas . . ."[21] When the Martins fall into bored slumber, the maid addresses the audience: "Elizabeth is not Elizabeth, Donald is not Donald. . . . It is in vain that he thinks he is Donald, it is in vain that she thinks she is Elizabeth. . . . But who is the true Donald?

Who is the true Elizabeth? Who has any interest in prolonging the confusion?"[22] Ionesco is telling us in this play that loss of self is loss of communication, and that loss of communication is loss of self. Where there is nothing to symbolize there are no symbols; there are only sounds to hide the terrifying emptiness, sounds that break the awful silence, and meaningless words that eliminate the necessity of thought. A play like "The Bald Soprano" may be regarded as a dramatic presentation of the Humean theory of an unconnected world. Things have no relation to other things—logically, causally, ontologically, or axiologically. Nothing means anything. Events necessitate no other events. The only cohesion among things is that which man supplies—if he is interested in supplying any. Both existentialism and language analysis are resultants of the Humean philosophy; but whereas the existentialists prefer to talk to take their minds off the meaninglessness of the world, the analysts prefer in the words of Wittgenstein "To say nothing except what can be said, i.e., the propositions of natural science. . . . Whereof one cannot speak, thereof one must be silent."[23]

John Macmurray in the Gifford Lectures of 1953-54[24] attempted to solve the problem of the self by taking the self out of the epistemological context of subject-object and putting it in the activity context of agent-object. But Macmurray's thesis that the self is actor rather than "spectator of all time and existence" does not do justice to man's humanness. Self-knowing is the *sine qua non* of man. Only the human animal is self-aware. In the words of Teilhard de Chardin "It is generally accepted that what distinguishes man psychologically from other living creatures is the power acquired by his consciousness of turning in upon itself. The animal knows, it has been said; but only man, among animals, knows that he knows."[25] Furthermore, contends Teilhard, qualitative distinctions among men are made upon the basis of self-knowledge: "The great superiority over Primitive Man which we have acquired and which will be enhanced by our descendents in a degree perhaps undreamed-of by ourselves, is in the realm of self-knowledge; in our growing capacity to situate ourselves in space and time, to the point of becoming conscious of our place and responsibility in relation to the Universe."[26] We should note here that one of the ideas common to all the six systems of orthodox Indian philosophy is that the difference between animal and man is the difference between mere consciousness and self-consciousness, and also that the difference between man-as-*jīva*, i.e., as limited self, and man-as-*Ātman*, i.e., as unlimited Self, is the difference between self-consciousness (*ahaṁkāra* or *ahaṁbuddhi*) and what is sometimes called "super-consciousness" (*chaitanyam* or *nirviśesacinmātram*). The lower animals are unaware of their own existence. God also is not self-aware, for God has no need of knowing self. The beast is wordless. God is the Word. But man—caught between beast and God—must know himself in order to be. The beast has no self; God is the Self; man attempts to become Self. Man in his middle position sometimes longs like Whitman to turn and live with animals, and sometimes he longs like Plotinus to take a flight of the alone to the Alone. But neither is possible. Man is an absurd beast with divine aspirations. He is conscious clay, a bewildering paradox, a mere perhaps. He is the only animal that can make a fool of itself. But when we attempt to define man, as Hannah Arendt has pointed out, we "almost invariably end with some construction of a deity."[27]

"You must know yourself," wrote Pascal, "even though that knowledge serves in no wise to find the truth."[28] I am contending that man must know himself in order to be man. But since man fails to know himself, I do not wish to conclude that he fails to be man! It is the *questing*, not the finding, that makes man man. And why the failure of the search? Why does he not know himself? There are two reasons for this failure. One has to do with the novel epistemological structure of self-knowing; the other has to do with the ontological duality of the epistemological object. We shall examine the epistemological structure first. The philosophical way of stating the problem would go like this: all knowledge includes a subject, an object, and an act—knower, known, and knowing. Whether one follows the argument of the realist that the object is unmodified in the act, or whether one follows the argument of the idealist that the object is modified ontologically by the knower in the act, the fact remains that within the total structure of knowing subject and object are distinct. The subject knows the object; the object is known by the subject. But when that which is known is the self, the problem becomes more complex. As some Indian philosophers love to say, the self is like the eye that seeks to see itself. The eye is the seer of the seen. But what happens when the object of seeing is itself the seeing subject? Can the knower of knowing be known? And if something is known in the act of self-knowing, is it really the knower? If I seek to know the I, do I end in knowing the I, or must I be content with knowing me?

The subject-object duality in self-knowing is poetically expressed in the *Ṛg Veda*, and is repeated in both the *Muṇḍaka Upaniṣad* and the *Śvetāśvatara Upaniṣad*: "Two birds associated together, and mutual friends, take refuge in the same tree: one of them eats the sweet fig; the other, abstaining from food, merely looks on."[29] The ancient commentator Śāyana, explained that the two birds are the vital spirit and the Supreme Spirit. This interpretation is shared by Advaita Vedāntists, but the Viśiṣṭādvaita Vedānta philosophers tend to treat this passage as referring to a duality within the constitution of man. The tree is the human body. The bird that eats the fruit is the active self which enters fully into the experiences of physical life: eating, drinking, waking, sleeping, breeding, suffering, and dying. The bird that does not eat the fruit but merely watches the activity of the other bird is the passive self, the witnessing self (*sākṣin*). It refrains from entanglement in bodily acts. It contemplates the life of physical activity; it does not censure the active self, but when the active self compares its own helplessness with the quiet strength of the passive self it grieves and turns from its life of sorrow and bondage. This duality of the self appears in various forms in the *Upaniṣads*; for example, in the *Kaṭha Upaniṣad* the two are called *buddhi* (the intellect) and *ākāśa* (the heart as enjoyer): "Two there are who dwell within the body, in the *buddhi*, the supreme *ākāśa* of the heart, enjoying the sure rewards of their own actions."[30] Whenever the concept of duality of the self is introduced in the *Upaniṣads*, reference is made to a tension between the selves. The lower or active self is so closely related to the body that "Whatever body he takes to himself, with that he becomes connected."[31] It brings difference to all it touches; it is the doer of the deeds which must be carried out to their fruition. Thus it is the carrier of *karma*. But the higher or passive self is the self that points the way to liberation.

The problem of self-knowing has been concisely and metaphorically stated by the contemporary existentialist author Simone de Beauvoir in *The Mandarins*: "It's easy to say 'I am I.' But who am I? Where find myself? I would have to be on the other side of every door, but when it's I who knock the others grow silent."[32] To know the self the self must be on both sides of the same door, but—alas—when the self knocks on the knower side of the door there is no one on the other side to open the door, and when there is a self on the other side of the door to open there is no self on the knower side of the door to knock! So what should one do? Some say, "Stop knocking!" But that is the way of the beast. Some say, "Climb over the transom!" But that is the way of God. Others say, "Keep on knocking!" And that is the way of man.

Man tries in two ways to overcome the epistemological dichotomy which is inherent in self-knowing. One way is to confine his knowing to objects of the world of the non-self. This way is to turn from self-knowledge as introverted, unsocial, abnormal, even perverted—a kind of intellectual masturbation. "None of us really wants to observe or know ourselves," writes Otto Rank. "Such observation is not natural to us."[33] "I'm neither virgin nor priest enough to play with the inner life,"[34] says Antoine Roquentin, the hero of Sartre's *Nausea*. How much of the pursuit of research in the natural sciences is motivated by the effort to keep our attention off ourselves? Subjectivity is eliminated when objective interests take over. Psychology—the *term* still means study of the soul—becomes the study of human behavior that can be quantitatively measured, experimentally tested, and linguistically expressed. The self is left for poets, mystics, theologians, and others who are slightly out of touch with reality as defined by the sciences. The ontological imperialism of scientific methodologies is a pressing danger. It is one matter to hold that if something cannot be known by scientific methods it cannot be *known*, but it is quite another matter to hold that if something cannot be known by scientific methods it does not *exist*. Occasionally a voice is raised for the importance of self-knowing in the midst of an objectively-oriented civilization. For example, Peter Viereck wrote in 1958, "Today Americans have no outer or geographic frontier left to conquer. This pushes us, instead, to increasingly inward conquests. . . . Therefore, let us stop being defensive, stop being apologetic about affirming the dignity and importance of the so-called impractical: namely, the humanistic and the spiritual studies."[35] Since 1958 Americans have found a new frontier, the frontier of space. Once again the inward conquests can be postponed. John Wilkinson of the Center for the Study of Democratic Institutions of The Fund for the Republic has recently proposed that some parts of the world ought to be kept deliberately "backward" as a refuge for individuals concerned for the inner life who would accept plain living as a condition for high thinking. If we establish sanctuaries for condors and whooping cranes, why not establish sanctuaries for a breed of men in danger of extermination? Wilkinson cautions, "The big problem would be, sooner or later, how to fend off the ravages of administrators, speculators, politicians, and other quantitative folk."[36] These are the people about whom René Guénon warned us in 1945 in his book *Le règne de la quantité et les signes des temps*.[37]

The second effort to overcome the subject-object dichotomy is the way of the mystic. The scientist *avoids* the problem of self-knowing; the mystic *transcends* the problem by attempting a form of knowing in which the knower and known are merged into a unit. There is no disputing that there are experiences in which the agent feels a unity with the object of his awareness. But is this feeling a form of knowing? I doubt that much meaning is left in the concept "knowledge" when it is divided into two species: direct knowledge and indirect knowledge. All knowledge is indirect. Knowledge is a salute, not an embrace. It is a representation, a symbolization, a universalization, an analysis. In a sense, knowing is a form of falsifying; for reality is concrete, particular, specific, unanalyzed. Were a Zen master suddenly to throw a bucket of cold water in my face in order to nudge me to *satori*, I would find it an arresting, commanding experience, but I contend that to experience water in this fashion is not to *know* water. Water *known* is not water in the face, rather it is H_2O, or the universal solvent, or a substance that swells when it freezes, or the stuff said by Thales to be the first stuff of all things. If these seem to be dry facts rather than wet experience that is because knowledge is the propositional designation of facts.

The second reason for man's failure to know the self has to do with the ontological duality of the epistemological object. Perhaps this is not a second reason but another aspect of the same reason. The self-as-known cannot be disentangled from the self-as-knower. From the point of view of the ontological status of the known object this problem is: Is the self-as-object a discovery or a creation? Do I *find* myself, or do I *form* myself? Plotinus, one of the greatest of the Western philosophers of the self, criticized Plato for writing ambiguously on the nature of the self: "Lastly, we have the divine Plato who said many beautiful things about the soul. In his discussions he often speaks of the arrival of the soul in this world. But unfortunately he does not everywhere say the same thing and so does not enable one easily to know his intent."[38] But Plotinus himself does not speak without confusion about the self. In particular, the salvation to which he directs his philosophy means both extinction of the individual soul and also the fullest realization of the individual soul. The One is both "not all things . . . not Intelligence . . . (and) not Being,"[39] and also the One is "the principle which he (a man) possesses within himself."[40] When Plotinus is thinking in the context of the Limited, salvation is the loss of what one is, and when he is thinking in terms of the Unlimited, salvation is the fulfillment of what one is.

In the West we have sought to avoid making contradictory statements about the self by attempting to limit the known self to the status of either a discovery or a creation. We have sought to know the self as an object in the order of things. Descartes said it is "a real thing, and really existent."[41] We have also sought to avoid contradiction by denying thinghood altogether. The self, said Hume, is "a bundle or collection of different perceptions."[42] One of Hume's better analogies is that of the theater. The self is a kind of theater where "perceptions successively make their appearance: pass, repass, glide away, and mingle in an infinite variety of postures and situations."[43] Hume, knowing that the fate of analogies is to be pushed too far, added that the self is not the theater as building but only the theater as spectacle. Not a *thing*, we might add, but an ever-changing array of color and sound. For Descartes the self is a discovered thing; for Hume the self is a created spectacle. The former view over-objectifies; the latter over-subjectifies. The former betrays the Unlimited; the latter betrays the Limited. Again man attempts to make himself into beast or God. But the self is no mere thing, and the self is not Being. It is a thing-aspiring-Being. The self is always infinitely more than it would be if it were only what it is.

The Judaeo-Christian tradition is puzzling in this respect. Here man is condemned for his desire to become God. Yet if we are right in holding that the passion for divinity is the essence of man, then man in Judaeo-Christianity is condemned for being himself. Man must either cease to desire to become God, and thus cease to be man, or he must continue his divine aspiration, and then stand condemned by Judaeo-Christianity. But perhaps the Christian view is that by ceasing to become God, the Christian throws himself on the mercy of his God. He loses himself. But he that loses self will find self, whereas he who continues to desire to be God will in his effort to preserve self lose self. Aurobindo has expressed this same doctrine of grace in self-knowing: "A complete self-knowledge in all things and at all moments is the gift of the supernatural gnosis."[44] This affirmation of the impotence of man and the placing of man's salvation upon the grace of God may be good Semitic theocracy, Vaiṣṇava yoga, and Calvinistic soteriology, but twentieth-century Western man has difficulty squaring this view of the self with his democratic presuppositions of the importance of the individual and his educational theories of self-expression and self-development.

In India the conflict between self-as-discovery and self-as-creation may be avoided by the doctrine of *māyā*. From the Limited point of view the attainment of *mokṣa* is a creative achievement by which the finite self through proper techniques reaches an identity with the Supreme Reality. From the Unlimited point of view *mokṣa* is the removal of confining perspectives which prevent the self from an existential awareness of its true nature. *Mokṣa* from the second point of view is the transcendence of phenomenalism. The two interpretations do not conflict. Works and grace do not cancel each other out. A Hindu myth relates that a tiger cub once became lost from its mother and was adopted by a flock of sheep. It was reared as a sheep. One day a tiger attacked the flock, and upon seeing the timid cub bleating among the sheep, asked, "What do you think you are?" "I'm a sheep," replied the cub. The tiger took the cub to a pond of water and forced the cub to look into the water to compare reflections. Then the tiger forced the nose of the cub into the warm bloody carcass of a recently slain sheep. "Now what are you?" asked the tiger. "I'm a tiger," replied the cub.

Man becomes what he is. His is-ness is his becoming. He is a becoming, not a being. His being is becoming-ness. Because his is-ness is always in process, he never is with the finality of beast or God. He creatively discovers what he is, and he discovers creatively what he can become.

The theory that man is a becoming is subject to modifications in the Advaita philosophy. According to these Vedāntic philosophers the self-that-becomes is the self considered from the Limited point of view, whereas from the Unlimited point of view the self is Reality-becoming only in the sense of losing its *māyā*-ness. The self-as-*jīva* is the Self-as-*Ātman* seen under the conditions of time and space. Becoming is the phenomenal description of Being. From a transcendent or non-phenomenal point of view there is Being but no becoming. Man becomes the Absolute only in the sense that a "snake" becomes a rope when the "snake" is recognized as rope-mistaken-for-a-snake.

Sartre has expressed the created-discovered issue in this fashion: "The ego is always surpassed by what it produces, although from another point of view, it *is* what it produces. Hence the classic surprise: 'I, I could do that!'—'I, I could hate my father!'—Here, evidently, the concrete totality of the *me* intuited up to this time weights down the productive I and holds it back a little from what the I has just produced."[45] In *Nausea* Roquentin asks, "Is it I who is going to live this mushroom existence?"[46] Again, in his essay *The Transcendence of the Ego*, Sartre speaking of the ego as passive object and as created object says, "However irrational it may be, this union is nonetheless the union noted in our intuition of the ego. And this is its meaning: the ego is an object apprehended, but also an object *conditioned*, by reflective consciousness."[47]

The self-as-object is both a discovery and a creation. Man is his becoming; his becoming is what he is. He is ever in process. Jaspers says he is "that creature which poses problems beyond his powers." In the words of Nietzsche, man is "the animal that is not yet established." I'd add, he is the animal that is never established. Buber holds that man can be defined only in terms of his relation to all beings. These relations, says Buber, are his relations to the world of things, his relations to the world of individuals, and his relations to the world of Being—call it Absolute or God. Buber speculates that there might be a fourth relation—a very special relation, i.e., man's relation to his self. But Buber withdraws from this possibility because, as he says, this relation cannot be completed nor perfected. But perfectionism has nothing to do with the nature of man. Wisely the Christian churches have seldom taken literally the admonition "Be ye therefore perfect, even as your Father which is in heaven is perfect." "Man is neither an angel nor a beast," wrote Pascal, "and it is his misfortune that he who seeks to play the role of the angels acts most like a beast."[48] Man is a great promise—a promise forever unfilled, but great in the complete persistence of his incompleteness whether expressed in St. Paul's "I press toward the mark for the prize of the high calling of God in Christ Jesus,"[49] or in Beckett's "I don't know, I'll never know, in the silence you don't know, you must go on, I can't go on, I can't go on, I'll go on."[50]

NOTES

1. Ernst Cassirer, *An Essay on Man*. Garden City, N.Y.: Doubleday and Co., 1944, pp. 18, 241, 16.
2. Charles I. Glicksberg, *The Self in Modern Literature*. University Park, Pennsylvania: The Pennsylvania State University Press, 1963, p. 50.
3. Lao-tzu, *Tao-Te-King*, xxxiii. Translated by Lin Yutang.
4. Bhagavan Śrī Rāmana Maharshi, *Who Am I?* Tiruvannamalai, India: Śrī Rāmanāsramam, 1955, p. 36.
5. Heraclitus, *On Nature*, Fragment 101. G. S. Kirk and J. E. Raven translation.
6. Augustine, *De vera religione*, XXIX, 72.
7. Kierkegaard, *Journals*, 22.
8. Susanne Langer, *Philosophy in a New Key*. New York: The New American Library of World Literature, 1948, p. 100.
9. Lewis Carroll, *Alice's Adventures in Wonderland*, ch. ii.
10. George Arthur Wilson, *The Self and Its World*. New York: The Macmillan Co., 1926, p. 275.
11. Rāmana Maharshi, *op. cit.*, p. 34.
12. *Immanuel Kant's Critique of Pure Reason*. Translated by Norman Kemp Smith. London: The Macmillan Co., 1950, Preface to First Edition, A XI, p. 9.
13. Jean-Paul Sartre, *Being and Nothingness*. Translated by Hazel G. Barnes. New York: The Philosophical Library, 1956, p. 615.
14. *Soliloquies*, Book I, Sec. 7. C. C. Starbuck translation.
15. *The City of God*, XI, 26.
16. *Sermon* XLIII, iii, 4; vii, 9.

17. *On the Free Will*, II, 6.
18. *Confessions*, X, 33.
19. David Hume, *A Treatise of Human Nature*, Vol. I. London: J. M. Dent and Sons, 1939, pp. 238-239.
20. *Ibid.*, Vol. II, pp. 317, 319.
21. Eugene Ionesco, *Four Plays*. Translated by Donald M. Allen. New York: Grove Press, 1958, pp. 39-40.
22. *Ibid.*, p. 19.
23. Ludwig Wittgenstein, *Tractatus Logico-Philosophicus*. New York: Harcourt, Brace and Co., 1933, p. 189.
24. John Macmurray, *The Form of the Personal*. New York: Harper and Brothers, 1957.
25. Pierre Teilhard de Chardin, *The Future of Man*. Translated by Norman Denny. New York and Evanston: Harper and Row, 1964, p. 158.
26. *Ibid.*, p. 16.
27. Hannah Arendt, *The Human Condition*. Garden City, N.Y.: Doubleday and Co., 1959, p. 12.
28. *The Thoughts*, 66.
29. *RV* 1. 22. 8. 20; *MU* 3. 1. 1; *SU* 4. 6. The form given is from H. H. Wilson's translation of the *Ṛg Veda*.
30. *Kaṭha Upaniṣad* 1. 3. 1. *Swāmi* Nikhilananda translation.
31. *Śvetāśvatara Upaniṣad* 5. 10. Robert Ernest Hume translation.
32. Simone de Beauvoir, *The Mandarins*. Translated by Leonard M. Friedman. Cleveland and New York: The World Publishing Co., 1960, p. 43.
33. Otto Rank, *Psychology and the Soul*. Translated by William D. Turner. New York: A. S. Barnes and Co., 1950, p. 6.
34. Jean-Paul Sartre, *Nausea*. Translated by Lloyd Alexander. Norfolk, Conn.: New Directions Books, 1959, p. 18.
35. Peter Viereck, "The Unadjusted Man," *Saturday Review*, Nov. 1, 1958, p. 13.
36. John Wilkinson, "The Quantitative Society, or What Are You to Do with Noodle?" An Occasional Paper on the Role of Technology in the Free Society. The Center for the Study of Democratic Institutions, 1964, p. 7.
37. Paris: Gallimard, 1945.
38. *Enneads* IV. 8. 1. Joseph Katz translation.
39. *Enneads* VI. 9. 2. Joseph Katz translation.
40. *Enneads* VI. 9. 3. Joseph Katz translation.
41. Descartes, *Meditations*. Translated by A. D. Lindsay. London: J. M. Dent and Sons, 1937, p. 88.
42. David Hume, *op. cit.*, p. 239.
43. *Ibid.*, pp. 239-240.
44. Aurobindo, *The Life Divine*. New York: The Greystone Press, 1949, p. 864.
45. Jean-Paul Sartre, *The Transcendence of the Ego*. Translated by Forrest Williams and Robert Kirkpatrick. New York: The Noonday Press, 1957, p. 80.
46. Jean-Paul Sartre, *Nausea*, p. 231.
47. Jean-Paul Sartre, *The Transcendence of the Ego*, pp. 80-81.
48. *The Thoughts*, 358.
49. Philippians 3:14. King James translation.
50. Samuel Beckett, *The Unnamable*. New York: Grove Press, 1958, p. 179.

—6—

*THE INDIVIDUAL IN EAST-WEST DISCUSSIONS**

The theme of the Fourth East-West Philosophers' Conference held during the summer of 1964 at the University of Hawaii was "The status of the individual in reality, thought, and culture in the East and West." One hundred and twenty-five philosophers met for six weeks discussing this topic without ever defining the term "individual"! The director of the conference on many occasions reminded the members of the theme. "What does this have to do with the status of the individual?" he asked. "How can we discuss the status of the individual when we do not know what we are talking about?" others asked. Yet no definition of the individual emerged. In the words of Confucius, the rectification of terms ought to be first on the agenda.

The Eastern philosophers at the conference thought the individual being discussed was the Jeffersonian individual, and further that this conception was being forced upon them. The efforts of the Indians and the Japanese to prove that the concept of the Jeffersonian was an essential element of their philosophies fostered among the Westerners emotions ranging from amusement to exasperation. Even though various members of the conference pointed out that the role of the individual in Western cultures is not fixed, that we in the West are bothered about the status of the individual, the Eastern

* Adapted from an article entitled "What is an Individual?" which was published in *International Philosophical Quarterly*, Vol. V, No. 4 (December, 1965), pp. 666-676. Reprinted by kind permission of the editor.

philosophers seemed to believe that this was play-acting. The Eastern philosophers did not grasp the profound dissatisfaction of the West with its own theory and practice of individualism. Books such as *The Lonely Crowd*, *The Organization Man*, *The Unadjusted Man*, and *Individualism Reconsidered* should have been required pre-conference reading for all Eastern members. Somehow the individual was never defined, and in the absence of a definition the discussions often failed to come to grips with questions which puzzle Westerners: Will India develop a democracy that encourages individual initiative? Can Confucian humanitarian ideals ever again pervade the Chinese mainland? Is Japanese democracy a thin veneer over Emperor worship? What is the future of the Judaeo-Christian conception of the worth of the individual in the impersonal life of European and American cities?

In view of the failure of the conference to define its theme, I offer as a framework for future discussions of the status of the individual in the East and West the following nine "individualisms."

1. *The Atomic Individual.* This is the unitary indivisible being. The atomic individual, as the Greek radical implies, is that which cannot be divided into more elementary units. It is the mathematical unit from which by addition all whole numbers are formed. In pluralistic cultures it is the person counted as one in statistical tables. Each one is like every other one in respect to his oneness, but each does not depend on the others for his being or nature. Each is universal unto himself, and, as an atom, cannot be classified or compared. St. Thomas' angels are perhaps the clearest example of the atomic individuals in a pluralistic society: each angel is a separate species. In monistic cultures, on the other hand, the atom is the Great Atom. The atomic individual is not ones, but the One, the Whole, the Totality. The ones are illusory. The One is real. The One may be The State, or The Blood, or The Absolute. Parmenides in the ancient Greek world, Śaṅkara in eighth century India, and Tillich in contemporary Protestantism have attempted to create systems in which the atomic individual is the All. Parmenides called it Being; Śaṅkara, Nirguṇa Brahman; and Tillich, the Ground of Being. Somewhere between the pluralists with their many ones and the monists with their One lie the efforts of men and societies to create familial units of social action: the joint families, the castes, the cults,

the clans, the communes, the cooperatives, and the unions. These are the atomic units which stress the indivisibility of the group in its oneness. Other examples are the churches, the political parties, and the fraternities whose leaders brainwash the members, ostensibly to create the spirit of the group but in fact consciously or unconsciously to cement the members into a oneness which transcends the wills of the members, and finally eliminates the ability of the members to protest.

2. *The Logical Individual.* In logical systems the individual is contrasted with the universal. The logical individual is often designated by the words "There is at least one" which distinguishes the existential interpretation of universal statements from the hypothetical interpretation: "All Xs—and there is at least one X—are Ys" and "All Xs—but we do not know there is an X—are Ys." The logical individual is the individual translated from logical symbols to common English in the modern Western logician's view of the Aristotelian particular statement, "Some Xs are Ys" as "At least one X, and maybe all Xs, are Ys." Furthermore, the logical individual may be either the individual as included in a class so that what is true of the class is true for the individuals making up the class, e.g., All dogs are mammals, and Fido is a dog, so Fido is a mammal; or the logical individual may be the individual as a member of a class so that what is true of the class is not necessarily true of the member, e.g., Dogs (as a class) are becoming more vicious, and Fido is a dog—but the increasing viciousness of Fido cannot be logically inferred. The logical individual need not be an existent individual.

The unit in logical discourse may have no reality outside the discourse itself. Non-existing three-eyed dogs appealed to in the factually false statement "Some three-eyed dogs are mammals" are logical individuals as much as are the dogs appealed to in the factually true statement "Some dogs are collies." Logical individuals mentioned within the framework of logical discourse need not have reality within time or space.

3. *The Epistemological Individual.* This is the knower in the knowing relationship. It is the subject in the experiences of believing, opining, perceiving, conceiving, etc. It is the "I" in all expressions of cognition beginning with some form of "I know . . ." Differing views as to the nature of the epistemological relationship

separate philosophers into a significant classification: the realists, who affirm that the object of knowledge is existentially independent of the knowing relationship, and the idealists, who affirm the dependence of the object upon the relationship. Stating the epistemological situation from the point of view of the knowing subject rather than of the object brings out another facet of the usefulness of this concept of the individual, particularly in intercultural studies. "Does the knowing subject retain its independent status in the act of knowing?" is a question which separates mystics and non-mystics. Mystics claim that the subject-object dichotomy vanishes in the highest and best form of knowing. To know plant, animal, or God is to become plant, animal, or God. But non-mystics of all shades deny the subject-object epistemological integration, contending that knowing is always the knowing *of* something. To "identify" with an object may create sympathetic values but not knowledge, say the non-mystics. Even in self-knowledge the object known, the "me," is not identical with the knower, the "I." For the non-mystic knowing is a form of falsifying—a transposing of living experiences into static words and sentences. If man is to know, he must transmogrify his solipsistic sensations into intersubjective symbols. Expression may murder the immediacy of the experience, but not to communicate symbolically is to settle for a world of windowless monads. Whereas Zenists and Bergsonians regard immediate sensations as the highest, the purest, the absolute form of knowledge, non-mystics of all persuasions hold that without the Word knowledge is impossible.

4. *The Psychological Individual.* This is the person distinguished from other persons by such factors as sex, color of skin, texture of hair, shape of head, weight, height, dispositional tendencies, intelligence, attitudes, personal values, commitments, etc. Psychological individuality is the individuality of difference; the more people are alike the less their individuality, and the more they differ the greater their individuality. The advice, "Be an individual! Be yourself!" is the recommendation to assert one's psychological individuality. In some cultures and times differences are prized; but in other cultures and times differences are not only disvalued but also believed to be illusory. Secure nations prize the individuality of their citizens; insecure nations fear the individuality of their citizens. Young people of most societies demand the right to differ but often

refrain from exercising the right once they have it. It is easier to demand the right of psychological individuality than to exercise the right. Kierkegaard, one of the rare men of all times, asked that the epitaph on his tomb be "That single one." Few men have struggled as hard as he against the conforming forces of social organizations, and few paid a higher price for non-conformity. Most of the "individuals" of history made face-saving, and sometimes life-saving, concessions to the group. Psychological individualism is sometimes referred to as rugged individualism, possibly because only the exceptionally courageous can achieve it in its fullest form. For the person who has developed his psychological individuality, social relationships are largely external to his being. The physiological aspects of psychological individualism are fixed by nature, but the psychological *per se* admit of a wide variety of modification. Mankind has not exhausted the possibilities of individual differences; the varieties of psychological individualism have not even been dreamed of.

5. *The Egalitarian Individual.* Whereas psychological individualism is based on the differences of persons, egalitarian individualism is based on the sameness of persons. Egalitarian individuals are alike. Each person is a unit of society, and each unit is like every other unit—no more and no less. Each counts as one: one before the law, one in the census, one in a military draft, one at the voting poll. Unfortunately, the concept of egalitarian individualism is often confusedly understood. Those who would ridicule "All men are created equal" by appeal to the obvious differences of persons fail to distinguish egalitarian individualism and psychological individualism. "In a democracy all men are created equal—and some are more equal than others" commits the same error. The notion of egalitarian individualism is inherent in Western democratic theory, regardless of what was in the mind of Jefferson when he coined the fine phrases of the Declaration of Independence. Where the notion of egalitarian individualism is not found, a double standard of justice develops. The relationship of lord and serf in feudal societies is a case in point. But more chronologically immediate is the problem of race relations in our world. The problem can be clearly stated in terms of psychological and egalitarian individualism: Should the members of the racially different minority groups be given the rights and privileges of egalitarian individualism before they have

achieved a desirable level of psychological individualism, or should the level of psychological individualism first be raised and then egalitarian individualism be conferred? The issue is often unclearly stated as "revolution or gradualism?" Some nations are today in the unhappy situation of *de jure* egalitarian individualism and *de facto* non-egalitarian individualism. To withhold civil rights from a people until they demonstrate civil responsibility is to demand a performance while withholding the means of the performance. Can one learn to swim without entering the water?

6. *The Soteriological Individual.* Religions claim to offer and to confer upon the person what is usually called salvation. Other terms for this desirable state are liberation, integration, wholeness, redemption, *nirvāṇa*, etc. The means may be either some form of personal effort or some form of unearned merit. The entity that is to experience this state is the soteriological individual. Whether this individual is more precisely identified as soul, spirit, self, psyche, *jīva*, *ātman*, *anātman*, or *jīvātman* is important, but more important is the belief that within the context of a religion this individual is the essential person. Gnostic religions contend that the soteriological individual is separate and separated from the corporeal body. Some of the non-gnostic religions hold that the soteriological individual includes the body in all its physicalness; and others attempt a compromise by distinguishing a physical body and a spiritual body—only the latter participating in the salvation. This recipient of salvation may be the breath of the living God, an immortal spirit, a spark of the divine, a phenomenal image of the Absolute, a ghostly presence, or a temporary collation of behavioristic tendencies. Christians have probably engaged in more religious imperialism in assuming the universal existence of a soul that is a potential candidate for Christian salvation than they have in their tendency to read the spiritual quest of other peoples as a quest for the Judaeo-Christian God who "left not himself without witness." But what this individual is within a religion must be determined only by a careful study of that religion within its cultural context. One observation can be made with certainty: the object of salvation is ultimately an individual however metaphysically conceived.

7. *The Humanitarian Individual.* Closely related to the individual as the object of religious salvation is the individual as the object

of enrichment through social institutions. This is the individual for whom the Sabbath was made according to the New Testament, the person to whom Social Security, welfare work, and even labor unions direct their benefactions. This is the citizen whose well-being is abetted in social legislation, whose education is the concern of the school, whose good is the goal of all eleemosynary activities. In democracies this individual is both determiner and receiver of political and economic benefits; in other forms of political and social life this individual may receive but not determine benefits. But in all political, economic, and social systems this is the individual whose welfare is the ultimate justification of the state. The humanitarian individual in different cultures and at different times is selected on the basis of such factors as sex, age, race, religion, heredity, economic status, land ownership, etc. Universal humanitarian individualism is an ideal yet to be realized.

8. *The Humanistic Individual.* The humanistic individual is the person as creator. He determines human culture through art, science, and religion. He is the active agent in human values. This individual is best exemplified in the lives of musicians, sculptors, painters, architects, scientists, poets, philosophers, and prophets who have added to the collective art, literature, technology, and wisdom of mankind. Most of these individuals have been forced to develop only one aspect of their natures and to leave undeveloped many other aspects. For each man of developed talents, such as da Vinci, Goethe, and Schweitzer, there have been a thousand who attained greatness at the cost of wholeness. Most potential musician-scientists or scientist-musicians have been obliged to neglect one talent in order to advance the other. The expected span of human life does not allow time for persons of many talents to develop all their talents. Hence, there is the musician who does not understand science, and the scientist with the undeveloped musical ear. With the increase of human knowledge the problem of knowing a little about a lot and a lot about a little will become crucial. The well-rounded individual—the Renaissance man—will become a rarity and finally an impossibility.

One implication of the humanistic individual is that educators need to make more allowances for the superior student. Some educators should be reminded of Descartes' teachers who allowed the young man to lie in bed in the morning when they found that he did his best mathematical thinking under these conditions. Those who have argued for a general education for every student must re-examine this demand. How much has been lost in forcing young geniuses to complete courses designed to foster the so-called "spread" in learning and interest. The humanistic individual—the creative person—needs the freedom to differ. Societies have much to learn about the importance of tolerance for these who are persons at their best. Pages of human history are marked by the graves, stakes, and crosses of humanistic individuals who have been denied their right to be individuals.

9. *The Libertarian Individual.* This individual has been anticipated in many of the other forms of individuality. This is the individual as self-determiner of action, and hence as one who can be held accountable. There are two sub-classes of the libertarian individual. One is the individual who is free to choose, i.e., the person who has the power or ability to choose and to act. This presupposes a certain degree of health, sanity, and intelligence. The paralyzed person cannot move his arm, the idiot cannot make change, and the illiterate cannot read a book. The second is the individual who is free from restraints. A society can deprive an otherwise free individual of his freedom by placing curbs on his free activity. Every society must restrain the individual in the interest of the whole. The completely free individual is neither an ideal nor a possibility. Yet how far and what kind of restraints are necessary for the public good is a matter upon which societies do not agree. The degrees and kinds of "free from" and "free to" are the chief problems of the relation of person and society. Intercultural conversations on these problems are crucial now that the role of the individual in society must be determined internationally rather than merely nationally.

—7—

THE AGE OF HOMINIZATION

The New American Library published during the 1950's a series of six brief anthologies entitled "The Mentor Philosophers." The series covered Western thought since the Middle Ages, largely by centuries. The volume on the Middle Ages was called *The Age of Belief.* The volume on the Renaissance was *The Age of Adventure.* The seventeenth century was *The Age of Reason*, the eighteenth *The Age of Enlightenment*, the nineteenth *The Age of Ideology*, and the twentieth *The Age of Analysis.* Of course it is presumptuous to summarize the thinking of a century in a single word. As we come to the closing decades of the twentieth century many would like to hope that we have accomplished more in these hundred years than analysis. A whole century of examining assumptions, methodologies, and arguments! Yet if asked to name the greatest achievement of our century, I should affirm that it is analysis, although I'd want to add that it is a *quantitative* analysis: we have discovered that we are one. This is the century in which we've found the world. It is the century of world wars and world peaces, of the first attempts to unite the nations in world courts and world leagues, of world travel and space travel, of recognition of world poverty and world overpopulation, of world health and world pollution, of world fairs and world Olympic contests, of world congresses of philosophy and world scientific research. We have made a great discovery: that which concerns any man anywhere concerns everyman everywhere. For example, nuclear testing in the heart of China affects the milk delivered at my doorstep in Ohio—and nuclear testing at the West Sands Testing Grounds in

New Mexico increases the radioactivity of the milk delivered in China. A curious benefit of the discovery of atomic fission, I have been told, is that our bodies will soon carry so much radioactivity that human flesh will be dangerous, even fatal, to other human beings. Cannibalism will then be impossible!

If the publishing house known as The New American Library is still functioning one hundred years from now, and if its editors wish to add a seventh volume to the series "The Mentor Philosophers," what will be its title? *The Age of* . . . what? Some Jeremiahs seem to think it might be *The Age of Extinction*; and I suppose there are a few Panglosses who think it will be *The Age of Utopia*. I submit, however, that it will be a second age of analysis. The twentieth century is an age of quantitative analysis; the twenty-first will be an age of qualitative analysis. Perhaps I ought not to say will be, but must be. In the twentieth century we are finding oneness; in the twenty-first we must find the nature of that oneness. Man must accomplish the simple, yet profound, awareness that the oneness is himself. An old Indian tale illuminates my meaning. Ten travelers once crossed a raging stream. After regrouping on the shore, they counted to determine if all had safely gotten across. But each traveler counted only nine. Their mourning for the drowned member of their party terminated when a passing stranger observed that each had forgotten to count himself. Man is the foolish traveler who has failed to count himself. The twenty-first century must be the age in which man discovers himself. I say "must" because I maintain there may not be a twenty-second if man does not shortly come to the realization that genocide of the human race will be the unplanned result of his failure to limit human population, to eliminate war as a method of settling national disputes, and to stop the pollution of earth, water, and air. So I submit as a title for the anthology on the twenty-first century *The Age of Qualitative Analysis*—or better, *The Age of Hominization*—the century in which the human race at last knows that man is the determiner of his destiny, the telos of his world, and the realizer of reality.

I can conceive of a certain type of person who would reject my alarmist observations about the future. If he is a Western man he might say, "The future will be much like the past. There is nothing really new under the sun." If he is a Hindu, he might mention that all knowledge and all technology have been anticipated in Vedic literature. And if he is a pious man, either Western or Indian, he might solve all issues with the mantra, "God is good." That in fact was the *deus ex machina* which I heard a devout Indian offer in a discussion sponsored by the United Nations at Ootacamund several years ago. Not only can I conceive of a person having such a reaction, but I can also empathize with this person, for I was like that in my younger more conservative years. But now that I am older and more radical I am in full agreement with Alfred North Whitehead when he said, "Our sociological theories, our political philosophy, our practical maxims of business, our political economy, and our doctrines of education, are derived from an unbroken tradition of great thinkers and of practical examples, from the age of Plato in the fifth century before Christ to the end of the last century. The whole of this tradition is warped by the vicious assumption that each generation will substantially live amid the conditions governing the lives of its fathers and will transmit those conditions to mould with equal force the lives of its children. We are living in the first period of human history for which this assumption is false."[1] I offer one emendation to Whitehead's observations: what he says about the falsity of the assumption of the contiguity of the generations is true for all modern peoples and for all peoples pressing into modernity. Perhaps it was Gandhi's horror of this state of affairs which prompted him to oppose the industrialization of India. I suggest, on the other hand, that this break with the past and future gives man the opportunity to live in the eternal present. It was such a life that Kālidāsa expressed in his lovely poem "Look to this Day."

> Look to this day!
> For it is life, the very breath of life.
> In its brief course lie all the varieties and realities
> of your existence:
> The bliss of growth;
> The glory of action;
> The splendor of beauty.
> For yesterday is already a dream, and tomorrow
> is only a vision.
> But today, well lived, makes every yesterday
> A dream of happiness, and every tomorrow a vision of hope.
> Look well, therefore, to this day.

We in the West sometimes jokingly refer to the Who-Who bird, the bird which flies backwards thinking that by seeing where it has been it will know where to go. How much of our formal education is Who-Who education! How often we are told to study history so we can understand the future. That cliché will not work any longer. We have entered upon an age of reconstruction in religion, in science, and in political thought. Both Dewey and Whitehead said this fifty years ago, but when we read these great philosophers of the first half of the twentieth century we have the strange feeling that they, like Moses, saw into the promised land but could not enter. They foresaw the need for fundamental change, and they themselves were prepared to change, but the nature of the change was beyond even their vision. My purpose is, if possible, to suggest what will be the center of that great change, and I have already suggested that it will be the discovery of the identity of the one which we have analyzed as one in the twentieth century.

The twenty-first century, I have said, must be the age of hominization. Now let us be specific about the concept of hominization. The term, to the best of my knowledge, was first coined by Pierre Teilhard de Chardin in his book, *The Phenomenon of Man*. Teilhard uses it as equivalent to spiritualization, but I depart completely from Teilhard's usage. The term comes from the Latin *homo*, *hominis*, which designates generic man, i.e., mankind, as distinguished from *vir*, which designates a particular man. It appears in such words as hominoid, hominiform, hominity, and hominivorous. The term does not appear in dictionaries I have consulted, but I think we can see that it is a proper extension of *homo*, *hominis*. When I refer to *The Age of Hominization* as an appropriate title for a volume dealing with the next century, I refer to the hominization of the universe itself, the interpretation of the universe in terms of generic man. Hominization, as I use the term, means

> *First*, that man—*homo*—is the culmination, consummation, apex, summit, of the cosmic evolutionary process.
>
> *Second*, that a new mode of evolutionary process begins with man, a mode in which man is involved as evolver.
>
> *Third*, that man can and must direct the evolutionary process toward the realization of his own highest values.

Hominization is strikingly consistent with the Sāṁkhya *darśana*, the oldest native philosophy of India, the philosophy which set the fundamental metaphysical problems for the later schools. According to the Sāṁkhya man is a product of the same modes of operations which produced the entire physical universe. His mind and body are the unfolding of the potentialities of *prakṛti*, the basic uncreated stuff from which all has evolved. Even his consciousness is an evolvent. In man *sat* has become *chit*, and because of this evolvement, all further evolution involves the functioning of an integrated *sat* and *chit*. *Chit* is telic in the sense that it can see, plan, and direct the continuing evolutionary activity. To be it must be purposive, and its purposes must be the attainment of the value (the *ānanda*) inherent in the line of operation by which *sat* became *satchit* with the ultimate goal of a fully creative integration, a *satchitānanda*.

The cosmos has evolved a self-aware being, an instrument of conscious value creation. Man is the cosmos creating. He is the cosmos consciously evolving new levels even as the cosmos has unconsciously evolved him. In him the cosmos has attained self-consciousness, and through him the cosmos may emerge into an age of hominization. Man must take on his own evolution and the evolution of all beings. He must become his own evolver. Man is the first emergent of a hominized universe. He is the growing edge of that universe. The paths of hominization do not lie clearly ahead, but the path of non-hominization is clear: it is the way of pluralization, of atomization, of total death. The energy which has brought life and consciousness into being can also bring death and unconsciousness. There is a future for the cosmic self-consciousness only if that cosmic self-consciousness realizes who he is, and if he now takes on consciously what the cosmos has heretofore done non-consciously. He must direct the nisus which brought him into being. His future, his survival, is in his hands. The universe must become hominized, and the twenty-first century may be either the century of hominization or the last century for the being who could have accomplished that hominization.

Man at the primitive level of his environment was a dualist. He placed himself against an external world and a transcendent being. As Arthur O. Lovejoy has argued in *The Revolt Against Dualism*, there is a natural and normal genesis for dualisms epistemological and psychological, and I would add, metaphysical or theological. In the epistemological dualistic syndrome men form certain preconceptions as to what an object of thought ought to be, and then, upon comparing the characteristics of the thing presented in their experience with their preconceptions, find that the two do not match. Hence there arises an almost universal faith that we live in the midst of realities which are not ourselves. These are the realities we can touch, taste, smell, hear, and see. They pass into and out of our experience. They maintain an existence of their own, independent of us and our awareness or non-awareness of them. Because of their fixed characteristics they are the public facts to which we refer in our intersubjective verifications. Of course we cannot experience them unexperienced, but our firm faith is that they maintain their identity when unperceived. They do not depend upon us. They are *sui generis*. The second dualism inherent in our unsophisticated experience is the psychophysical. We form some notions of what characteristics existent objects ought to possess were they parts of the physical world, and then discover that parts of the content of our experience do not satisfy the specifications. Or was it the other way around—did men first discover the inner world of dreams, imagination, thoughts, and feelings? Whichever came first, primitive man believed he lived in a world of doubles: the self that went forth by day hunting and gathering food and the self that went forth by night hunting ghostly animals and fighting ghostly enemies. Each man, each tree, each animal was thought to be two, one seen and one unseen. The third dualism is the metaphysical. Perhaps the unseen world of doubles was reified into a transcendent reality. Perhaps it was an expression of men's feelings of finitude, dependence, and helplessness. Imperfection required perfection, finite demanded infinite, temporality suggested eternity, the part needed the whole. Thus came the gods into the minds of men. Longings for unity remained, and the nature that longing took is one of the clues in distinguishing the East and the West. In the West man has sought unity as the harmonization of real dualities: matter and spirit, body and mind, earth and heaven, time and eternity, man and God. Augustine's great book, *The City of God*, is the classic expression of this view. Conflict between the City of God and the City of Man is the theme of history, a conflict which can be resolved only by the total victory of the City of

God and the total destruction of the City of Man. Christianity in the West today is experiencing a crisis in the symbol structure which it inherited from Augustine. One of the signs of the crisis is the appearance of a type of theology known as the Death of God theology. This theology is a symptom of the disease; it is not a cure, although it may point the direction in which healing can take place. That direction is the human. For example, Harvey Cox, although not a Death of God theologian, acknowledges his own debt to the movement: "My own response to the dead-end signaled by the 'death of God' mood is to continue to move away from any spatial symbolization of God and from all forms of metaphysical dualism. I am trying to edge cautiously toward a secular theology, a mode of thinking whose horizon is human history and whose idiom is 'political' in the widest Aristotelian sense of that term, i.e., the context in which man becomes truly man."[2] In the East man has sought unity by attempting to find the oneness which lies behind the twoness; in other words, the duality is a phenomenal manifesting of a noumenal one. This one is Tao, or Chi, or Adi Buddha, or Śūnyata, or Nirguṇa Brahman.

Primitive man lived in a world of doubles, but as he became sophisticated he attempted to overcome his dualities, he revolted against dualism. One of the first steps in his liberation from duality was inherent in his conception of gods. A god supposedly eliminated certain mysteries, overcame some dualities, offered a few consolations, and established harmonies. But the god-human dichotomy has never been complete. Primitive man was anthropomorphic in his speculation about gods. He animated the inanimate, psychologized the physical, spiritualized the material, and humanized the divine. The scientific man has converted three of the above: he has inanimated the animate, physicalized the psychological, and materialized the spiritual. Both primitive man and scientific man are reductionists; the former reduces to psychical terms, the latter to physical terms. But both agree in humanizing the divine; both would make God human. But they do not agree as to the manner in which the divine is to be humanized. Whereas primitive man humanizes God by making God a superman with human emotions, volitions, thoughts, and even appearances, modern scientific man, finding no God up, out, or beyond, is making the amazing discovery that the absolute values, the efficient causes, and the telic factors which have been attributed to transcendent entities are immanent in the cosmic self-consciousness which is himself. Religious reality which formerly was defined in terms of gods must be defined in terms of human attitudes and responses. The divine is the human realized. Our myths of *avatāras* and divine incarnations are symbolically correct, but we miss their thrusts. They are ascents, not descents. They are prophetic of the *sarvamukti* (universal salvation), that eschatological state when shall be realized the Hebrew vision "Ye are gods and all of you sons of the Most High" (Psalm 82:6), the Christian "Ye therefore shall be perfect, as your heavenly Father is perfect" (Matt. 5: 48), and the Upaniṣadic "*Tat tvam asi.*"

Man is the being who has become the conscious creator of values. The process of hominization is to discover that the power to become, to become aware, and to become the determiner of values is within. Man is that power. In his earlier days man assigned that power to gods above, below, and within. Now he realizes his error of mislocation, and he discovers with awesome ecstasy that the power is himself. His religions are shifting from the role of protector of inherited ways of acting and thinking to the role of innovator in new ways. Priests are once again giving way to prophets. Theologians are trying to think "the unthinkable thoughts" and to dream "the impossible dreams." Some religious leaders are trying to be the *avant-garde* of social action, and some wonder if religious organizations can be the vanguard of change. Can temple, mosque, synagogue, and church become the centers of intellectual, social, and moral revolutions? Can priest, rabbi, and *swāmi* be innovators of the new day? Can that which has been the opium become the catalyst? Or will the new wine break the old wine skins?

Let us now pass from the institutions of possible hominization to another fundamental question: Is the world teleological? Is there a direction of cosmic evolution and of organic evolution? To ask "Is nature teleological?" is not to ask if nature has purposes. Rather it is to ask questions like these: Does nature act in such a manner that from our point of view it is purposive? Are there ends of natural events so that if nature were psychic, as we are psychic, nature would be said to be a kingdom of ends? The question is almost anathema to scientists. One reason for their opposition, I believe, is they forget that they themselves are natural and teleological. As Whitehead has said, "Scientists animated by the purpose of proving they are purposeless constitute an interesting subject for study."[3] We do not need to go into the theories of teleology. All that is needed for our purposes here is to recognize that the universe is such that this solar system has come into being with the planet earth on which life, mind, and consciousness have appeared. The cosmos is like that. The self-knowing animal has evolved. Hypotheses of factors accounting for his appearance ranging from his special creation at the hands of a god to a chance meeting of wandering atoms do not alter the fact of what has happened. Man is! He has come into existence. The processes which evolved him cannot be the same again, because as long as man as self-knower continues he is part of the evolving. Whether the forces operating before the arrival of man were divine or natural, at least they operated to produce man. Now this creature of evolvement is part of the continued evolution. The direction and the tempo are partly in his control. Power is not snatched from the divine, rather man has become the divine in that he now, whether he wishes it or not, is on the board of directors. His vote counts—and counts heavily—in determining the future. His is the anxiety resulting from foreknowledge. If genocide by means of human warfare, or by disruptions of ecology, or by pollution of his natural environment comes about, to this is added the horrors of the knowledge that he is the doer. Man is the being who can commit suicide, and also the being who can anticipate his own suicide. He is the two birds in the tree—both the eater of the sweet fruit and the watcher of the eating.

The universe has evolved solar systems, solar systems have evolved planets, at least one planet has produced life, and one form of life has evolved self-consciousness. The processes by which man has risen may be correctly viewed as a battle. Bergson regarded the lines of evolution as a conflict between intellect and instinct. Loren Eisley has suggested this conflict in a humorous essay "The Squirrels are Watching You" in which he argues that the squirrels are waiting for man to make a fatal mistake so they can take over. There is little reason for sentimentalizing on the harmony of the manifold forms of life. Instead, as Darwin saw, conflict is the principle of evolution. Conflict will continue to be the principle.

Hominization requires that plants and lower animals be subordinate and ancillary to man and man's own evolution. The doctrine of *jīvas* ought not to be interpreted to imply that plants and lower animals are undeveloped men. They are on a different line. It is we who have become self-conscious. That does not give us the right to abuse animals—Jainism and societies for preventing cruelty to dumb animals are correct in demanding humane treatment of these creatures—but this does not mean that we regard them as self-aware beings. Their good is the promotion of human good. Hominization means that all values come into focus in human values. The ultimate test of good is the degree to which processes and substances enhance the nisus which has brought man into being. To say they have lost out to man in the race to mind, consciousness, and value assumes unwarrentedly that hominization is the only way in which the universe might have evolved its meaningfulness. Instead we need to recognize that the way things are is the way they have become. We must tell it as it is and accord our lives and our thoughts to the nature of things. Man has evolved. His evolution may have been the work of an evil demiurge, or of a benevolent deity, or of chance actions of natural forces; but the important fact is that he has evolved. A self-aware being has appeared, and it can and must take over the lines of evolution which brought itself into being. He who is the universe evolved must now become the universe evolving. The direction and the tempo are now in his hands. Life or death, heaven or hell, immortality or genocide, beauty or ugliness, order or chaos—these are his choices. That which he formerly thought was on the knees of the gods is now in his own lap. Glorious opportunity or hideous responsibility! The determiner of destiny is he. There is no fate, but there is a fateful task before man. This task cannot be avoided, for in this case surely not to act is to act.

In India there is a belief that the nearer a man approaches to the state of liberation the shorter does the time seem. A year for a fully-liberated man seems to require no time at all for its passage. All of us as we grow older experience this acceleration. How slowly a year passes for a seven-year-old child! How quickly for a seventy-year-old man! So it is in our group experience. Some have estimated that more changes have taken place in human experience in the last one hundred years than in all previous human history. But that is a difficult statement to confirm or refute. The twentieth century has been a century of increasing tempo of change—changes in technology, ideology, sciences, arts, and religion. The twenty-first century must be a century of direction. The third eye of Śiva is symbolic of the direction in which man must move. Man must discover himself. No longer can he trust implicitly to the outward look. Both scientific objectivity and theological transcendency must give way to the *advaita Ātman* (the non-dual self). The *sarvamukti* of man is the full realization of the *upaniṣad* of the *Mahābhārata*: "There is no status that is superior to that of humanity."[4]

NOTES

1. Alfred North Whitehead, *Adventures of Ideas*. New York: The Macmillan Co., 1933, p. 117.
2. Harvey Cox, "The Death of God and the Future of Theology" in *New Theology No. 4*. Edited by Martin E. Marty and Dean G. Peerman. New York: The Macmillan Co., 1967, pp. 246-247.
3. Alfred North Whitehead, *The Function of Reason*. Princeton: Princeton University Press, 1929, p. 12.
4. *Śānti Parva*, Section 300. *The Mahabharata*, Vol. IX. P. C. Roy edition. Calcutta: Oriental Publishing Co., no date, p. 404.

—8—

THE HINDU MAN

Hinduism is a unique creation. In the three or four thousand years of its development it has manifested almost every form of religion, philosophy, and social structure, yet it is not merely religion, nor philosophy, nor social structure. It is a life style which has been focused essentially and existentially on the fundamental human problem—the problem of being human. Knowing the external world and building the ideal social order have in Hinduism been secondary to actualizing the potentialities of man.

Hindu Sādhana

Scholars, both Indian and non-Indian, have tried unsuccessfully to fit Hinduism into the Western categories of religion and philosophy. How often in a volume on Hinduism, the author, if he is a philosopher, will say "Hinduism is a philosophy, but it is a *religious* philosophy, that is, it is a way of *living* as well as a way of thinking." If the author is a student of the history of religions he will say "Hinduism is a religion, but it is a *philosophical* religion, that is, it is a way of *thinking*, as well as a way of living." Heinrich Zimmer, for example, wrote, "Oriental philosophy is accompanied and supported by the practice of a way of life."[1] Louis Renou said that Hinduism "is not a religion in quite the same sense in which we use the word in the West . . . On one side it is inseparable from philosophy; on another, from communal and social life."[2] Franklin Edgerton observed, "Philosophy in India has always been practical in its nature. And its practical motive has been what we should call religious."[3] Some Indians talk out of both sides of the mouth, for example, G. R. Malkani of the Indian Philosophical Institute says, "Hinduism . . . is a religion that cannot be divorced from philosophy, and is in fact the highest form of philosophy."[4] *Swāmi* Nikhilananda identifies the goals of the two: "The goal of philosophy may be Truth, and the goal of religion, God; but in the final experience God and Truth are one and the same Reality."[5] Nalini Kanta Brahma says in the preface to his book, *Philosophy of Hindu Sadhana*, that it is "a presentation of the practical side of Hindu Philosophy,"[6] but S. Radhakrishnan says in the foreword, "In 'Hindu Sadhana' Dr. Nalini Kanta Brahma contributes a highly interesting and important work to the literature of Hindu Thought and Religion . . . a book which will be invaluable to all students of Religion."[7] T. M. P. Mahadevan has analyzed the problem of Indian philosophy and religion as follows: "It has puzzled many a Western student of Indian thought how and why there has been maintained in India a close alliance between religion and philosophy. Generally speaking, the preacher and the philosopher alike in the West deplore this alliance for quite opposite reasons. To the preacher, it would appear that Hinduism is too philosophical to be a religion. He finds in it a cold intellectualism, not an appeal to life in all its aspects, but an appeal to logic. To the philosopher, Indian philosophy seems to be overweighted on the side of intuition because of its association with religion."[8] A young Indian philosopher, B. K. Matilal, launched in the spring of 1970 a new periodical entitled *Journal of Indian Philosophy*. The announcement of the new journal states "The field of our contributions will be bound by the limits of rational inquiry: we will avoid questions that lie in the fields of theology and mystical experience. . . . Our aim will be to attract professional philosophers rather than professional internationalists." Matilal continues, "We make this statement not in a spirit of snobbery but out of regret at the long neglect of Indian philosophy by those professionals in the West who might best have put it to creative use." Matilal says the *Upaniṣads* and the *Gītā* are philosophy only in an "etymological sense." I share Matilal's concern, and I agree that the *Upaniṣads* and the *Gītā* are more speculation than philosophical argument, but I contend that when one studies Indian Philosophy "without recourse to religion or ontological commitment" (Matilal's words) what one is studying is only that portion of Hinduism which satisfies the Western criterion of philosophy. It is not inappropriate to note that the editorial office of the new journal is located in the West.

Part of the difficulty is that the Indian—be he Hindu, Jain, or Buddhist—does not do philosophy as we do philosophy in the West. For him philosophy is essentially a quest for values. For example, L. C. Gupta in a paper delivered at the 28th Indian Philosophical Congress (1953) said, "A philosophy which is merely an enquiry into the ultimate nature of the spatio-temporal world or the nature of consciousness as such and is thus merely a philosophy of being is a truncated thing." Gupta argued that "no philosophical theory can be wholly true unless it is based on and shaped by our deepest experiences involving active interaction between ourselves and the objective world. It should be a reflection of the whole of our life and not simply a fraction of it."[9] Whereas philosophy in the West began in wonder and seeks above all to make ideas clear, philosophy in India began as a way to eliminate suffering and to integrate man with his total environment. Even the classical logical treatise, the *Nyāya Sūtra*, opens with the observations that logic is offered as a means to "supreme felicity."

Rather than trying to classify Hinduism into religious slots like pantheism, henotheism, theism, or atheism or into philosophical slots like monism, dualism, rationalism, intuitionism, naturalism, or idealism, a wiser course would be to recognize it as a unique life style concerned primarily with developing the candidate for humanity into the paradigmatic self-aware man. Hinduism is *sādhana*. But unfortunately the English language has no word synonymous with *sādhana*. The term comes from the root *sādha* meaning to reach one's goal, to accomplish an aim, to guide aright, to fulfill, to subdue, to gain power over. It is the process of the perfecting of man. It is the liberating of dormant powers, the fulfilling of potentialities. *Sādhana* is not simply the notion of the full development of the individual man since it keeps man in the social context, for man is to be redeemed both in the physical world and in society. He is not saved from matter nor from his inter-personal relationships and obligations, because only in matter and in society can man realize his being. *Sādhana* is the healing of the hiatus between theory and practice. It is a becoming of being, a realizing of what we are, a perfecting of latent perfections. It is the existential achievement-discovery of man's essence.

When Hinduism is interpreted as *sādhana* the student is able to discuss Hindu "religion" and Hindu "philosophy" without the usual constant reminder that religion in Hinduism is not like Western religion, and philosophy in Hinduism is not like Western philosophy. Consider, for example, the plight of Betty Heimann when she wrote in her book, *Facets of Indian Thought*, "Two ways are thus open to Hindu religion and philosophy. The way of concrete cult and contact between the beings in heaven and earth—and the other, the higher way, of abstract speculation on the ever unmanifestable fullness of the Divine."[10] Miss Heimann revealed her problem by referring to the ways of "cult" and "speculation" as two ways of "Hindu religion and philosophy." She was not able to separate the two, yet she undoubtedly knew that they are separable though related. Surely she did not mean that there are four distinct ways: (1) cult in religion, (2) speculation in religion, (3) cult in philosophy, and (4) speculation in philosophy. What she needed was the concept of *sādhana*. Then she could have referred to cult and speculation as the religious and the philosophical aspects of *sādhana*.

Hindu *sādhana* is both goal and means to the goal, truth and way to truth. Hinduism does not leave the attainment of the devotee to his own devices; rather it offers to him a variety of techniques for implementation. Existentialism did not need to appear in Hinduism, disrupting the ideology of the system, since in Hinduism existence is part of the total pattern. In the words of René Guénon, "In all doctrines that are metaphysically complete, as those of the East, theory is always accompanied or followed by an effective realization, for which it merely provides the necessary basis; no realization can be embarked upon without a sufficient theoretical preparation, but theory is ordained entirely with a view to this realization as the means towards the end, and this point of view is presupposed, or at least tacitly implied, even in the exterior expression of the doctrine."[11] This is why—to use Western categories—Hindu philosophy has not been able to dissociate itself from religious tendencies. Hindu "philosophy" and Hindu "religion" are but aspects of the realizing of the highest ends of life. *Sādhana* is the tenor of human life to the attainment of an ideal goal.

The Ātmansiddhi Ideal

The goal of *sādhana* has many names. One of the most descriptive is *ātmansiddhi* (the perfection of the essential nature of man). Others are *puruṣārtha* (a person of riches) and *uttamapuruṣa* (a superior person). The *ātmansiddhi* ideal has been variously conceived within Hinduism. In the *Ṛg Veda* the *ātmansiddha* is the pious man, the man faithful in recitation of *mantras* and in sacrifice of ghee and soma to the *devas*. The *Brāhmaṇas* mark a change; the ceremonies had become so complicated that the head of the family or of the clan could no longer perform them. Proper performance required a professional. The *ātmansiddha* was the sacerdotal man, the priest who could conduct the ritual without error. In the Upaniṣadic period the knowledge of esoteric doctrines was added to the perfection ideal. The *ātmansiddha* was the *ṛṣi*, the sage who possessed secret learning and was able to transmit it to the pupil ready to receive it. In the *Dharma Śāstras* the ideal man is the regal man, the man mature enough to assume the duties of the tribal assembly, the man who has undergone the training and received the instruction requisite for leadership in the community. And in other periods and contexts the *ātmansiddha* is the *bhakti* man (the man devoted to his chosen deity), or the *dhyāna* man (the adept in meditative practices), or the yogic man (the man whose body and mind are fully controlled by his volition). In the *Bhagavad Gītā* the Perfected Man is the man of stabilized wisdom (*sthitiprajñā*).[12] According to Lord Kṛṣṇa he is the man who has overcome the desires of the flesh, who is at peace with himself, who is stoically indifferent to pleasure and pain, who has no selfish aims or personal hopes, and who makes no demands on others. This is the man, says Kṛṣṇa, who attains peace.[13] The *ātmansiddha* has been viewed in still other ways in recent years. For Ramakrishna he was the mystic lost in his adoration of his deity, for Aurobindo the yogi proficient in meditation, for Gandhi the *satyāgraha* steadfastly loyal to truth and expressing his loyalty in active participation in social improvement, for Tagore the Supreme Man "infinite in his essence . . . finite in his manifestation,"[14] and for Radhakrishnan the free spirit.[15] Despite the variety of conceptions two presuppositions prevail in all the views: (1) *ātmansiddhi* is a moral phenomenon with emotional, intellectual, and spiritual overtones, and (2) it begins with man turning inward but it finds fulfillment only by turning outward towards the world and the needs of fellow beings.

There have been attempts to spell out in concrete and simple outline the exact qualities of the Perfected Man, e.g., Viśiṣṭādvaita Vedāntists have listed seven qualities:[16]

1. *viveka* (purification of mind resulting from the taking of only pure food)
2. *vimoka* (the leaving of all desires)
3. *abhyāsa* (the ability to contemplate an object without interruption)
4. *kriyā* (the habit of doing one's own duties)
5. *kalyāna* (the habit of speaking the truth)
6. *anavasāda* (not being disturbed by physical miseries)
7. *anuddharasa* (satisfaction with one's own condition)

The ideal has sometimes been misinterpreted as either a legalism or a Gnosticism, but it is neither a form of obedience to ceremonial or moral law nor a God-intoxication, a turning from life, a killing of the body, or an other-worldly dreaming. It is an exalted humanism which holds before man a noble ideal for approximation.

Although the *ātmansiddha* is described both as a *videhamukta* and as a *jīvanmukta*—the former denoting the being on the other side of death who has attained the state of elimination of all *karma* and the latter the being who is liberated but who is still living in the flesh—we shall consider only the *jīvanmukta*. His *mokṣa* is not postponed until death. For him death does not count. His state is adumbrated in Islam as "Dying before you die" and in Christianity as "O death, where is thy victory? O death, where is thy sting?"[17] There are no definite rules for the life of the *jīvanmukta*. Some forsake the active life; some lead a life of useful service; some are indifferent to the world; some are motivated by sympathy for all creation. In other words, part of the freedom of the free man is the freedom to be himself. He is free because there is no longer a self to bind him. He is conscious only of the *Ātman*. There is no loss of self, only an enlargement. The "I" and the "Thou" are taken up in a comprehensive reality in which nothing is lost. The *jīvanmukta* no longer makes distinctions between himself and the other self. His value distinctions are timeless; his liberation is now, the eternal now. *Mokṣa* is now, for it cannot be at any other time. It is always *now* when *mokṣa* is. Time does not limit nor contain *mokṣa*. It is whenever man is ready for it. His liberation is fundamentally a new perspective. Nothing happens. Nothing needs to happen. The new is a new orientation. He now *sees* what before he merely was.

The belief that the *jīvanmukta* is beyond good and evil has been both prized and despised by Hindus. Radhakrishnan praises the notion: "The pure and perfect are laws unto themselves. The imperfect have to accept laws made by others and recognized by society."[18] Mahendranath Sircar, recognizing the condition and offering no criticism, says that the *jīvanmukta* "has no virtues nor vices, no good nor evil; rights, duties and values are categories that have no meaning for him. He is an onlooker of life and its claims. . . . But no definite law can be laid down how a *jīvanmukta* should behave himself. Theoretically he is open to no influences."[19] Rāmānuja rejected the *jīvanmukti* concept. According to him the liberated is a mode of Brahman, yet it is also a monad standing in the relation of fellowship and equality to Brahman.[20] *Mukti* is always *videha* for Rāmānuja. The liberated one passes into a state of actual communion with Īśvara, a condition which is not possible before forsaking the vital and bodily sheaths of the soul. R. C. Bose severely criticizes the conception of *jīvanmukti*: "The system has proved a refuge of lies to many a hardened sinner. The perplexed minds which have found shelter in its solution of the problem of existence are few indeed, but the number of wicked hearts which have been composed to sleep by the opiate of its false hope, is incalculable."[21] Identification of the hypocrites would be most difficult. In any case Bose's criticism is wide of the mark, because abuse of a system is not necessarily an indictment of the system. What seems to be implicit in the doctrine of *jīvanmukti* is that the person in this state is impervious to the requirements and restrictions of common morality not because he is a violator of this morality but because he conforms to it without benefit of the sanctions which influence the lives of ordinary men, e.g., fear of punishment, desire for social approval, and hope of reward.

The *ātmansiddhi* ideal is open to three serious misunderstandings.

The first is the problem of putting the state in time, and yet not making it a time-bound state. It is an eternal condition which may or may not be in time. This is what is meant by the distinction between *jīvanmukti* and *videhamukti*, but this distinction must not be overemphasized. It is rather a way of proclaiming that the Perfected One is indifferent to the presence or absence of the physical conditions of earthly life. The quality of a complete value experience does not depend upon its temporal extension. The limiting conditions of space and time neither add nor detract from the highest values.

A second misunderstanding is in making a sharp distinction between the Perfected Man as *jīva* and the Perfected Man as *ātman*. Much of the language about the Perfected Man implies that it is the individual man who is perfected, but the Hindu ideal is not the ideal of the Renaissance Man, that is, he is not an individual in isolation from social and cosmic contexts. Radhakrishnan, in what can only be explained as a moment of unguarded enthusiasm, once wrote that the aim of Hinduism is to make all men prophets.[22] But a prophet is a man against the group, the prophet sets himself as it were outside his social environment, and from this detached point of view levels his criticism upon it. On the other hand, there is also the monistic absorptionist tradition in Hinduism which would identify all Hinduism with Advaita Vedāntism. For example, Betty Heimann writes, "In fully developed Hinduism, no personal survival of liberated man is ever hoped for, nor does Hinduism rely on the constant support of any God-person."[23] Miss Heimann's statement is consistent with her assumption, evident in many essays that Śaṅkara's Vedānta is "fully developed Hinduism." Her writings would lead to the conclusion that believers in personal survival or in a supporting deity are cases of arrested development! However, the doctrine of the Perfected Man is the view that nothing of value is lost. The true individuality remains; the false distinctions which separate men from each other are seen for what they are. The Universal Man (*Viśvātman*)—to use a term favored by Tagore—or the Gnostic Being in the terminology of Aurobindo, does not slough off matter or spirit. The Perfected finds himself, knows himself, and fulfills himself. He becomes humanized; he learns to empathize with others so that he respects, tolerates, aids, and loves others. He becomes hominized; he becomes the generic man, unable to set himself apart from other men. He becomes divinized; he sees the Godhead in all and embraces God-in-man. He becomes Brahmanized; the gods fade away as he intuits the unity of being and value.

The third misunderstanding arises out of translating *ātmansiddhi* as "the perfection of man" and *ātmansiddha* as "the perfected man." If *ātmansiddhi* is, as we have suggested, the telos of Hindu *sādhana*, it is an ideal which never seems to be realized, for the literature of Hinduism does not present to us any human paradigm. In the epics one would expect to find an example of the Perfected Man, but there are flaws in the moral character of all the heroes in the *Rāmāyaṇa* and the *Mahābhārata*. Rāma is too easily moved by gossip, is stubborn beyond all reason, pontificates on the duty of others, and causes great suffering in order to keep the letter of the foolish words of his father; Sītā is usually a model of humble obedience to her husband, but she lacks Draupadī's spirited confidence in action; Draupadī, on the other hand, is far too swayed by the emotion of revenge; Yudhiṣṭhira tells a complete lie to bring about the death of his *guru*; Bhīma kills Duryodhana by a foul blow which violates the basic rules of fair fighting; Arjuna kills Bhīṣma by shooting him while hiding behind an effeminate warrior with whom Bhīṣma will not fight. Strangely enough, Bhīṣma, the grandsire of the villainous Kauravas, comes as close as anyone in either epic to being the Perfected Man. It is he through whom the lengthy moralizing of the *Mahābhārata* is given, yet he renounces marriage and the throne to gratify a whim of his aged father. The curious anti-heroic character of the heroic Pāṇḍavas and the heroic character of some of the Kauravas prompted Adolph Holtzmann to contend that the original Mahābhārata had glorified the Kauravas but was altered when the figure of Kṛṣṇa became magnified in later centuries. This theory, which E. Washburn Hopkins called the "Inversion Theory," was given up by its supporters when it became clearer from epigraphic evidence that the epic had been extant in about its present form several centuries before the fourth century A.D.[24]

The non-realization of the *ātmansiddhi* ideal is an extremely important fact in Hinduism. The ideal remains an ideal; it is beyond being but not beyond imagination. Man's potentiality exceeds his actuality. He is never all that he can be; or to state this in a different form, were man to become what he potentially is, he would cease to be man. His being as man is his eternal becoming. Man is the being that includes the potentiality of becoming more than his status as man. Man Perfected is more than man. As Kṛṣṇa says,

> Rid of passion, fear, and wrath,
> Made of Me, taking refuge in Me,
> Many by the austerity of knowledge
> Purified, have come to My estate.[25]

If there were a concept of *hybris* in Hinduism, it would not be the overweening pride of man, but the jealousy of gods directed toward man, the being who can attain the divine estate. A god is a god, but a man is more than a man!

Ātmansiddhi, the goal of Hindu *sādhana*, turns out to be not Perfected Man but Perfect*ing* Man. Hinduism is not a Donatism, demanding that man become perfect; rather it is concerned with the melioristic direction of man's life, individually and generically. "The individual's aim of perfection" writes Radhakamal Mukerjee "is the same as the group's aim of culture, complete, balanced and practical—the realization of the Universal Self and the Universal Community."[26] That is to say, perfection is to the individual as culture is to the group, a process of becoming rather than a state of being. The individual seeks perfecting as society seeks "culturing." Miss Heimann correctly analyzes the perfectionism of Hinduism: "The ideal of the final goal of Perfection is a Western postulate, not an Indian one. The West thinks on results, believes in facts which ultimately can be reached and fulfilled . . . the Western ideal rests in perfection, the fulfilment of a distinct aim which can be accomplished by limitation and selection only. The end, ideal, is static and changeless in its perfected individuality. By contrast, the Indian is never satisfied with any static end. . . . For him there cannot be a resting-place in a personal perfection, in a distinct single survival. The end of development is for all phenomena a final re-flow and inflow into the general receptacle of the 'Ocean,' the Brahman, the universal reservoir out of which all forms sprang forth and into which all of them, in the end, are reabsorbed."[27]

Mokṣa or *mukti* is a process. Part of the difficulty Westerners have in understanding Hinduism is rooted in the fact that static categories of Western essentialism miss the dynamic character of Indian thought. Hindu soteriology is progressive. Christianity, having rooted its atonement in a historical event, is constantly puzzling as to whether salvation is a reality already accomplished or an invitation to assist in a saving process. Hinduism, having no one historical soteriological event, has less difficulty in making salvation a process. The life of each man is an evolution, a *pravṛtti mārga*, a path of progress. Albert Schweitzer conceived of ethics as "the maintenance of one's own life at the highest level of becoming more and more in spirit,"[28] yet because of his conviction that Indian thought is "world and life negation," he was unable to perceive the degree to which Hinduism approximated his own definition.

Hinduism is a pursuit, an endeavor, a striving. According to the *Mahābhārata* immortality is the "pursuit of Brahman or self-knowledge."[29] The drive to fulfillment is a promise which forever falls short of the goal, but it ought not to generate despair. Mysore Hiriyanna once expressed his view on this as follows: "Some Indian thinkers admit *jīvanmukti*, which means that the goal of life can be reached here on this earth; others do not recognize it and so make it realisable hereafter—in a future existence. If I may conclude by expressing a personal opinion, the question whether the highest value is attainable is not of much consequence. We may grant that it is not finally attained and that man's reach will always exceed his grasp. What really matters is the deliberate choosing of it as the ideal to be pursued, and thereafter making a persistent and continued advance toward it."[30]

The Perfecting Man is a man of forward-looking enthusiasm. Whereas the ancient Greeks advised moderation in all things, the Indians seek to derive the full worth of each idea, each value, each *mārga*, by pushing it to what Aurobindo has called "a fine excess." He speaks of "a tendency of the Indian mind which is common in all its activities, the impulse to follow each motive, each specialization of motive even, spiritual, intellectual, ethical, vital, to its extreme point and to sound its utmost possibility."[31] Self-assertion is pushed to dissatisfied regality, self-denial to satisfied nudity. Yet this is not the end, for in the extremes the Indian seeks for a rule which will result in a measure of harmony and balance. The Buddha is a classical example of this existential dialectic. As a young prince he lived in three palaces, one for each season of the year. A retinue of servants, mistresses, and a doting father were ready to satisfy his desires. When he turned from this life style, he wrenched the hair from his head, changed his royal robes with the first begger he met, and finally, according to the legends, reduced his diet to a few grains of rice a day. After his enlightenment he established the Middle Way, the way that avoided the extremes of pleasure and asceticism. The Indian makes distinctions only to turn upon them and to deny all distinctions. To quote again from Aurobindo: "Balance and rhythm which the Greeks arrived at by self-limitation, India arrived at by its sense of intellectual, ethical and aesthetic order and the synthetic impulses of its mind and life."[32] The life of Keshub Chunder Sen is a good example of "fine excess." Two years before his death he said, "I am partial to the doctrine of enthusiasm. To me a state of being on fire is the state of salvation. . . . Coldness and hell have always been the same to my mind. Around my own life, around the society in which I lived, I always kept burning the flame of enthusiasm."[33] P. C. Mozoomdar comments, "The entire society of the Brahmo Samāj was exceeding fervid in his [i.e., Keshub Chunder Sen's] time. His disciples were distinguished not so much by intellect, as by a certain emotion, by an intense enthusiasm, the best impulses of his nature kept always aglow."[34] One of his disciples, Devendranath Tagore, wrote, "God does not reckon what portion of His infinite work is performed by individuals. Let everyone use the powers given him, without reservation; this is God's ordinance."[35]

Ātmansiddhi is a programmatic telos, a direction for moving, not a goal for reaching. The Perfecting Man is the reality to be attained; the Perfected Man is the ideal to be approximated. The aim is progression toward an ever receding goal of perfection. According to the *Aitareya Āraṇyaka*, "Whatever he [man] reaches, he wishes to go beyond. If he reaches the sky, he wishes to go beyond. If he reaches the heavenly world, he would wish to go beyond."[36] Gandhi also expressed this idea. "The goal ever recedes from us. The greater the progress the greater the recognition of our unworthiness. Satisfaction lies in the effort, not in the attainment. Full effort is full victory."[37] On another occasion Gandhi described man as "a spiritual unit . . . launched on a pilgrimage to perfection."[38] Hinduism glorifies man as the being who is capable of knowing and living in accord with the highest truths and deepest values. In the *Mahābhārata* the dying Bhīṣma at last discloses the *upaniṣad* which transcends all *upaniṣads*: "This is the secret and supreme doctrine. There is nothing in the universe higher than man."[39] And in the *Rāmāyaṇa* Tulsīdāsa observes, "The devotee of Rāma is greater than Rāma."[40] The real atheism in Hinduism is not to have faith in man.

The Yogic Way

Hinduism as *sādhana* not only sets forth the *ātmansiddhi* ideal but also presents the method for the attainment of the ideal. This is known by the generic term *yoga*. However, *yoga* has been so badly misunderstood that one almost hesitates to use it. *Yoga* need not involve postures, special breathing, unusual foods, nor any of the other features so often associated with *yoga*. Rather *yoga* may be said to have three hallmarks: human, normal, and telic. First, *yoga* is human activity. No animal lower than man can engage in it. All myths of gods performing *yoga* are to be interpreted analogically. Second, *yoga* is normal activity. One may set aside certain times of the day and certain modes of behavior as particularly yogic, but in the last analysis these so-called yogic acts are overtly the same as acts that are non-yogic. Third, *yoga* is telic activity, that is, it is activity done for a particular purpose or goal. This goal is inherently bound up in the entire human enterprise.

By identifying *yoga* as human activity the intention is to emphasize *yoga* as peculiarly the activity of man. Aristotle divided the psychical activities of man into three types: the plant-like, the animal-like, and the uniquely human. Each man lives a life which may be characterized as vegetative, or animalistic, or human. Aristotle did not mean that any man can be only a vegetable, or only an animal, or only human; rather he meant that each man places emphasis existentially on one of the three. The man whose life values are centered on food, drink and sex—the nutritive-reproductive psyche according to Aristotle—is "the vegetable man." This is not to despise the enjoyment of the palate nor of sexual activity—Aristotle was no puritan—but it was to remind us that these activities are the necessary, rather than the sufficient, acts of man. Secondly, the man whose life values are rooted in physical movement, who enjoys the hunt and the chase, who goes to the games as either participant or spectator, and who relishes sound and color in music and art was called by Aristotle "the animal man." His life is compared to that of an animal constantly on the move, and it is contrasted to that of a plant with its roots fixed in the earth. The third sort of man is the individual who places his highest values on the life of reason. His psyche is rational, rather than nutritive or sensitive. He is "the rational man." Aristotle in his typical realistic manner granted that individual men must engage in nutritive, reproductive, and sensitive behavior, but he held that he who limited himself to these modes of behavior would be less than human. The manual laborer, which for him was the slave, is not human; he is a living tool. The life of active thought, of contemplation, is the truly human life. When Aristotle attempted to depict the life of his God, he said that God is always in that good state in which men sometimes are, that is, God eternally engages in contemplating the highest values and the fundamental realities. Mortals do this only rarely and incompletely. Aristotle's words are beautifully illuminating: the divine life "is a life such as the best which we enjoy, and enjoy for a short time;" it is a thinking which "deals with that which is best in itself;" it is the contemplating of "what is most pleasant and best."[41] When Aristotle attempted to analyze the nature of this highest activity, he said it is a thinking that is a thinking on thinking.[42] To interpret this as an expression of solipsism is to reduce a profound insight to absurdity. The fully human act—and hence for this great Greek humanist the divine act—is the act of self-awareness.

Yoga is human activity, peculiarly human activity. It is that form of acting which cannot be done by any form of life lower than man, and it is that form of acting in which a man becomes aware of himself. *Yoga* is man waking up to his nature as man. Man is plant-like in his dependence upon nutrition and reproduction; he is animal-like in his physical activities and in his life of the senses. He is both plant and animal, but he is not just plant and animal, for he is aware that he is plant and animal and this no mere plant nor animal can be. By being aware of his plant-like and animal-like nature and activities, he is more than plant and animal. A plant or animal that knows it is plant or animal is no mere plant or animal. Man is that being. Self-awareness is his blessing and his curse. It is a blessing in that he is not captive to his external environment, and it is a curse in that he catches glimpses of potential perfections he cannot actualize. He is an earthbound creature who dreams of that which is impossible for the earthbound.

Yoga as human activity is man aware of himself as human; it is man seeing through his plant and animal nature to the self which transcends the necessary conditions of his life on this planet, a self which transcends individual selves, a self which transcends the divisions of nationality, race, and religion. But care must be taken not to make a yogic act a specific identifiable act of man. This would demean the ordinary life of man. One does not exalt *yoga* by suggesting that yogic activity is superior to any form of the everyday acts of man. *Yoga* is human activity of a quite ordinary nature. Any human act can be yogic.

Yoga is normal activity. Yet when one is known as a yogi the common assumption is that he does things which are unusual or even bizarre. Does he place his legs in painful positions? Does he hold his breath for long periods of time? Does he stare at the sun until almost blind? Does he eat strange foods and drink strange drinks? Hindus are partially to blame for these ideas. Most Hindu teachers of *yoga* from Patañjali to the present day have said a good deal about these matters. It is small wonder that the layman is convinced of the supreme importance of posture, breathing, and diet. If the half-lotus position is good, then the full lotus position is twice as good! If nothing happens in an eight-to-sixteen sequence of inhalation and exhalation, then maybe one should try a ten-to-thirty sequence! If a diet of vegetables and milk is good, maybe a diet of only vegetables would be still better! How often means and ends, techniques and outcomes, secondary and primary become confused in the writings of Hindu yogis and Indophiles.

Buddhists—particularly Zen Buddhists—are much more sensible about *yoga*. They stress the commonplace character of *yoga*. For example, the historical koans and mondos are full of emphases on the everyday acts of people: the drinking of a cup of tea, the eating of a meal, the washing of plates, the cultivating of plants, the chopping of wood, the mending of clothes, the making of music, and the engaging in small talk. These are yogic acts. To do *yoga* one does not step outside the normal routines of life. This is not to affirm that every act done by any person at any time is a yogic act, but it is to call our attention to the fact that the most ordinary act can be one in which "the scent soaks into the robe." Most human acts are done, and then forgotten. What were you doing at 10 A.M. on October 15, 1965? Not many of us could say. For most of us that moment is gone, and it cannot be brought back; its fragrance did not scent the robe. On the other hand, each can recall seemingly insignificant events of years ago which for some reason have stayed in the mind, not merely events which led to great consequences but also events which led to nothing more than a pleasant association. How many have pleasant associations with a certain species of flower, or with a specific shade of color, or with a phrase in an aria, but have lost completely the original which produced the association. The scent has soaked into the robe, the event left its mark, but the event itself is hidden in the limbo of the past.

The yogic act need not, and probably did not, have at the time of its appearance any distinctive marks. A yogic event is all gray; it has no psychedelic colors. On the surface the act looks very commonplace. *Yoga* may be done on street corners, in buses, in railway stations, and at airports. The yogic act is the ordinary act, either private or public, which is outwardly no different from the non-yogic act. Two men eat at a restaurant. Mr. A enters, orders, eats, pays, and leaves; Mr. B enters, orders, eats, pays, and leaves. For A the series of events are almost automatic; they become a part of his historic self which will never again be raised to consciousness. But for B the series of events have a meaning and significance such that they are yogic.

Yogic activity is goal-seeking activity, but not all goal-seeking activity is yogic. There is a particular telos involved in *yoga*, and this is the goal which is uniquely human. There are many ways to describe the uniqueness of man: he is called the time-binder, the one who is self aware, conscious clay, the God-intoxicated. According to Hinduism man is the finite seeking infinite, the incomplete longing for wholeness, the imperfect in quest of perfection.

Hinduism has grasped the uniqueness of the human. According to Hinduism man is unique because man, and only man, engages in *sādhana*. *Sādhana* encompasses all the acts, thoughts, volitions, and feelings related to the search for the fulfilling of the potentialities latent in man. Man is the being whose reach exceeds his grasp. In him all reality comes to a focus. He is the growing edge of the entire value-reality complex. The telos of man—the goal toward which he unconsciously moves—is *satchitānanda*, the integration of being, consciousness, and value. According to Hinduism man relates to this telos in four ways or *mārgas*: (1) he clarifies it intellectually (*jñāna mārga*); (2) he feels it emotionally (*bhakti mārga*); (3) he labors for it overtly (*karma mārga*); (4) he disciplines himself volitionally for its realization (*yoga mārga*). The four *mārgas* are not as separate or separable as a listing suggests. *Yoga mārga*, in particular, cannot be isolated from the other *mārgas*, for it denotes all the thinking, the feeling, the willing, and the acting which attempt the complete realization of the possibilities in man. It is cosmic and organic evolution risen to the level of consciousness. In each person the plural manifestations of the universe are witnessed, and in each the integrative possibilities are attained. No one can say what is *yoga* and what is not *yoga* for another. Each must do his own *dharma*, as the *Gitā* says.

Yogic behavior may not even be consciously telic. An unplanned act can become the doorway to self-realization. But it is more realistic to admit that most yogic acts are programmed by a set of mind and emotions of an individual. A yogi is not a strange abnormality. He is a human being who understands what is the meaning and value of being human. His life is an expression of gratitude that cosmic forces have evolved the human. He through karmic forces dimly grasps his becoming a member of the human species. The yogic person is the *human* person. Non-yogic persons are sleeping monads—men and women whose self-awareness seems to be but slightly more developed than the self-awareness of the lower animals. They count the days and months and years, but they see no sense in their passage, and they come to the end of their earthly pilgrimages almost blind to the human condition. Yogic persons are awake to their nature and to the opportunities afforded them as creatures capable of self-awareness. They have discovered who they are and have progressed toward the divine goal of human fulfillment. Yogic people possess *kausala* (skill, cleverness, experience). They are skillful in the art of being human. They seek immortality by means of the mortal, perfection by means of the imperfect, spirit by means of flesh, the divine by means of the human. They seek to transform themselves and their society by a self-directed evolution in harmony with the dynamic integration of reality and value which we denote mythologically by "God."

Max Eastman in his essay, "Poetic People," claimed that mankind can be divided into the poetic and the non-poetic. The poetic are those who go on deck of a ferry crossing a river; the non-poetic stay below. The poetic wish to enjoy the trip, but the non-poetic merely want to get to the other shore. Yogic people are obviously among the poetic. But we can go further in this analysis. Joseph Campbell says the poetic people can be divided into three classes: (1) those in whom poetry is underdone, (2) those in whom poetry is overdone, and (3) those in whom poetry is done to death.[43] "Poetry underdone" refers to the sentimentalists who rest happily among the whimsies of personal joy, surprise, or anguish. "Poetry overdone" refers to the prophets who turn the poetic vision into a message of salvation. They develop cults and attempt to duplicate themselves in the lives of others. "Poetry done to death" refers to the priests who reduce the poetic vision to clichés. They institutionalize, creedalize, and finally fossilize the original vision. The poets try to preserve the original freshness of the vision, but they make no use of it; the prophets and the priests attempt to utilize the vision, but they destroy its vitality and finally slay it. The yogic people are a fourth category. They are not poets, nor prophets, nor priests. They use the vision, and do not slay it. The poetic man is a man of process. His telos is one of growth rather than attainment. He is ever on the way. His state is the state of becoming. He is *mārgayāta*, a wayfarer. The yogic man reminds us that the glory of man is not in his attainments but in his aspirations. In him poetry is not underdone, nor overdone, nor done to death; it is being done.

The Hindu is distinguished by a *sādhana* in which he pursues *ātmansiddhi* by yogic means. He detects a general psychic evolution from fragmentation to integration, from disorganization to unity, from parts to whole, but he chooses to bypass this slow evolutionary development via chosen paths of growth to the fullest realization of the human potential. His prayer that he may be led from the unreal to the real, from darkness to light, from death to immortality summarizes the direction of his *sādhana*. The Hindu man is man self-aware. He is man consciously questing to become truly human. Other cultures have in varying degrees encouraged men to actualize human potentialities, but none has surpassed Hinduism in its singular dedication to the perfection of man.

NOTES

1. Heinrich Zimmer, *Philosophies of India*. Cleveland and New York: The World Publishing Co., 1956, p. 50.
2. Louis Renou, *The Nature of Hinduism*. Translated by Patrick Evans. New York: Walker and Co., 1962, p. 32.
3. Franklin Edgerton, "The Meaning of Sāṅkhya and Yoga," *American Journal of Philology*, Vol. XLV (1924), p. 1.
4. G. R. Malkani, "The Synthetic View of Vedānta" in *A. R. Wadia: Essays Presented in His Honour*. Edited by S. Radhakrishnan and others. Madras, 1954, p. 186.
5. *Swāmi* Nikhilananda, *Self-Knowledge*. Mylapore, Madras: Sri Ramakrishna Math, 1947, p. 19.
6. Nalini Kanta Brahma, *Philosophy of Hindu Sādhanā*. London: Kegan Paul, Trench, Trübner and Co., 1932, p. xi.
7. *Ibid*., p. ix.
8. T. M. P. Mahadevan, "The Religio-Philosophic Culture of India" in *The Cultural Heritage of India*, Vol. I. Calcutta: The Ramakrishna Mission, 1958, p. 164.
9. Proceedings of the 28th Indian Philosophical Congress (1953), pp. 27-28.
10. Betty Heimann, *Facets of Indian Thought*. New York: Schocken Books, 1964, p. 32.
11. René Guénon, *Introduction to the Study of the Hindu Doctrines*. Translated by Marco Pallio. London: Luzac and Co., 1945, pp. 171-172.
12. *Bhagavad Gītā* 2. 54.
13. *Bhagavad Gītā* 2. 72.
14. Rabindranath Tagore, *The Religion of Man*. London: George Allen and Unwin, 1931, p. 118.
15. *The Philosophy of Radhakrishnan*. Edited by Paul Schilpp. New York: Tudor Publishing Co., 1952, p. 65.
16. M. Rangacharlu Garu, "Visishtadvaitism: What It Teaches Us." *The Vaishnavite*, Vol. I (1898), pp. 69-73.
17. I Corinthians 15:55. Revised Standard Version.
18. Sarvepalli Radhakrishnan, *Indian Philosophy*, Vol. I. London: George Allen and Unwin, 1923, p. 507.
19. Mahendranath Sircar, *Comparative Studies in Vedāntism*. Bombay: Oxford University Press, 1927, p. 271.
20. See his commentaries on *Vedānta Sūtras* 4. 4. 4.
21. Quoted by W. S. Urquhart, *The Vedānta and Modern Thought*. London: Oxford University Press, 1928, pp. 174-175.
22. Sarvepalli Radhakrishnan, *The Heart of Hindusthan*. Madras: G. A. Nateson and Co., 1945, p. 22.

23. Betty Heimann, *op. cit.*, p. 61.
24. See V. S. Sukthankar, *On the Meaning of the Mahābhārata*. Bombay: The Asiatic Society of Bombay, 1947, pp. 13-15.
25. *Bhagavad Gītā* 4. 10. Franklin Edgerton translation.
26. Radhakamal Mukerjee, *The Culture and Art of India*. London: George Allen and Unwin, 1959, p. 18.
27. Betty Heimann, *op. cit.*, pp. 142-143.
28. Albert Schweitzer, *Indian Thought and Its Development*. Translated by Mrs. Charles E. B. Russell. Boston: The Beacon Press, 1936, p. 260.
29. *Udyoga Parva*, Section 42. *The Mahabharata*, Vol. IV. P. C. Roy edition. Calcutta: Oriental Publishing Co., no date, p. 96 (of *Udyoga Parva*).
30. Mysore Hiriyanna, *The Quest after Perfection*. Mysore: Kavyalaya Publishers, 1952, p. 35.
31. Aurobindo, *The Renaissance in India*. Calcutta: Arya Publishing House, 1946, p. 19.
32. *Ibid.*, p. 23.
33. P. C. Mozoomdar, *Keshub Chunder Sen and His Times*. Calcutta: Baptist Mission Press, 1887, pp. 14-15.
34. *Ibid.*, p. 16.
35. *The Autobiography of Maharashi Devendranath Tagore*. Calcutta: S. K. Lahiri and Co., 1909, p. 193.
36. *Aitareya Āraṇyaka* 2. 3. 1, 2. F. Max Müller translation.
37. *Selections from Gandhi*. Edited by Nirmal Kumar Bose. Ahmedabad: Nirajivan Publishing House, 1948, p. 30.
38. Quoted by R. R. Diawakar, *Gandhi: A Practical Philosopher*. Bombay: Bharatiya Vidya Bhavan, 1965, p. 45.
39. *Śānti Parva*, Section 300.
40. *Dohāvalī* 3.
41. *Metaphysics* 1072 b 15, 17, 23. W. D. Ross translation.
42. *Metaphysics* 1074 b 34.
43. Joseph Campbell, *The Masks of God: Occidental Mythology*. New York: The Viking Press, 1964, p. 518.

—9—

*DEMOCRACY AND VARṆA**

The term "democracy" is the transliteration of a Greek word meaning popular government, literally "people-rule." It is either a disparaging or a eulogizing term depending on whether "people" denotes mob or everyman. Aristotle, having the usual Greek intellectualistic prejudices about the common man, regarded democracy as the most tolerable of the inferior forms of government; but the eighteenth- and nineteenth-century European and American revolutionists equated virtue with commoner and vice with royalty. Democracy means rule by the people. It also means rule for the sake of the people. Perhaps Abraham Lincoln's expression "government of, by and for the people" is one of the best concise descriptions of democracy.

Democracy means more than a form of government. It is also a form of state and a form of society. Therefore, a complete definition of democracy would include the notions of rule by the majority, of sovereignty in the hands of the citizens, and of polity determined directly or indirectly by the citizens. Democracy as a form of government, state, and society is based on a high regard for man. It assumes that man is a being of such dignity that he should wherever possible be the determiner of his own actions. It assumes that this dignity is sufficiently uniform that the gains of commonwealths should be essentially mass gains to be shared as equally as possible among the citizens. It assumes that man is a dynamic being, and

* This essay first appeared in modified form in *Darshana International*, Vol. IX, No. 4, (October, 1969), pp. 51-60.

therefore that changes in government are constantly required as man readjusts his values.

The ideals of democracy are four: Freedom, Equality, Individualism, and General Welfare. The worth of any democratic system is judged by its approximation of these ideals. Freedom includes freedom of expression, freedom of assembly, freedom of travel, freedom to enter a vocation, freedom of worship, etc. Equality denotes equality of treatment before the law, equality of economic and social opportunity, equality of franchise, etc. Individualism refers to such items as the right to own private property, to move about unmolested, to protest when one objects to treatment meted out to him, to protection against those who might do one harm in person or property, etc. General welfare is the right to form organizations, to be protected as a group against the violence of other groups or individuals, to expect as a member of the majority to prevail in policy making, etc. But to leave these ideals in this form would belie the heart of democratic ideals, for democratic ideals are rights counterbalanced by obligations. Each right the democratic man claims for himself is countered by his obligation to respect the similar rights of others. The democratic man cannot claim for himself what he is unwilling to grant to another. The reciprocal nature of rights and obligations is unique to democracy. This feature is often interpreted to mean that equality is the chief of the democratic ideals. This, I believe, is a false understanding of democracy, and this is why I think that the caste ideal is an essential ingredient in the theory and practice of democracy.

I have intimated the reciprocity of rights and obligations. They are two sides of the same coin. One might suppose that a similar reciprocity subsists among the four ideals. But this is not the case. The relation among the ideals is not mutual dependence or cooperation—it is conflict. To be more specific, the four ideals pair off in polar opposition. Freedom and equality form one pair. If, desiring to achieve equality, we constrain the strong in the interest of making them equal with the weak, the strong may justifiably claim that they have lost their freedom. In that prophesied time of peace when the wolf and the lamb, the leopard and the goat, and the lion and the calf shall be bedfellows, does it not occur to you that the wolf, the leopard, and the lion have been denied their freedom to seize an easy meal? Again, if in the interest to achieve the maximum of freedom, the same freedom is granted to the weak and to the strong, the lambs, goats, and calves may justifiably claim that they have lost their freedom. Liberty for the pike is death for the minnow, said Tawney.

A similar conflict subsists between individualism and general welfare. If the legislator decides in the interest of a private citizen, he may mitigate against the interests of the group; and if he acts in favor of the best interests of all, he may constrain the wishes of individuals. Capitalistic countries are constantly confronted with the problem of balancing the exploitation of natural resources by private interests and the necessity of conserving the natural resources for coming generations. Regulations regarding mining, fishing, lumbering, and agriculture constantly face this problem of the welfare of individuals and the welfare of groups.

Democratic practice requires constant adjustment of checks and balances between these two pairs of polar opposition. At various times a democratic government must make different decisions with respect to these ideals. This is why administrators, legislators, and judicators cannot go on holiday. And this is why a democracy cannot be defined in terms of a hierarchy of the four ideals. Rather let us say there are four democracies: (1) individual libertarian democracy, (2) individual egalitarian democracy, (3) social libertarian democracy, and (4) social egalitarian democracy.

Individual libertarian democracy is based on the principle that each individual should be allowed the maximum degree of freedom commensurate with social order. People recently freed from the hands of a despot believe that all that is needed is to set men free, that the chief function of government is to protect the liberties of individuals, and that the less a government interferes with the lives of individuals the better is the government. "That government is best which governs least," said Thomas Jefferson, and Thoreau went him one better with "That government is best which governs not at all." However, Jefferson had a different view when he assumed the office of President of the United States. Although he had affirmed before taking office that there ought to be a revolution every ten years, he did not hesitate to call out the national militia to stop a revolution in the state of Pennsylvania. The chief difficulty in this form of democracy is the determination of which individual freedoms are unessential and/or dangerous. For example, there are some in the United States who believe that the freedom to bear arms is an essential liberty for individuals, whereas in the United Kingdom there is almost no demand to possess arms, and few of the police carry weapons more lethal than a nightstick.

Individual egalitarian democracy attempts to organize the checks and balances so that no individual has more rights, privileges, freedoms, or duties than any other individual. Losers in the rough and tumble of the economic life of a nation are especially likely to think of democracy in this fashion. They would lose in the open market. This is the form of democracy which has appealed to many political leaders in the West. The original form of the American Declaration of Independence made this ideal the basic one from which the others are derived: "All men are created equal, and from that equal creation they derive rights inherent and inalienable, among which are the preservation of life and liberty and the pursuit of happiness." Jefferson's colleagues demanded that the words "from that equal creation they derive" be struck out and that in their place be substituted the high-sounding pious phrase "they are endowed by the Creator with." A psychologically effective reference to divinity thus replaced a logically organized set of ideals. The priority of equality in democracy has been a common theme in the West. "All that democracy means is as equal a participation in rights as is practicable" (James Fenimore Cooper); "For the new democratic theory liberty is necessarily a function of equality" (Harold Laski); "Equality is the basis of any real democracy" (James Truslow Adams); "I will accept nothing which all cannot have their counterpart of on the same terms." (Walt Whitman).

Democracy is claimed in the American constitution to be a means for the promotion of the general welfare, but in America as in other nations trying to implement the democratic ideals there is no agreement as to whether the general welfare is enhanced by liberty or by equality. Hence democracy may take on either the form of social libertarianism or social equalitarianism. Those who think in these terms speak of the conflict between rulers and ruled, or between management and labor, or between the proletariat and the bourgeoisie, or between ethnic, religious, and language groups; and they define that conflict either in terms of the need for liberty or for equality. Today there seems to be common agreement that only through an organization—a union, a federation, or an association—can results be obtained. The pressure brought upon legislators by lobbied interests in modern democracies is more than most of us can imagine. These group efforts are usually defended as the means by which the individual can achieve his freedom and/or equality. But, as so often happens, the means tend to become the ends, and the individual is lost in the group.

The American constitution gives priority to equality. What about the Indian constitution? The preamble to the Constitution of India begins with these words:

> We the people of India, having solemnly resolved to constitute India into a sovereign democratic republic and to secure to all its citizens:
>
> JUSTICE: social, economic and political;
>
> LIBERTY of thought, expression, belief, faith and worship;
>
> EQUALITY of status and of opportunity; and to promote among them all
>
> FRATERNITY assuring the dignity of the individual and the unity of the Nation . . .

The Constitution of India thus far does not establish a priority of democratic ideals. But, after Part I of the Constitution, which defines the union, and Part II which identifies the citizen, there follows Part III on "Fundamental Rights," and it is significant that the first right named is the "Right to Equality." The statement is "The State shall not discriminate against any citizen on grounds of religion, race, caste, sex, place of birth or any of them." Following the full itemization of rights, including Section 17 which states that Untouchability is abolished and its practice in any form is forbidden, the other rights are named: "Right to Freedom," "Right against Exploitation," "Right to Freedom of Religion," "Cultural and Educational Rights," "Right to Property," and "Right to Constitutional Remedies." We can conclude that India and the United States both give priority to equality in their constitutions.

When equality is the prior ideal, democracy may be said to be founded on the principle that when all persons are free then each person is free both as an individual and as a member of a group. My contention is that the application of this principle leads to uniformity and mediocrity. Conformity is sanctified. Variety is suspected.

He who seeks to excel is pressured to conform to the standard of average attainment. Labor unions specify the number of bricks which the mason may lay per day. College students exert social pressure on the good student lest he become a disturber of the average level of achievement. In some professions the one who pays excessive attention to his duties may suffer ostracism, e.g., in many communities doctors agree that none shall make house calls. These egalitarianisms are, I believe, a misinterpretation of democracy.

The problem is the reconciling of the egalitarian ideal with the qualitative differences in the natural capacities and the intellectual and moral attainments of individuals. Democratic societies delude themselves in supposing that these qualitative differences are irrelevant in such citizenship activities as voting, serving on juries, and holding public offices. Political figures are not above the "just common folks" touch. Perhaps the best example in American history was that of F. D. Roosevelt, the son of wealth and privilege, who throughout the darkest days of the economic depression spoke regularly to the American people in "fireside chats" beginning always with the salutation "My friends." This motif was exhibited in India by the lawyer from the London Inns of Court who returned to India and exchanged his striped pants for a loin cloth.

Democracy's greatest need is respect for quality. William James once said that the wise man is not necessarily the man who knows but the man who knows who knows or who knows where to get knowledge. We recognize expertise in technology, art, and science, but in the area of government we tend to fear the expert and to glorify the common man. I shall not speak for India, but in the United States anyone who has made a name in medicine, business, the movies, the military, or other areas equally removed from government is deemed qualified to run for even the highest positions. We in the West glorify Greece as the home of democracy, and we admire the achievements of fifth-century Athens, forgetting that this city-state became in the words of Edith Hamilton "a little center of white-hot spiritual energy" partly because of the selective process of requiring midwives to allow only healthy, well-formed babies to live and partly because a slave-free ratio of ten-to-one gave the citizens leisure for the arts, letters, sciences, and philosophy. Quality in individual lives and in civilizations does not result from a leveling to the lowest common denominator of mediocrity.

Let us consider this need for quality in another fashion. In a representative democracy the elected officials are caught between two motivations: one idealistic and one realistic. The idealistic motivation is to act in accord with their own best judgment; the realistic motivation is to act in accord with the wishes of their constituents. When these motivations are in conflict, the elected official has several options open to him. Let us suppose he must cast his vote on a controversial issue. What are his options?

1. He may vote as he thinks best without regard for the opinions of his constituents.
2. He may vote as he thinks best and attempt to educate his constituents so they can see the rationale for his vote.
3. He may vote in accord with the wishes of the majority of his constituents even though it conflicts with his own best judgment.
4. He may vote in accord with the wishes of the majority of his constituents and then seek some sort of justification or rationale for this position.
5. He may attempt a variety of compromises—including not voting at all.

The issue I am raising is a hornet's nest! On the one hand, a representative of the people is elected to represent the people, not to express his own values and prejudices; on the other hand, the elected official is elected because he has information and insight beyond that of the majority of his constituents, and he is empowered to act in accord with his best informed judgment. However, in the practice of representative government the elected official is usually so motivated by the anxiety of re-election that he is more concerned about what people think than in what is the right and proper decision. Thus a "good" lawmaker, a "good" executive, and even a "good" judge tends to be one who acts in accord with the majority opinion. Majority opinion becomes a quick and easy approach to ultimate truth and ultimate value. What progress would have been made in the sciences if scientific issues had been decided on the basis of public opinion?

At this point in the argument I wish to introduce the conception of caste. The term "caste" comes from a Portuguese word meaning pure race. Such a concept is nonsense in the ancient melting pot which is South Asia. We are, in fact, concerned with the ancient four-fold classification in Hindu society known as *varṇa*, and not with the vocational distinctions (*jātis*) which have crept into the classification. The *varṇa* principle can be stated in three propositions:

1. There are qualitative differences among people.
2. These differences are the result of the acts of each person.
3. Each person ought to seek his fullest development.

Radhakrishnan in his volume, *The Heart of Hindusthan*, in the context of his discussion of *varṇa* writes, "The ideal of the Hindu *dharma* is to make all men Brahmins." (p. 22) This statement is open to diverse interpretations depending upon what one means by the term *Brahmin*. If *Brahmin* denotes those whose *gotra* indicates they have descended from Vedic *ṛṣis* and who therefore observe strict rules about intermarriage and interdining, then I maintain the statement badly misrepresents the *varṇa* ideal. But if the term *Brahmin* in this statement is used to designate a person who has made much progress in the development of his human potentialities, then this is an excellent statement of the *varṇa* ideal. In terms of the second possible interpretation, we can say that the ideal aim of human society is to create those conditions within which every individual is given the opportunity to become brahminized.

Democracy needs this ideal of the actualization of man's potencies symbolized in the term *Brahmin*. For example, if one asks "Why ought there to be a balance of the ideals of equality, freedom, individualism, and general welfare in democracy?" the answer is "Because that is the best way to create a situation in which each individual can be challenged, encouraged, and assisted in the fullest realization of the human potential latent in him." The *varṇa* ideal adds a third dimension to the ideals of democracy. Without this ideal the four polar ideals are ideals of Flatland rather than the ideals of a full human situation. How this ideal of the third dimension is to be implemented is another problem. It certainly calls for creative imagination. But much is gained if we think of democracy in terms of rule by popular election. This, I suggest, is one of the means which often becomes confused with the proper ends of democracy.

We often read in *smṛti* literature that one of the marks of Kali

Yuga is that *Brahmin* women marry and have children by *Śūdras* and outcastes. In the *Dharma Śāstras* the mixing of castes is considered the most appalling sin, especially that form of exogamy in which a *Brahmin* woman has a child by a *Śūdra*. The child of such a union becomes the lowest of the low. Social pressure against *varṇa* mixing is frequently grossly misunderstood both in and out of India. Restrictions on marriage, for example, ought not to be interpreted that the *Brahmins* have a good thing going and that they ought to hang on to it. Rather I interpret the restrictions of intercaste marriage as being based on the opinion that the people of qualitative attainment ought to take that attainment into consideration in the matter of selecting a spouse, and that they ought to regard proper marriage as an integral part of their existential striving toward the realization of the full human potential.

To be a member of the twice-born is not an accident; rather each birth is determined by karmic powers of which the person is the determiner. If we assume reincarnation, *varṇa* distinctions are the proper and just results of causes largely under the control of the person; if we do not assume reincarnation, *varṇa* distinctions are perniciously unjust. I plead therefore for Hindus to be charitable to non-Hindus who evaluate Hinduism in a context which rejects reincarnation, and I plead also for non-Hindus to consider the vast difference which the conception of reincarnation makes in the interpretation of *varṇa*. But however one views *varṇa*—from a point of view which accepts reincarnation or one which rejects reincarnation—the *varṇa* distinctions must become less rigid if they are to be appropriate in a democracy. Specifically, the terms *Brahmin*, *Kṣatriya*, *Vaiśya*, and *Śūdra* must be altered to designate levels of attainment in the business of becoming truly human.

Democracy needs the *varṇa* ideal, but the *varṇa* ideal it needs is one which provides for social mobility. *Varṇa* must be modified so the attainment of the highest qualitative levels symbolized by the term *Brahmin* is possible for everyone within a single life span. Furthermore, democracy should provide the opportunities for this attainment. In a democratic society in which the doctrine of reincarnation is assumed, the terms for the four *varṇas* should indicate without prejudice both those whose birth indicates attainment over many generations and those who attain the *Brahmin* status within the present incarnation. I confess there is a likelihood of a feeling of "first class twice-born" and "second class twice-born," but such distinctions are facts with which all societies have to cope. My contention is, that in spite of the difficulties in implementation, the qualitative distinctions which traditional Hindu society expresses in the *varṇa* system are needed in democracy. Respect for quality tempers an excessive emphasis on the ideal of equality and also gives direction to all the ideals of democracy. The conception of equality on which the United States of America was founded must be radically altered, and the direction in which it needs to be changed is indicated in the *varṇa* ideal. I therefore suggest to those who form Indian internal policy that it may not be altogether wise to attempt to reorganize Indian society without *varṇa*. In eliminating the objectionable features which have crept into the *varṇa* system care should be taken not to throw out the rice with the husks and gravel. India can make an important contribution to democratic theory and practice if she can demonstrate to the world how it is possible to develop a democratic nation which preserves, honors, and implements the qualitative attainments of individuals within the democratic forms of government, state, and society. Democratic theory should be reformed so the supreme ideal is not equality, nor liberty, nor individualism, nor general welfare but the fullest development of persons both individually and collectively. Democratic practice should be a *sarvamukti* (universal salvation). A democracy should offer to all the opportunity to become a *puruṣārtha* (person of riches), an *ātmansiddha* (person whose essential nature is perfected). The brahminization or aryanization of each person should be the ideal of democracy, and this ideal is a contribution *varṇa* can make to democracy.

I cannot close this brief essay on democracy and *varṇa* without some reference to the economic realm. Nothing is of greater concern and of greater difficulty to the modern nation of India. Those of us who watch India from the outside are frequently puzzled by the way in which she mixes socialism and capitalism. How do socialism and capitalism relate to equality and quality? Socialism is often thought to be equality at work in economics, and capitalism is believed to be essentially competitive; ergo, it results in inequalities. Capitalism is thought to encourage quality through its open markets, and socialism the opposite by its removal of competition. But, on the other hand, a socialist economy can set national qualitative goals and establish rewards for differences of achievements among its citizens, and, while capitalism may encourage individual enterprise, it may also foster shoddy workmanship because of its stress on productivity. Socialism and capitalism may not be as opposed as we sometimes assume, and India may be on the right track in trying to find a balance between the two economies.

—10—

*THE BURDEN OF TRADITION**

In March, 1959, a small group of Indians and Americans met at Ootacamund under the auspices of UNESCO to discuss the topic "Traditional Values of India and the United States." On the second day, when it became obvious to me that from the Americans' point of view entirely too much emphasis was being placed on the traditionality of values, I put the following question to the group: "Would it not be better if the leaders of the Indian nation were to ask 'How much of our cultural heritage can we eliminate?' rather than 'How much of our cultural heritage can we save?' " The Indians were horrified by my question. "Surely you are jesting," the chairman observed. "After all you are a philosopher." I replied, "Yes, but I am a pragmatic philosopher." But I was not jesting, and I am not jesting now when I reopen the question. This problem seems to me to be one that India must face. India has a vast cultural tradition. In fact, she has the longest continuous cultural history of any modern nation. China's may be as long, but the continuity was broken many times. In the five thousand or six thousand years of Indian tradition her artists, poets, and philosophers have produced a prodigious quantity of material. Much of this has been lost, but that which remains is greater in bulk than similar products of any other people. At the same time India is young, a very young nation. Her culture may prove to be a liability. Tradition can become a burden.

* This essay first appeared in a slightly different form in *The Mother*, Vol. II, No. 4, (December, 1959), pp. 180-182. *The Mother* is a journal honoring the modern Hindu holy man Śri Śri Sitārāmdas Omkārnāth.

Tradition can become a burden either due to its sheer quantity or due to the uses which are made of it. Let us consider the problem of quantity first, and, following the example of Plato, begin by looking at the life of the individual. Memory is to the person as tradition is to the society. Every person has at times been embarrassed by the fraility of memory. How frequently we fail to recall a name, a fact, or an experience. Western psychologists have worked out a curve of forgetting which shows that we forget about 90 per cent of what we read in a few minutes. Some practical psychologists have attempted to formulate techniques for the improvement of memory. Yet let us not forget the blessedness of forgetting. Imagine a person who forgets nothing. After forty or fifty years his mind would be so filled with memories both useful and useless that he would find his great gift a great burden. For one thing, he would not be able to enjoy the present moment. The present would lose its freshness. For him there would be nothing new under the sun. Again, such a person would find difficulty in thinking or acting decisively because he would feel obligated to scan through the channels of memory to find clues for the solution of each theoretical and practical problem. I have been told there are some holy men in India who can recall their previous incarnations, but upon questioning I have found that what was meant was that these men had vague feelings that their present life is in some sense a repetition. Imagine the burden of a man whose memory included the infinite details not only of one life span but of thousands!

Now consider a mythical society which kept alive *all* its music, *all* its poetry, *all* its mythology, *all* its philosophy, and *all* its science. I mean by "kept alive" not that this material was incarcerated in museums, archives, galleries, and libraries where the erudite student might examine it, but that the cultural achievements were vital influences on the daily life of the people. The resulting conflicting and confusing chaos would create a social stalemate which would check and counter-check almost every move made in the society. A study of Pandurang Vaman Kane's five volume *History of Dharmashastra* causes the average Westerner to ask if India is in danger of becoming that mythical society. In India old age, not youth, is believed to possess the greater values. The young person is made to feel apologetic for his youth. This evaluation, I find, is carried over in the thinking about India as a nation. When I observe that India is a young nation, I am invariably reminded by my Indian friends that India is ancient in culture, and I am to infer that this in itself is high praise.

This leads to my second point about tradition. Tradition can become a burden when tradition is used scholastically. Tradition is used scholastically when an authority—say the *Ṛg Veda* or an *Upaniṣad*—is quoted as the final authority in politics, or education, or agriculture, or medicine, or even religion. I can illustrate by the appeals to the name of Gandhi. I have heard Gandhi quoted as the infallible authority on the question of the proposed industrialization of India's economy, on the proper form of education for modern young people, on matters of health and diet, on etiquette, etc. Please note I am saying that Gandhi's opinions were expressed not as an aid for the solution of the problem but as the final solution of the problem. This is a method which the Scholastics of the Western world identified as *ipse dixit* (he himself says so). They customarily settled issues during the Middle Ages in Europe by seeking exactly what Aristotle, or Holy Writ, or a Church Father said about the matter in question. I do not intend to cast doubt on the greatness of Gandhi, but I wish to point out that a solution made by Gandhi or an opinion expressed by Gandhi is not necessarily apropos to a related problem or even to the same problem today. The memory of Gandhi is not honored in making him an infallible authority. In fact to do so would be very un-Gandhian. For example, when Gandhi was once asked what he would do were he to attend a certain series of meetings to be held in London, he replied that he could not say for he did not know in advance what he would do or say. He found his solutions, he said, in a kind of intuition which came to him at the moment when the problem arose. How inappropriate it is to utilize the opinions of this great man to solve problems which Gandhi himself would not solve until he faced them.

Advance in human affairs often consists in cutting the umbilical cord of tradition. Man did not learn to write, or to till the soil, or to fly in the air until he was willing to make a break with the past. Henry Ford overstated the case when he said, "All history is bunk," but he caught the necessary spirit. Once on a visit to a village in West Bengal I was told that this was one of the most progressive villages in the area. One of the villagers showed me around the village, and with great pride he told me that his village had two hundred tanks. I was not impressed with this form of progress. Greater progress, I thought, would have been shown by the village if it had cooperated in putting down a deep well in order that it might have a dependable source of pure water. If India chooses to take her place among the developed nations of the modern world, she will have to reconsider the role of tradition. Many of the traditional mores and folkways will need examination in the light of this new nation's aspirations. Can India march forward by looking backward? Such sights as a jet plane flying in the sky over a bullock cart on a dusty road, a young man in the city trying to keep ties with his joint family in a village, electric lights burning in a mud hut, and an educated family keeping ancient customs because the grandmother wants it that way are illustrations of the ambiguous situation of a people puzzled about its cultural tradition. The best clue to a solution is that admonition of the Buddha on his death bed when he advised his disciples not to follow the old ways of thought and action but to launch out on their own: "Work out your own salvation with diligence." Jawaharlal Nehru saw the situation clearly when he wrote, "The extreme tolerance of every kind of belief and practice, every superstition and folly, had its injurious side also, for this perpetuated many an evil custom and prevented people from getting rid of the traditional burdens that prevented growth. . . . India must break with much of her past and not allow it to dominate the present."[1]

NOTES

1. Jawaharlal Nehru, *The Discovery of India.* Edited by Robert I. Crane. Garden City, N.Y.: Doubleday and Co., 1960, pp. 61, 387.

—11—

*THE BONDAGE OF NATIONALISM**

> In the West, a real anxiety and effort of their higher mind to rise superior to business considerations is beginning to be seen. I have come across many there whom this desire has imbued with the true spirit of the sannyasin, making them renounce their home-world in order to achieve the unity of man, by destroying the bondage of nationalism; men who have within their own soul realized the advaita of humanity.
>
> Rabindranath Tagore, "The Call of Truth," *Modern Review*, Vol. XXX, No. 4, p. 433.

One of the surprises in studying early Greek philosophy is discovering that the first philosophers of the Western world had no conception of space. Being is, and being is all there is, observed the Eleatics. The opposite of being is a name—"non-being"—but it stands for nothing. According to the Atomists there is void between atoms, but there is nothing which can be occupied either by atoms or void. Thus, neither the Eleatics nor the Atomists had the notion of things as space-occupying. Aristotle refers once to space (*chōra*) as a continuous quantity,[1] but he does not develop this idea into a full theory of space. On the other hand, he has much to say about place (*topos*), the innermost boundary of a containing body. But he was unaware that his definition of place required him either to admit that the cosmos is in no place or to develop a theory of space.

Modern scientists have pushed far beyond the early Greek intellectuals in their understanding of the up-down-ness, forward-back-

* This essay appears in *Cohesion*, Vol. III, No. 1, (January-June, 1972), pp. 2-8. *Cohesion* is the journal of The Nehru Institute of National Integration.

ness, and right-left-ness which we designate as "space," but at one crucial point they agree with the Greeks, viz., space implies limits. To the average man who puzzles over Einstein's "expanding universe" as the universe of space moving out into a nothing which must somehow also be a something, an astronomer has warned, "If our instinct is to ask, 'How can space expand when there is nothing outside for it to expand into?' we must again remember that the idea must be interpreted in terms of operation only. Put somewhat graphically, it means this and nothing more: if we measure the greatest possible distance by which two bodies can be separated, we shall get a certain result; if we perform the same operation tomorrow we shall get a larger result. There is no need to court insanity by trying to imagine expansion into a vacuity which isn't there."[2] The primitive divisions of our spatial universe into earth, air, fire, and water—or hot, cold, wet, and dry—were based on the supposition that the limits of each were distinct and recognizable. Occasionally this supposition was challenged, e.g., in the myth of Indra's slaying of the dragon Vṛtra the lethal weapon was a column of sea foam, i.e., an object neither wet nor dry and thus consistent with the compact not to use a weapon that was wet or dry. Some of the limits or boundaries on the surface of our planet are natural demarcations easily recognized. Such are seashores, rivers, mountain ranges, and canyons. When these were insufficient for man's purposes, he made artificial boundaries by means of canals, breakwaters, hedges, walls, fences, and roads. Thus he separated his fields, confined his domestic animals, and attempted to restrain his warring neighbors. The Chinese Wall, Hadrian's Wall, and the Maginot Line come to mind as boundaries to keep out enemies. But besides these physical barriers men have erected non-physical barriers. The most striking of these non-physical limitations of space are national boundaries. They may follow a river or a range of mountains, but often they are completely invisible, following no river, fence, or wall. They are denoted by lines on maps. A national boundary, however, is a very real spatial limit, and the crossing of such boundaries can be a serious transaction involving passports, visas, entrance requirements, exit permits, immigration certifications, health examinations, vaccinations and innoculations, police registrations, money exchanges, political declarations, tariffs, etc. Reasonable men know that a barrier like the Berlin Wall is demeaning and dehumanizing, but sometimes they forget that all barriers set between nations are demeaning and dehumanizing.

Nations came into existence with the crumbling of feudal societies in Europe and of empires throughout the world. The process of nation formation is still going on. Nations were first supposed to be bodies of people connected by blood ties. Later, the unifying force was thought to be similarity of customs. And finally the nation was justified solely on the principle of political sovereignty. These three reasons constitute the rationale for the creation and preservation of nations. Today in over a hundred national states children are conditioned to cherish the preservation of their nation more than their own lives. As Tagore observed in the quotation at the head of this essay, he had met Western people who, seeking a common humanity, found it necessary to destroy the bondage of nationalism. We should like to know just whom he had in mind who had renounced a "home-world" to achieve "the unity of man," and we should like to know how it was accomplished. An individual can change his citizenship, or he can become a dropout in his nation, but how can he become a citizen of no nation? Where is the Shangri-La for those who seek to escape the bondage of nationalism?

At the end of World War I the leaders of many Western nations, recognizing the dangers inherent in the doctrine of absolute sovereignty of nations, established the League of Nations and the World Court. Again at the conclusion of World War II, when atomic weapons made more imperative the implementation of reason in place of military might, the United Nations was formed and a Universal Declaration of the Rights of Man was prepared. In a sense these efforts following military conflicts were extensions of earlier national revolutions, especially the American and the French. The meliorative endeavors of these international organizations are not to be minimized, but the fact remains that they have operated within the framework of a nationalistic mentality. Although international, their existence stresses the importance of nations, and they have been contributing factors to the formation of more nations. Over fifty new nations have come into existence since the establishment of the United Nations. Again, despite the efforts of the United Nations to promote cooperation and mutual assistance among the nations, each nation still remains an independent entity manifesting absolute self-righteousness and engaging in acts which at the personal level are usually punishable by incarceration or death. Self-preservation remains the *summum bonum* of national morality. Self-sacrifice is never a national ideal. Lies, theft, and murder "on a grand scale," to use Plato's expression, are sometimes great national virtues. Patriotism, perhaps the highest virtue in the context of the nation, demands doing for one's nation that which if done by the same individual for another nation is the worst of all evils—treason.

The United Nations has done much to stop conflicts and to foster good relations in the last quarter-century, but it has failed to encourage men and women to examine the national ideal itself. It may even be charged with petrifying the habit of thinking of the importance of sovereign nations. This set of mind is deeply rooted in even the most forward-looking and creative persons in the West today. A striking example is Norman Cousins. Cousins sees the danger in the existence of nations as sovereign states, but he offers no original nor challenging solution. "Here, then, is the tragic flaw in the organization of human society. The ultimate need on earth is for the protection and preservation of life. Yet, no workable authority exists beyond the nation. The nation arrogates to itself the authority and the power to decide what it does not only inside but outside its borders."[3] He adds that "there is no legal process by which human destiny can be protected and served." Cousins, who has often been rebuked and praised for his radical opinions, cannot bring himself to think beyond the national structure: "The beginning of the age of civilized man, when it comes, will be marked by his political, philosophical, and spiritual awareness of himself as a member of a world species with world needs and with the capacity and desire to create world institutions to meet these needs. Humankind need not sacrifice the nation to create such institutions. It need only recognize and assert an allegiance of humans to one another beyond national boundaries and to do those things in the human interest that the nation as an organization is incapable of doing." According to Cousins the nation is a viable institution, and even though "the present mode of life on earth is madness," somehow by sufficient willing man can elevate and enlarge his nation-mindedness to world-mindedness: "Rational existence is possible, but it calls for a world consciousness and a world design. People who develop the habit of thinking of themselves as world citizens are fulfilling the first requirement of sanity in our time." One cannot but be disappointed that a thinker of this caliber falls into the old stereotype of imagining men can change their habits of thinking without changing their institutions or can change their habits of thinking before changing their institutions, rather than recognizing that "thinking" is a panegyric given to the process by which we defend the manner of living which is determined for us by our institutions. How can Cousins believe that people living within the nation, the institution which "arrogates to itself the authority and the power to decide what it does, not only inside but outside its borders," will somehow "develop the habit of thinking of themselves as world citizens?" He laments that "no workable authority exists beyond the nation," and that our "present mode of life on earth is madness, which is nonetheless lethal for being legal," yet he cannot move in imagination to the next step, which is the formation of world institutions of law and coercion which could within a generation or two create the habit of thinking as world citizens and of regarding with amazed wonder the former structures as we today regard the feudal structure of medieval Europe.

The failure of Cousins to think "unthinkable thoughts" and to dream "impossible dreams" points up a suspicion that we can no longer look to the West for creative insights in the area of politics. As a Western man I admit this regretfully, but I rejoice that we can look hopefully for healing ideas and actions from the ancient culture and the new nation known as India. In considering ideas first, I propose to confine attention to two great Indians of this century, Rabindranath Tagore and Aurobindo Ghosh. In bypassing Mohandas Gandhi I do not wish to diminish the importance of his ideas, ideals, and achievements, but he was primarily an activist, a pragmatist, and even an opportunist. He was the right man for his time. Many have attempted to state Gandhi's philosophy, ethics, and religion. But philosophical consistency was not his forte. His words, as he stated over and over again, were chosen for particular situations, not for all times and places. Despite what Gandhi wrote about Truth as his God, the fact is that Gandhi was faithful to truth as he saw it at any given moment rather than a timeless eternal Truth. The only unchanging article in his practical faith was his trust in his own conscience. He did not hesitate to contradict himself when he felt that the current situation demanded a changed posture. Consequently, Gandhi does not come off well in a philosophical scrutiny. Tagore and Aurobindo, on the other hand, are intellectuals whom India and the world can profitably study more closely.

"We have no word for 'Nation' in our language," wrote Tagore. "When we borrow this word from other people, it never fits us."[4] Nationalism, he claimed, is foreign to the tradition of India. Yet he confessed that from earliest years he had been subjected to attempts to instill national-mindedness in him: "Even though from childhood I had been taught that idolatry of the nation is almost better than reverence for God and humanity, I believe I have outgrown that teaching, and it is my conviction that my countrymen will truly gain their India by fighting against the education which teaches them that a country is greater than the ideals of humanity."[5]

What went wrong in India? According to Tagore, India neglected the cult of "Anna Brahma," which found the infinite manifested in the material world, and sought reality and value in the spiritual to the neglect of the material. India's contact with the West offered her an opportunity to remedy the malady of excessive and exclusive spirituality, but unfortunately India did not distinguish "the spirit of the West" and "the Nation of the West." India, not realizing she could have the former without the latter, embraced both. By "the spirit of the West" Tagore meant the active productivity, the energetic mode of life characteristic of the West; by "the Nation of the West" Tagore meant the entire apparatus of government which stresses equality and uniformity. The nation, he said, is like a power-loom in contrast with a hand-loom. Both are modes of production, but the power-loom is "relentlessly lifeless and accurate and monotonous in its production."[6] As a consequence of India's exposure to the Nation of the West, "The present civilization of India has the constraining power of the mould. It squeezes man in the grip of rigid regulations, and its repression of individual freedom makes it only too easy for men to be forced into submission of all kinds and degrees."[7] Tagore concluded after an extensive visit to China and Japan that China had been poisoned by contact with the Nation of the

West, but that Japan had been able to absorb the spirit of the West and to resist the Nation of the West. He feared that India would not show the strength displayed by Japan, that India would adopt the ways of conflict and conquest which is the core of Western nationalism, and that India, deserting her destiny, i.e., "to raise the history of man from the muddy level of physical conflict to the higher moral attitude,"[8] would seek to develop like other nations a civilization of power.

Tagore turned all his poetic emotions against the concept of the nation and the ideal of devotion to the nation. He warned against "the fierce self-idolatry of nation-worship."[9] His short essay entitled "The Nation" is a tirade of accusations against nationalism. The nation is "the survival of that part of man which is the least living."[10] Nations do not create, rather "they merely produce and destroy . . . they crowd away into a corner the living man who creates."[11] In the growth of nationalism "man has become the greatest menace to man."[12] The nation is ever watching to take advantage of the crowd mind, "this enormous power of darkness."[13] Nationalism is a thing of "gigantic vanity and selfishness."[14] But there is one ray of hope: the Age of Nationalism is "only a passing phase of civilization."[15]

Tagore's life was saddened almost unendurably in his last two years by the outbreak of war between the British and the Nazis. "I had at one time believed that the springs of civilization would issue out of the heart of Europe," he confessed in the last year of his life. "But today when I am about to quit the world that faith has gone bankrupt altogether. Today I live in the hope that the Saviour is coming—that he will be born in this poverty-stricken land that is India. . . . As I look around I see the crumbling ruins of a proud civilization strewn like a vast heap of futility. And yet I shall not commit the grievous sin of losing faith in Man."[16]

Aurobindo, like Tagore, was subjected in his youth to the propaganda of nationalism but in a vastly different fashion. While Tagore was taught to idolize the nation in his Calcutta home and schools, Aurobindo was sent to England with instructions that he be reared as an Englishman. The orders were that he not be allowed to make acquaintance with any Indian or undergo any Indian influence. These orders were carried out as far as possible during the fourteen years of his life in England, but the plans of his father to have only

English sons were not to be realized. Six months after his return to India he published a series of articles called "New Lamps for Old" on the feebleness of the activities of the Indian National Congress. The National Congress, he said, was not really national. Specifically, he charged that the Congress failed to offer a plan of action which would appeal to the distressed and ignorant masses. Already Aurobindo was planning techniques of armed rebellion, a rebellion which culminated in his arrest on May 2, 1908, for complicity in a bombing at Muzaffarpur in Bihar and incarceration in Alipur jail for one year. During the years of his militant activity he regarded nationalism as a religion: "The movement of Nationalism in Bengal is a religion by which we are trying to realize God in the nation, in our fellow-countrymen."[17] Again, "Nationalism is an Avatar. . . . It is divinely-appointed Shakti and must do its God-given work before it returns to the bosom of Universal Energy from which it came."[18] Nationalism was a "mission" to recover "Indian thought, Indian character, Indian perceptions, Indian energy, Indian greatness, and to solve the problems that perplex the world in an Indian spirit and from the Indian standpoint."[19] Aurobindo at this time displayed the narrow zeal characteristic of the new convert. However, the redeeming feature of Aurobindo's nationalism, even in those years of his youthful enthusiasms, was that India's existence as a free nation was not for India's sake alone, but for the world: "India must have *Swaraj* [self-rule] in order to live; she must have *Swaraj* in order to live for the world, not as a slave for the material and political benefit of a single purse-proud and selfish nation, but as a free people for the spiritual and intellectual benefit of the human race."[20] "Our ideal of patriotism proceeds on the basis of love and brotherhood and it looks beyond the unity of the nation and envisages the ultimate unity of mankind."[21]

During the trial Aurobindo was prophetically described by his defender, Chittaranjan Das, as "the poet of nationalism . . . the lover of humanity." His year in Alipur jail—which Aurobindo called "Alipur Ashram"—brought about a significant change in the young revolutionist. Nationalism was now a *sanātana dharma* (an eternal religion). India's work was the world's work. India possessed the key to the progress of humanity. The liberation India sought was not India's liberation but the liberation of mankind. He retired to

Pondicherry to spend the rest of his life working out the implications of the larger liberation. But the British were not convinced that Aurobindo had forsworn violence, and for twenty-eight years Aurobindo and his ashramites were shadowed by the police who year after year described them as "a dangerous gang of bomb-makers."

Aurobindo, like Tagore, appeared to have doubts about the nationalism of India as he watched the progress of the independence movement. He also feared that India might imitate the West in structure and miss the spirit: "Either India will be nationalised and industrialised out of all recognition and she will be no longer India or else she will be the leader in a new world-phase, aid by her example and cultural infiltration the new tendencies of the West and spiritualise the human race."[22] Finally, in his Independence Day Declaration issued on August 15, 1947, while rejoicing in the liberation of India from the British, he cautioned that the nation must be only a transition to more valuable governmental organizations: "But an outward basis is not enough; there must grow an international spirit and outlook, international forms and institutions must appear, perhaps such developments as dual or multilateral citizenship, willed interchange or voluntary fusion of cultures. Nationalism will have fulfilled itself and lost its militancy and would no longer find these things incompatible with self-preservation and the integrality of outlook. A new spirit of oneness will take hold of the human race."[23] Thus the nationalism of Aurobindo, like the nationalism of Tagore, turned into an internationalism. Aurobindo dreamed "of individual perfection and a perfect society." Tagore proclaimed, "The great sky resounds with hallelujahs to the Coming of Man."

Of course, neither lived to see the fulfillment of his dreams. No man does! The fruit is never as sweet as anticipated. India in the years of her nationhood has been confronted with economic, social, political, religious, and linguistic problems which have brought her close to civil war. Boundary disputes have resulted in armed conflicts. Poverty, overpopulation, and underemployment keep a large percentage of her people on the border of starvation. India's situation is so desperate, and the ability of the world to help is so limited, that one author—Paul Ehrlich in *The Population Bomb*—has advised the employment of the concept of "triage," i.e., the separation of the needy into three classes: (1) those who will die regardless of treatment, (2) those who will survive regardless of treatment, and (3) those who can survive only if given treatment. Ehrlich singles out India as an example of the first class, and he recommends that India be written off as a nation and as a people. Those of us in the West who have learned to love India and Indians, and who are appalled by the inhumanity of this suggestion, do recognize that the Indian nation is in serious trouble. This may be a good time for Indians to rethink what Tagore and Aurobindo said about the nation as a transitional stage and to reconsider Tagore's "country of the No-Nation." India's policy of non-alignment has been a remarkable witness to her unwillingness to play the game of nationalism. Unfortunately, India's conflicts with Pakistan and China have forced her to maintain a far larger military force than her economy can support or her tradition of tolerance justifies. Circumstances have forced India to stress nation-mindedness rather than the human-mindedness of Tagore and Aurobindo. Can India reverse her actions so that she labors not for the old pattern of national conflicts but for Aurobindo's dream of "a world-union forming the outer basis of a fairer, brighter and nobler life for all mankind?"[24]

It is not for me to answer the last question, but a few suggestions might be offered about how any nation might begin to break the cycle of problems inherent in the national syndrome. Today we do have a "world-union" which forms the outer basis of a brighter life for all mankind. This is the United Nations. It has not worked as well as was hoped, and it has not worked as was planned. But it has survived. Secretary-General U Thant upon the termination of his tenure in that office in 1971 pleaded that the United Nations be given more responsibility. My suggestion is that some nation take him at his word. That nation can begin by abolishing its militia. It may then, after a vote of its citizens, resign from the United Nations, abandon its government, renounce sovereignty, and hand itself over to the United Nations as a ward. Thus it would become a "country of No-Nation." This suggestion will sound ridiculous to minds trained to think in accustomed ways. A few may recall the observation of Socrates: "Those who have passed their days in the pursuit of philosophy are ridiculously at fault when they have to appear and speak in court."[25] But some people must begin to act as well as to talk about the unity of mankind. Some nation must break the bondage of nationalism.

NOTES

1. *Categories* 5 a 6.
2. Herbert Dingle, "Astronomy and Scientific Ideas" in *Science for a New World.* Planned and arranged by Sir J. A. Thomson. New York: Harper and Brothers, 1934, p. 283.
3. The quotations from Cousins appear in an editorial in the *Saturday Review*, September 25, 1971, p. 30.
4. From a letter written to C. F. Andrews. *Sources of Indian Tradition*, Vol. II. Edited by William Theodore De Bary. New York and London: Columbia University Press, 1958, pp. 239-240.
5. *A Tagore Reader.* Edited by Amiya Chakravarty. New York: The Macmillan Co., 1961, p. 200.
6. "Nationalism" in *Sources of Indian Tradition*, Vol. II, p. 236.
7. "The Spirit of Freedom" in *Creative Unity*. London: Macmillan and Co., 1922, p. 140.
8. From a letter written to C. F. Andrews. *Op. cit.*, p. 239.
9. "Nationalism" in *A Tagore Reader*, p. 199.
10. "The Nation" in *Creative Unity*, p. 139.
11. *Ibid.*, p. 146.
12. *Ibid.*, p. 142.
13. *Ibid.*, p. 143.
14. *Ibid.*, p. 144.
15. *Ibid.*
16. "Crisis in Civilization" in *Faith of a Poet*. Edited by Sisirkumar Ghose. Bombay: Bharatiya Vidya Bhavan, 1964, p. 55.
17. *Speeches*, p. 24. Quoted in *The Liberator* by Sisirkumar Mitra. Delhi, Bombay, and Calcutta: Jaico Publishing House, 1954, pp. 102-3.
18. *Bande Mataram*, May 3, 1908. *The Liberator*, p. 104.
19. *Ibid.*, March 29, 1908. *The Liberator*, p. 105.
20. *Weekly Bande Mataram*, July 7, 1907. *The Liberator*, p. 106.
21. *Speeches*, p. 175. *The Liberator*, p. 109.
22. Aurobindo, *The Foundations of Indian Culture*. New York: The Sri Aurobindo Library, 1933, pp. 14-15.
23. *The Liberator*, p. 190.
24. *Ibid.*, p. 189.
25. *Theaetetus* 172C. Jowett translation.

-12-

THE ANATOMY OF VIOLENCE*

One of man's most persistent self-delusions is that he is the rational animal. The non-rational animals—the lower animals—are red in tooth and claw, but man uses the intellect to solve problems. This we like to believe. Yet with the exception of the deer, the dove, the Siamese fighting fish and a few others, the lower animals do no serious physical harm upon other members of their own species. The human animal on the other hand has been involved in internecine warfare during much of his appearance on the earth. Although man supposes that to be rational is to be human, one could more truthfully state that to be violent is to be human.

Violence refers to acts. Thoughts or feelings may be said to be violent only if they lead to violent acts. Violent acts form a subclass of acts done directly or indirectly upon beings capable of sensation and consciousness. To speak of breaking rocks violently or slapping water violently is to speak animistically. Destruction of property may be said to be violent only in the sense that it is an act against the owner of the property. A violent act is always an act in which the actor imposes his will upon another without regard for the will and desire of the one upon whom the act is directed. A dog may be treated violently; a dogwood tree probably cannot be treated violently; a piece of wood certainly cannot be so treated. Violence may be characterized as an act of a sentient being upon another sentient being

* This essay appears in *The Personalist*, Vol. LI, No. 4 (Autumn, 1970), pp. 417-433. Reprinted by kind permission of the editor.

without regard for that being's feelings or wishes. A violent act imposes the will of the actor upon another. The intent may be either good or evil.

Non-violence has been praised almost universally by religious and moral teachers. Peace, good will, harmlessness, compassion, charity, and love are the chief masks non-violence wears in various cultures. But man has not heeded his prophets and seers. While giving lip service to the virtue of non-violence, he has not felt secure without a weapon in hand, a weapon ranging from fist axe to hydrogen bomb.

Man's moral evolution from savage to savant is believed to be a passage from passion to reason. Civilization is thought to be the desertion of the old ways of violence and the inauguration of the non-violent techniques for promoting orderly change. Hebrew moral law, Greek philosophy, Christian theology, and Roman politics were civilizing influences in the development of Western culture. The doctrine of *ahiṁsā* has been variously interpreted as non-injury, compassion, pacifism, and vegetarianism in Hinduism, Buddhism, and Jainism. Yet both in East and West the rejection of the ways of violence has been neither widespread nor lasting. In India at the time when Gandhi was pleading for non-violence in the effort to push the British out, Shaheed Suhrarwardy, the Chief Minister of Bengal, wrote, "Bloodshed and disorder are not necessarily evil in themselves, if resorted to for a noble cause."[1] At the same time B. R. Ambedkar, the Chairman of the Constitution Committee, offered the admonition, "Non-violence wherever possible; violence wherever necessary."[2] One of the most beautiful apologies for violence couched in the language of the Enlightenment begins with these words: "When in the course of human events, it becomes necessary for one people to dissolve the political bands which have connected them with another, and to assume among the powers of the earth, the separate and equal station to which the Laws of Nature and Nature's God entitle them, a decent respect to the opinions of mankind requires that they should declare the causes which impel them to the separation." This document, like the words of Suhrarwardy and Ambedkar, recognizes the necessity of the resort to violence: "We must, therefore, acquiesce in the necessity, which denounces our Separation, and hold them, as we hold the rest of mankind, Enemies in War, in peace, Friends." The rational animal must have reason for his irrationality! He must find some causes which require him to act violently.

Although the United States of America was conceived in violence, the new nation became a haven of freedom, opportunity, and security for millions of oppressed peoples. The Statue of Liberty's invitation

> Give me your tired, your poor,
> Your huddled masses yearning to breathe free,
> The wretched refuse of your teeming shore,
> Send these, the homeless, tempest-tossed to me:
> I lift my lamp beside the golden door.

symbolized the hopes and aspirations of those who came to this land. The more energetic Europeans emigrated to America. Hence it is not surprising that it was these people who drove the Amerindians from their land and who fought one of the most savage civil wars of all time. In the twentieth century America has engaged in two World Wars, a Korean war, a Vietnam war, and several lesser armed conflicts, but in spite of these military ventures she has consistently preserved her self-image as that of a peaceful nation. At the same time her leaders insist that she not allow other nations to surpass her in military might. "Bargaining from a position of strength" is a favored cliché of her politicians. In addition to her stockpile of atomic weapons the United States has stored sufficient nerve gas to kill the human population of the world thirty times over. Other gases kept in reserve include vast quantities of vomit gas, tear gas, and incapacitating gas. Also in the "peace-keeping arsenal" are agents to induce anthrax, tularemia, Q-fever, and psittacosis. Work progresses on techniques for inducing plagues of undulant fever, coccidioidomycosis, botulism, cholera, encephalitis, Rocky Mountain spotted fever, and other diseases. Yet the United States agreed to the 1966 United Nations' resolution outlawing the use of chemical-biological weapons. She has given notice on several occasions that she will not be the first to use chemical-biological weapons, but the peoples of the world cannot forget that the United States is the only nation that has used atomic bombs—nor can they forget that the bombs were dropped on Oriental cities.

The violence syndrome is coming to a head in America. How explain to black ghetto dwellers, Amerindians, and college students that total warfare is approved as foreign policy but not as instrument of internal social pressure? That violence is allowable for a nation but not for the people of the nation? That unconditional surrender may be demanded of foreign enemies, but that non-negotiable demands have no place in domestic conflicts? That violence is an unfortunate necessity internationally, but that law and order must be maintained on streets and campuses? That what a nation wants may be secured by violence, but that what a group within the nation wants must be secured by legal means?

If man must find convincing arguments for violence, so also he must give reasons for those occasions when he acts non-violently. When is non-violence a virtue? When may we justifiably be asked to turn the other cheek, to go the second mile, to share a loaf of bread, and to give cloak and coat? The answer may shock at first, for it may not be what the man of good will expected. In simplest terms it is this: benevolent acts may be done and benevolent gifts may be given to a member of the secondary group only when doing so does not deprive one of performing the proper acts toward those of the primary group. If giving food and clothing to a stranger takes food away from one's child, then giving aid to the stranger is not virtuous. Non-violence in this respect is like benevolence. Acting non-violently is virtuous only when this way of acting does not conflict with what society considers to be primary obligations. Who would praise the man who gave away his family's food supply when there was no food available to replace it? Who would call virtuous the man who offered no resistance to the kidnapping of his child? Non-violence is a prodigality of affluence. The rich do not need to act violently; and with bread and circuses, dole and social security, they may induce the poor not to seize more than they have. But the good earth is not boundless in resources for life. The time will come when mines are exhausted, when rivers, lakes, and oceans can no longer support aquatic life, and when the land can no longer produce enough food for the human population. Will non-violence then be a virtue? Long before living space per person has shrunk to the spatial limitations of the human body we shall have given up the view of non-violence as a virtue. In order to preserve human life on this planet we shall need to declare some violent acts virtuous. Specifically we shall need to limit births. Voluntary limitation has not worked thus far, and we see little hope that it will work in the future. The time will come when sterilization, abortion, infanticide, mercy slaying, and other techniques of limiting the number of human beings on this planet must be imposed without consideration for individual wishes. These acts will be violent, and they will be done because they will be virtuous.

We who love democracy and cherish the liberal tradition may not wish to contemplate the collapse of our freedom, our egalitarianism, and our individualism, but human survival on this planet and on any planet capable of supporting human life depends upon the control of human population. Society will ultimately be based on forced controls. The best that lovers of democracy can hope is that the inevitable be postponed as long as possible. We must ask ourselves if we are approaching the end of the fruitfulness of the Hebrew-Greek-Christian-Roman tradition of the West and of the Buddhist-Taoist-Confucian-Hindu tradition of the East. Man's continued existence on this globe will depend either upon ways of behaving far different from any he has been able to muster in social situations other than those in a monastery or convent, or upon what we have chosen to call violence. The former seems highly improbable; the latter unavoidable—unless man chooses genocide. Looking at the future of the human species from the point of view of a secular eschatology gives us little ground for hoping we can escape violence. There is only the remotest possibility that we can discipline our self-destructive propensities in time to stave off ultimate destruction. The programs and sanctions of religion—the Buddhist middle path, the Hindu tolerance, the Hebrew law, and the Christian charity—will be completely inadequate under the ultimate conditions even as they are of limited adequacy under penultimate conditions. The time approaches when the preservation of the human race may depend upon a few in whom wisdom dwells controlling violently the acts of others. For example, all male children will conceivably be sterilized at birth save for a few breeders who will be the source of sperm to fertilize under laboratory conditions ova selected for development into human replacements. Death will probably be as regulated as birth. Few of us today are prepared to accept such a world, but given man's power to adjust, we can conceive of our descendents accepting modes of birth and death remote from those we today regard as normal and proper. We can at least prepare ourselves for the future state of our race by examining the anatomy of violence.

Violence appears in three forms: the hedonic, the frustrated, and the committed. These may be thought of as motivations of the act. The three are different emphases. Any violent act will be marked more by one than by either of the other two. Seldom, if ever, does one form appear in the total absence of the others. Let us consider as an example one of the favorite tactics of militant minorities—arson. Churches, libraries, business houses, post offices, buses, railway coaches, apartment houses, shops, and private dwellings have been burned by protesting minorities. But to what end? What appears to the majority as senseless destruction may appear to the minority as essential and meaningful. A specific act of arson may be planned by the minority as a symbol of its dedication to a social ideal: the old must go in order that the new may come. The act may in addition reflect the frustration of the minority caught in what appears to be a hopeless situation, and it may also be an effort to experience the hedonic satisfaction of destroying something the minority would like to possess. This plurality of motives may come in the arsonists' analysis of the act. It is described as an act of commitment in their appearance in a court of law, as an act of frustration in their conversation with a social worker, and as a fun act in the reliving of the event among their peers.

Hedonic Violence

In recent years much of the violence in American slums and ghettos has occurred in the "long, hot summer." While some have attempted to account for this as the impact of heat and humidity on bodies, the better explanation is that summer is the dull time of the year for dwellers in the inner city. The schools are not in session, the children are on the streets, young people are home from college, and it is slack time in factories and industries with vacations for men and women who have no place to go but their flats or the streets. It is a time of boredom in which a bit of excitement is a welcome change from the dull monotony of the days. A fist fight, a car accident, or a broken shop window are welcome breaks in a humdrum day. Violence can be fun both for the participant and for the onlooker. Car thieves, bank robbers, kidnappers, and even murderers when brought to trial try to rationalize why they did what they did, when the truth is that there may have been no well-thought-out motivation. It seemed like fun at the time. But to say "I did it just for kicks" is not the explanation one wants to give in a courtroom, so the hedonic event is couched in fine-sounding words about social justice, protest movements, community frustrations, and economic pressures.

Violence is enjoyable. This is one reason why people enjoy spectator sports such as cockfights, bullfights, boxing, wrestling, football, hockey, auto races, and roller-skating derbies. These are emotional equivalents for war, the most thrilling "sport" of all the combat sports. General George Patton observed at the close of World War II, "War is hell—and how I love it!"

The component parts of hedonic violence are four. The first is relief of monotony. Any human activity pursued for a long period of time must be broken. The coffee break is based on the sound principle of alternation in human life. Human effort, physical or mental, must be interrupted or there is a noticeable loss of efficiency, creativity, and enjoyment. Examples are numerous: the athlete must occasionally break training lest he overtrain; the Zen master terminates a long period of meditation with the order "Let us laugh!"; the Epicureans supplanted their simple diet of bread and gruel with a banquet once each month; the Lenten season is often divided by a day in which restrictions are rescinded; the Holi festival is a time when the twice-born act like *Śūdras*. Moral holidays, emotional outbursts, laughs over a simple joke, and violent acts have one common denominator: they serve to ease the strain, concentration, and dullness of a single way of acting, thinking, or evaluating.

A second component of hedonic violence is its unpredictability. Probability or statistical predictability is the rule of all human life. The farmer who sows his seed knows that if he does not sow he will not reap, but he also knows that sowing is no guarantee that there will be a reaping. Acts of violence are even more unpredictable. War, which is violence in the extreme, has been characterized as a science, but the truth is that it bears greater resemblance to art. Victory in war is not merely a matter of materiel and strategy; it depends still more on the intangibles of determination, the will to fight, the desire for victory, the consciousness of destiny, and other highly unpredictable psychological factors. All violent acts are like that. Violent acts are, as we have said, the imposition of the will of one sentient being on the will of another sentient being. The response of persons to violence is not predictable either. One person offers resistance at one time, acquiescence at another. This is part of the tantalizing nature of the violent act.

A third feature of hedonic violence is the thrill of destruction. The enjoyment of destroying is noticed early in the life of the human infant. The child soon experiences the excitement of knocking down piles of blocks and smashing sand castles. Why such acts are enjoyable is difficult to say. Perhaps there is satisfaction in the feeling of mastery and domination over inanimate objects. The phenomenon appears in adult years in watching a four-alarm fire in an apartment building, a free-standing chimney dropped by a dynamite blast, a demolition ball smash a brick wall, and a bulldozer push over trees. How much of the violence in the streets of Watts and Detroit was the result of the fun of destroying something? Destruction has not been incorporated into the philosophies and religions of the Establishment in the West. We keep the devil out of the godhead. Not so in India. The Trimūrti (three forms) of the godhead in Hinduism is Creation (Brahmā), Preservation (Viṣṇu), and Destruction (Śiva). This is probably more in accord with the nature of things; it is certainly more in accord with the nature of the human psyche. It is fun to destroy.

The last component of hedonic violence is what may be called the fascination of the terrible. John Bunyan, writes J. B. Pratt, was "extremely suggestible and peculiarly subject to the fascination of the terrible.' "[3] Bunyan, having read about the unpardonable sin, concluded it consisted of certain words which if spoken would bring eternal damnation. Bunyan became attracted by the heinousness of this sin, and was so fascinated by the thought of saying a word which would produce everlasting punishment that he found himself saying certain blasphemous words over and over again. In *Grace Abounding* Bunyan says, "And in so strong a measure was this temptation upon me that often I have been ready to clap my hand under my chin to hold my mouth from opening, and to that end also I have thought other times to leap with my head downwards into some muck-hill hole or other, to keep my mouth from speaking."[4] Bunyan wanted to do the terrible. Plato gives an example of desire to see the terrible in *The Republic*: "Leontius, the son of Aglaion, coming up one day from the Piraeus, under the north wall on the outside, observed some dead bodies lying on the ground at the place of execution. He felt a desire to see them, and also a dread and abhorrence of them; for a time he struggled and covered his eyes, but at length the desire got the better of him and forcing them open, he ran to the dead bodies, saying, 'Look, ye wretches, take your fill of the fair sight.' "[5] Man is fascinated by the unusual, the ugly, the tragic, the perverse, the grotesque, the hideous, and the evil.

A violent act may be repulsive to the actor and to the observer, but both may find a strange attraction for it. This attraction need not be an aberration. This fascination for the terrible is inherent in the animal that seeks to experience and to know.

Thus far we have had limited success in rooting hedonic violence out of human behavior. Nor is it clear why such an alteration would be desirable if possible. "I found them witless and gave them the use of their wits and made them masters of their minds," boasted the arrogant Prometheus.[6] He gave them something else: the Promethean enthusiasm which expresses itself in the will to live, the will to dominate, and the will to endure, and in the enjoyment of the unusual, the unpredictable, the destructive, and the terrible.

Violence of Frustration

Violence of frustration and violence of commitment are distinguished from hedonic violence in that they are motivated externally rather than internally. They are directed either against or in favor of a specific thing, person, plan, or existing form of behavior. The violence of frustration is negative in the sense that it is primarily aimed at stopping a state of affairs; the violence of commitment is positive in the sense that it is primarily aimed at originating a different state of affairs. An act of frustration, though negative, may be extremely effective in uniting a group of people in a common cause. The Boston Tea Party focused the attention of the American colonists on their common opposition to taxation without representation. Later, after winning a military victory over the British forces, the colonists found great difficulty in attaining the liberty propounded by Patrick Henry and the egalitarianism of Thomas Jefferson. In Germany in July, 1944, a group of men united in planning one violent act: the assassination of Adolf Hitler. Some of these men were discouraged Nazi officers who believed Hitler had lost the war and some were church leaders who opposed National Socialism on the grounds of justice, goodness, and decency, but all had come to the conclusion that Hitler must be killed. The plotters were discovered and executed. Among them was the Protestant theologian Dietrich Bonhoeffer. Preparation for violence growing out of their frustrations had brought them together. We cannot imagine what they would have done next had they succeeded, for their aspirations for Germany and the German people were widely divergent.

Three features of the violence of frustration are to be considered: it springs out of despair, it may serve as a catharsis of emotions, and it is a protest rather than a plan for positive action. This form of violence stands midway between the other two forms with respect to its motivation. If hedonic violence springs from boredom, and if violence of commitment springs from hope of improvement, violence of frustration may be said to spring out of such emotions as defeat, impotence, futility, anguish, and distress. It is the act of the person who does not like what he sees, has no power to change it, and lacks all the facts needed to formulate an alternative plan. During the 1930's and 1940's many Americans were asking why the Germans allowed the Nazi system to develop, and why they did not do something to stop it. But many Americans have found themselves in similar situations. How can an individual citizen register his opposition to a military draft? March in peace parades? Refuse to pay part of the federal income tax? Join peace organizations? Carry a sign reading "Hell no! I won't go!"? Write letters to Congressmen? Emigrate to Australia? Register as a conscientious objector? Most of these ways are expressions of frustration rather than techniques for improving the situation.

The violence of frustration is a climate in which martyrs are made. The individual may engage in acts against the Establishment which in our terminology will have to be called "non-violent violence." He may lie down in front of a bulldozer to prevent the destruction of a low-income residence, or parade for civil rights without a permit, or burn his draft card. In such acts he is saying to the Establishment, "Stop doing what you are doing!" Or the individual may express his frustration by an act on his body which calls attention to the depth of his anguish: fasting or self-immolation are examples. In these acts he is saying, "See how much I am opposed to this." Gandhi's fasts are classic examples. An act of violence of frustration may be chiefly a ceremonial act. It is not designed to improve or to change the object. It celebrates frustration. How much exhibitionism or masochism is involved in these acts is difficult to determine. But even so, it is a serious mistake to underestimate the importance of an act of violence as symbolic of the utter frustration of the person.

An act of violence of frustration may serve as a catharsis of emotions. A person in a helpless and hopeless situation continues to build up emotional resentment unless there is a means by which the emotion can be expended. A ceremonial act of violence can be the means for such release. A parade in the streets may not solve the problem, but it may diminish the emotional buildup. Wise administrators provide suggestion boxes for their employees. Even though the usable suggestions are very few, the box serves its purpose by providing employees a way to express complaints and recommendations. The ceremonial act, however, will lose its therapeutic value if it is known to be only therapeutical, even as prayer ceases to be meaningful for the average person when he realizes that prayer is a monologue rather than a dialogue.

An act of violence of frustration is essentially a protest, a disapproval of the status quo. Protest angers the Establishment. "Don't complain unless you have a better solution to offer," say those in power. But this is to ignore the fact that raising objections may prepare the way for desirable change. The Protestant Reformation was triggered by a list of ninety-five complaints. The violence of frustration is the first expression of dislike of things as they are. Two cautions may be appropriate. One is that there are professional complainers who find fault with everything on principle. They may be ignored. The other is that violence of frustration is a symptom of life and concern. While the words and acts of the protester may irritate the Establishment man, he, unless he be a tyrant, ought to be grateful that some care enough to protest. In modern democratic societies it is not the protesters who are social liabilities, rather it is those who do not care. If democracy weakens and dies, the onus is to be placed on the vast indifferent majority. Appeal to the "silent majority" is an artifice of demagogues.

Violence of Commitment

We have defined violence as any act in which the actor imposes his will upon another without regard for the will and the desires of the other being. The act may be motivated by the desire to seek a pleasant relief from boredom, or by frustration, or by commitment. The third form is the most significant. When John Dewey defined the religious quality as "any activity pursued in behalf of an ideal and against obstacles and in spite of threats of personal loss because of conviction of its general enduring value"[7] he was also giving a definition of what we have called the violence of commitment. Likewise T. R. V. Murti's statement on philosophy can be regarded as a characterization of the violence of commitment: "Philosophy, when cultivated seriously and systematically leads to interminable and total conflict."[8] It is a rare war that is not defended by its supporters as demanding total dedication because of the good which will spring from victory. Violence of commitment is action to make that which matters most prevail. Such action has highest priority. "Give me this, or give me death!" is the voice of the violence of commitment.

Violence of commitment is the ultimate proof of the degree to which one holds a belief. It is existential conviction, pragmatic affirmation, overt evidence. If one is fully dedicated to a program of thought and action, one will act to make that program operative. One will cease from such action only when this action is in conflict with another program which is placed higher in the hierarchy of beliefs and actions. A belief which will be given up intellectually and existentially when shown to be in conflict with another belief we shall call a contingent belief. A belief which transcends all contingent beliefs, one for which no other belief will cause us to cease our efforts to advance it, we shall call an absolute belief. Absolute beliefs are absolutely valued. Any act which will make an absolute belief triumph is justified. Such a belief is the end which justifies any means. We moderns think that absolutism was a medieval notion which we have outgrown, but in truth it is we who are the absolutists. The fanaticism of the Nazis was matched by the fanaticism of the allied forces. Hitler could not have asked for greater dedication to the Third Reich than that which Churchill asked of the British. The concept of total war with the bombing of cities, the eliminating of distinction between combatant and non-combatant, and, finally, the dropping of atomic bombs on civilians thrust mankind into the era of violence, the era of total commitment.

The paradox of absolute commitment is that the violence inherent in the commitment itself may be in conflict with violence. We Americans have found ourselves several times in this century in the position of inflicting violence upon people in order that peace, love, good will, brotherhood, and harmony will characterize the affairs of mankind. We have attempted to advance love hatefully, peace aggressively, good will evilly, moderation immoderately, and life murderously!

What is to be done? Two possibilities are open. One is to continue to seek the Good beyond good which is worthy of ultimate commitment, confident that it will be found and that it can be translated into human action. Fundamentally this is the idealistic tradition stemming from Plato in the West and from the Upaniṣadic tradition as interpreted by Śaṅkara in India. The other possibility is to desist from seeking the Good beyond good, and to advise men to cease playing God. Leave ultimacy to the gods! If anyone has ultimate truth, ultimate goodness, and ultimate beauty, it is they. Our speculations about the real and the valuable are human constructions subject to human limitations. This is the realistic tradition rooted in the West in Aristotle and in the East in Confucius. This tradition reminds us of the importance of incorporating metaphilosophical insights into our philosophical systems and metareligious insights into our religions. If we wish to keep the concept of deity in our systems, let us make God the consolation prize we award to ourselves when we discover our finitude. The only absolute is that there is no absolute. Let us recognize with the Hindu *tat tvam asi* (The That is you), with the Buddhist *saṃsāra* is *nirvāṇa* (The phenomenal is the Real), and with the Christian "*This* is eternal life."

John R. Platt of the University of Chicago has been quoted as saying, "The world has become too dangerous for anything less than utopias."[9] The saving grace of his statement is the fact that he has put the word "utopia" in the plural. There is no Utopia; there are only utopias, i.e., various conceptions of the good life. Man, the creature in whom has evolved self-consciousness, now takes on his own evolution. "He makes his own soul throughout all his earthly days," said Teilhard de Chardin.[10] But the optimism of the pluralistic possibilities of man and the world must not cloud from our minds the ugly truth that man must now include genocide among those possibilities. Life is a necessary condition of any good life. And the future existence of man on the earth is problematical.

The early Christians looked hopefully to the end of earthly condition of man. They were a waiting community. They were waiting for the immanent end of history and the beginning of a new dimension of reality. The medieval Christians may be said to have been an expectant community. They expected that there would be an end of history, but in the meanwhile they were preparing themselves both for the possibility of a full life on earth and a later entrance into heaven. Both the early and the medieval Christians held that somehow their God would save them.[11] Today some Christian theologians are inaugurating a new theology called "the theology of hope." They have even coined a new word—"mellontology"—to displace the term "eschatology." This is to suggest the shift from a study of last things to a study of possibilities. They want Christians to look forward eagerly and optimistically rather than apprehensively. But is this whistling in the dark? Perhaps a more realistic view based on the present overkill weapons stocked by some of the large nations is a secular eschatology which holds that there will be no future for the human animal unless worldwide controls of the most rigid nature are clamped on the stocking of doomsday weapons.

Human civilization is in a race with time. Can we control men and nations before we destroy each other and our world? The race is not merely between education and catastrophe, for there is a third contestant. This is coercion, enlightened force, violence of commitment, or whatever label may be applied to that situation described by Plato when wisdom and strength are united. Those of us reared in genteel traditions who had hoped that the liberal democratic tradition would through education and the popular ballot bring mankind into

Elysian fields may not be happy about the conclusions to which we must come. We should like to believe that through the slow and tortuous democratic processes of decision-making a social and political system will evolve in which each citizen of the world community has an opportunity to express his opinion. We should like to believe that rule will be by consent of the governed, and that persuasion will be by education and rational argument. We should like to believe that the day will come when each individual's intelligence, rights, and freedom will be respected. But the hopes for such a day are fading. Our world is rapidly moving into that state of urgency when action must be taken which cannot wait for a head count. The slow, wasteful, and cumbersome democratic processes are luxuries tolerable only as long as there is more land, more water, more air, and more space than is necessary for the support of the people now on the earth. But when there will be scarcely enough land, water, air, and space to sustain the human race, then the democratic ways will be drastically modified by the ways of violence. We foresee the approach of that terrible condition. The depletion of the natural resources of the planet and the multiplication of the human population will bring us to that awful day when we must decide between extinction or preservation of our species. If human beings cannot be educated to restrain voluntarily their exploitation of natural resources, warfare among nations, and sex relations leading to births, then a Grand Inquisitor policy must enter the human scene.

Those appalled by the revolutionary ideas of Marx and Engels may well prepare themselves for other ideas far more revolutionary. Marx saw through the gunsmoke of the revolution to the classless society and the withering away of the state. But the anatomy of violence offers no such utopia. There is no age of peace in the offing when the lion and the lamb will lie down together. The age of violence is not a threshold to an age of peace. It is the necessary condition of human survival. Violence may be not only part of the soteriological process but also part of the only possible heaven on earth. Violence may be the religion of the future. The preservation of the rational animal on the face of this planet depends upon the rational uses of violence. An alternative is to follow the ways of human behavior which are turning earth into a slag heap.

NOTES

1. *The Statesman* (Calcutta), August 5, 1946.
2. Quoted by Dhananjay Keer in *Dr. Ambedkar, Life and Mission*. Bombay: A. V. Keer, 1954, p. 87.
3. J. B. Pratt, *The Religious Consciousness*. New York: The Macmillan Co., 1923, p. 142. See also Troy Organ, "The Fascination of the Terrible," *Religion in Life*, Vol. X, No. 3 (Summer, 1941), pp. 372-379.
4. *Grace Abounding*, Section 104.
5. *The Republic* 439E. Jowett translation.
6. Aeschylus, *Prometheus Bound*, line 442. Translated by David Grene.
7. John Dewey, *A Common Faith*. New Haven: Yale University Press, 1934, p. 27.
8. T. R. V. Murti, *The Central Philosophy of Buddhism*. London: George Allen and Unwin, 1960, p. 126.
9. *The New York Times*, March 27, 1968, Section E, p. 12.
10. Pierre Teilhard de Chardin, *Le Milieu Divin*. Translated by Bernard Wall. London: Collins, Fontana Books, 1964, p. 61.
11. Cf. "From the gods who sit in grandeur grace comes somehow violent." Aeschylus, *Agamemnon*, line 182. Translated by Richard Lattimore.

—13—

GOD-TALK AND BEYOND *

Religious language is strange language. Its terms and expressions are notoriously confusing. Words such as "god,"[1] "salvation," "sin," "spirit," "inspiration," "belief," "faith," and "revelation" slip from one meaning to another. "God is a spirit," announces the Fourth Gospel, and then in the same sentence admonishes the worshiper to worship "in spirit and in truth." (John 4:24) Even philosophers slip in using the word "spirit." For example, note what happens to "spirit" in this quotation from R. G. Collingwood: "It is only when we reach the higher religions that we make the discovery that God is a spirit, and that the spirit of our acts is in his eyes more important than their conventional orderliness."[2] In a passage in the New Testament the term "love" is both property and substance: "Love is of God; . . . for God is love." (I John 4:7-8) But most puzzling of all is the language about god. I shall call it "god-talk." The examination of god-talk is one of the excellent services the philosophy of language analysis can perform.

As Western philosophy began to break from authoritarian theology, arguments for the existence of the Christian God were central concerns. Four major arguments came into being, each associated with a philosopher who is regarded as the first to give definitive structure to the argument: the ontological of Anselm, the cosmological of Aquinas, the teleological of Paley, and the moral of Kant. Since the time of the formation of these arguments philosophers

* This essay originally appeared in *Quest*, October-December, 1970, pp. 39-46.

have debated their validity. Often philosophers have been strangely unphilosophical in failing to examine the nature of the God whose existence the arguments seek to establish. Both the defenders and the critics of the arguments have for the most part assumed the nature of the god whose existence is established by the arguments. And as long as the arguments did not stray from the Judaeo-Christian-Moslem tradition this assumption was partially justified. The exposure to Eastern religions has changed this. Today philosophers of religion realize that before examining an argument for the existence of a god, they must examine the nature of the god whose existence is being argued for. And now, thanks to modern language analysis, philosophers know that prior to both an examination of the validity of the arguments and an examination of the assumptions about the nature of the god they must attempt to comprehend the god-talk, the language used to describe god and the relation of man and god.

The first of the analysts of language in our generation were the logical positivists. We now find it hard to believe that positivists in the 1930's and 1940's actually thought they could divide all language into the formal, the factual, and the emotional. A sentence according to this analysis establishes a structure, or states a fact, or expresses an emotion. So sentences in god-talk such as "God is love" or "I believe in God" must be a factual statement like "This patch is yellow," or a formal statement like "If A is greater than B, than B is less than A," or some form of emotional language like "Ouch!" or "Wow!" The positivists ignored the social matrix of language. They forgot that language is a tool with many functions. Thus they arrived at a simple reductionist classification of the uses of language. No philosopher of language today would dare claim he could enumerate all the uses of language. Instead he might call attention to some of the uses such as the hedonic, mystificational, emotional, imaginative, pictorial, illustrative, metaphorical, analogical, anagogical, interrogative. directive, motivational, prescriptive, pragmatic, persuasive, moral, soteriological, intentional, decisional, determinational, performative, formal, factual, reportative, symbolical, and representational.

Let us now demonstrate the use of language analysis upon god-talk. Consider four samples:

1. "God has his eyes upon you, and he hears what you say."
2. "God loves man."
3. "God is being."
4. "I believe in God."

The first sentence, "God has his eyes upon you, and he hears what you say," is, first of all, anthropomorphic. If God has eyes, are his eyes like ours, with conjunctiva, cornea, iris, retina, optic nerve, etc.? How many eyes does God have? Just two? Or does he have many? Or is one divine eye sufficient? Does he hear with ears? Even the most unphilosophic person will cry halt to such questions. We really do not mean that God has eyes and ears when we say God sees and hears. We must not literalize such talk; we must *de*literalize it. This sentence is poetic mythology and must be kept in the poetic idiom. A Hindu counterpart is Book 10 of the *Bhāgavata Purāṇa* with its accounts of the exploits of Kṛṣṇa.

The second sentence, "God loves man," is also anthropomorphic, but it is anthropomorphic more with respect to function than to physiology. If the first sentence is mythologically anthropomorphic, the second sentence may be said to be analogically anthropomorphic. It indicates a functional likeness of the relation of God to man and a type of man's relations to man. Of course we need to know whether God's love for man is like the love of sweethearts, or of parent and child, or of spouses, or of a man for his home, or of a patriot for his country, etc. Then we have to determine whether the analogy is one of attribution or of proportionality, that is, does love belong formally and properly to one of the analogates and only relatively and derivatively to the other, and does it belong perfectly to one and imperfectly to the other?

A third example is "God is being." Note it is "God is being," not "God is a being." Paul Tillich has said this is the only nonsymbolic statement that can be made about God. But if it is a factual statement, it is a strange sort of fact. Factual language requires a criterion by which one can determine its factuality. Usually the criterion is some form of verification. If I say, "The liquid in that test tube is acid," you know how to verify the truth of that statement by the use of litmus paper. But "God is being" does not lend itself to a verificational test. There is no litmus paper to determine whether God is not being. The sentence seems instead to have a decisional or determinational quality: "I've decided to affirm that God is being." In the case of Tillich it may even be a tautology, since his definition of God is the Ground of Being.

The last example is "I believe in God." Is this a cautious factual statement like "I believe his telephone number is 84621"? Or is it an expression of confidence like "I believe in my banker"? Or is it an affirmation of the ontological reality of what for others may be figments of the imagination like "I believe in ghosts"? N. H. G. Robinson in an essay entitled "The Logic of Religious Language" says, "When, for example, the religious believer declares 'I believe in God the Father Almighty' or 'We acknowledge Thee to be the Lord,' it is clear that whatever he is doing he is not simply giving his assent to a proposition. His words have something of a performative character comparable to that which attaches to the words of a returning officer at a parliamentary election when he declares a particular candidate to be the duly elected member of parliament for the constituency."[3] In a performative use of language the words do it, e.g., "I sentence you to thirty days in jail," or "I pronounce you husband and wife." But what is it that the words do in "I believe in God"? Robinson contends that the sentence "I believe in God" does more than create a state of belief. But he also contends that "I believe in God" does not actually create God. Then how is it performative? What does it do? He offers the suggestion that the words have "*something* of a performative character." He says also, "In an epistemological sense, or perhaps more accurately, in a responsive sense, they (i.e., the words of the sentence "I believe in God") do make him God who ontologically was already God."[4] I find it difficult to understand how saying "I believe in God" does anything epistemologically or responsively to the reality of God. Robinson may have in mind that when the believer says "I believe in God" he makes God real for him, but that would not justify the puzzling conclusions that the words "do make him God who ontologically was already God."

Perhaps these four examples at least illustrate my opening statement: "Religious language is strange language."

I have already said that prior to examining the arguments for the existence of a god we ought to ask the question "What is the nature of the god whose existence the arguments attempt to establish?" I have also said that prior to an examination of the nature of god we ought to ask "How do we talk about god?" Now I want to affirm that even prior to examining the ways we talk about god we ought to ask "Why do we use god-talk?" And it is to this question we now turn.

Why do we use the god-concept? Note we are not asking why people postulate the existence of god, nor the uses to which god is put. Rather we are asking a language question: Why do we interject god-talk into our language? One reason, I suppose, is because we think in this way we clear up mysteries. Thus we use sentences like "God knows," or "God must want it that way," or "It must have been the will of God" to avoid using sentences like "I don't know," or "I have no explanation," or "I am totally ignorant," or "It was a chance event." The fact that we appeal to a mystery to explain a mystery will not be pointed out to us by most people because their critical faculties are blunted by our pious appeal to deity. Only a philosopher, or some other cantankerous person, will call our attention to the emptiness of our way of removing mysteries.

Another reason for introducing god-talk is the positive side of what we have just said. Language is not merely a sophisticated means of communication. It is the content of much of our environment. Besides the environment of water, earth, and air, of continents, oceans, heavenly bodies, and the environment which we share with the lower animals there is a peculiarly human environment of ideas and values, of arts and sciences, of literature and law, of morality and religion. This environment is the resultant of language. This is man's own world. This world we have because we have language. God-talk enhances that world. By god-talk man expands his own finitude; he relates himself to the infinite. By god-talk he makes the infinite manageable by making god the first cause and the final goal. By god-talk he alters his I-It experiences to an I-Thou, thus easing some of the estrangement he feels as a self-knower in a world where everything other than man seems to be a non-self-knower. He uses mantras, prayers, hymns, and other devotional devices to convince himself that he can conduct dialogue with the universe.

A third reason for the use of god-talk is rooted in man's moral experience. He uses religious language both to justify his moral law and to supply a sanction for his obedience to it. His moral rules and obligations are often couched in the symbols incorporating god, but more important pragmatically is the use of god-talk to supply a reason for obedience to law. Man seems to need to symbolize a moral sanction in his linguistic environment. Talk about god is the *deus ex machina* which saves him the effort and anxiety of establishing a morality of duty, self-realization, utilitarianism, or hedonism. If I may be harsher in my indictment, god-talk supplies a scapegoat which enables man to live with inhumane, cruel, discriminating morals, laws, and practices. Marx was indeed correct when he said religion is the opium of the people. God-talk can lull human sensibilities so both the oppressors and the oppressed use language which supports the status quo. Ossified god-talk—I suppose this is a loose equivalent for *śruti*—must on occasion be demolished by those sensitive men and women who seek the nutmeat in the shell, as Eckhart put it. Thus Gandhi openly admitted he rejected the *Dharma Śāstras* when he found them in conflict with his own moral sensibilities. Socrates capitulated to the decision of the Athenian assembly upon trumped-up charges because he was a "good citizen." Gandhi marched to a different tune. His allegiance was to eternal law (*sanātana dharma*), not to *varṇa dharma* nor to *āśrama dharma*.

The fourth reason for god-talk is that such language seems required to express the persistent optimism of man. Hope triumphs over despair. Evil predominates, but good will prevail. Is this mere whistling in the dark? It may be so. But thus far the human mammal feeds on tomorrow and tomorrow. The life of man was compared by Bede to the flight of a swallow from the darkness of night into a lighted room and out into the dark again. But man will not have it so. Our present may be a *Kali Yuga*, but we insist that although we have lost a paradise, someday we shall regain it. We do not move from darkness to light to darkness again but from light to darkness to light again. God-talk is the language of ultimate optimism. These, I submit, are some of the reasons why we use god-talk.

Has man always used god-talk? Have references to a god been a part of human language ever since man has been a user of language? Students of language once believed that man was a silent animal before becoming a speaking animal. Likewise some have thought man was first without the god-concept, and then began to refer to a god.

Today, however, we question just what meaning those last two sentences have. Imagine a wealthy man who hires a corps of field anthropologists to find a tribe of primitive people who have no conception of a god. If these anthropologists were as wise as they ought to be, I suspect they would never take to the field, because they would realize the impossibility of determining the techniques by which a parallel of the god concept in a specific civilization could be discovered in a primitive society. We sometimes need to be reminded that, while we cannot locate perceptually or conceptually the origin of the god concept in the history of man, we do know the concept denoted one of the preternatural entities with which the fertile imagination of early man populated his world. In addition to gods there were angels, baghests, banshees, bogies, boggarts, bugabooes, centaurs, demons, devils, dibbuks, doppelgängers, dragons, dryads, elves, fairies, fauns, fiends, fulgjur, furies, garudas, genie, ghosts, ghouls, goblins, griffins, hamadryads, hamingjur, harpies, hobgoblins, incubi, jinn, kelpies, kobolds, lamias, lycanthropes, maruts, mermaids, naiads, nereids, nymphs, ogres, oreads, peries, pixies, poltergeists, salamanders, sirens, spirits, sprites, spooks, sylphs, succubi, trolls, undines, vampires, warlocks, werewolves, witches, wraiths, yatus, and many more. I call these "preternatural entities," i.e., entities beyond the natural but in one sense they are not beyond the natural; their locus of operation is the natural. What is preternatural about them is that they are not as subject to empirical observation as are natural entities. They are the reification of powers. Take one example: an ancient oak tree is a thing of mystery. It was in existence before the birth of the oldest person in the community; it seems to be a member of the community; its shade has become the place for the taking of oaths. What could be more natural than to speak of the spirit of this oak tree—a dryad—as the power of life and awareness of the tree?

In Roget's *Thesaurus of the English Language* you will find that these words which denote preternatural entities are listed as words denoting "mythical entities." Mythology is being carefully scrutinized by modern students of religion and philosophy. All connotations of falsity are removed. A myth is "a non-discursive symbolism" (Susanne K. Langer); "an autonomous act of creation by the mind," (Mircea Eliade); "a pragmatic character of primitive faith and moral wisdom." (Bronislaw Malinowski). Myths are of the genus of analogy; they attempt to make the unfamiliar familiar. But I think we forget that primitive men did not fashion "mythologies" as that term is understood by the modern scholar. We today still speak in mythical language, for example, we talk about "sunrises" and "sunsets" rather than about an illusion created by the rotating of the earth on its axis, of "stars in the sky" even though we know that the "star" is a beam of light now hitting our eyes after years or thousands of years of traveling from a source perhaps no longer in existence, and we know there is no entity "sky." Our language is filled with mythic terms. They are conceptual shorthand. But not so the "myths" of primitive man. For him a dryad was no symbol for the life functioning of the oak tree; a dryad was the being in the tree which made this a *live* oak tree—yes, a *sensing* oak tree. The term "dryad" was for him no mythic term; it was the class name for spirits that live in oak trees.

The word "god" was used by primitive man not as metaphor or analogy but as denoter of a functioner. A god was a doer of something. A god was a power made into a thing. For example, the Sanskrit word *deva* comes from a root meaning "to give." A *deva* is that which gives something. *Ṛṣis* give wisdom, *gurus* give guidance, *sādhus* give *praśada*, guests give pleasure, and all are *devas*. The Aryans who invaded the subcontinent of Asia in the second millenium B.C. referred to the heavenly bodies as givers of light and warmth, and in time *deva* took on the form of the bright and shining ones. *Deva* was a functional concept. *Devas* were the things as acting. The heavenly *devas* brought rain, storm, lightning, thunder, light, and darkness. Among the earthly *devas* were fire, water, and earth with power to burn, to drown, to destroy, and to make things grow. We do not have to appeal to early human history to illustrate that "god" denotes a functioner. A good illustration comes from the seventeenth century. From 1643-1647 the so-called Westminster Assembly of Presbyterians, Congregationalists, and Episcopalians met to create a definite statement of Protestant beliefs. Their definition of the Christian God is interesting: "God is a spirit . . ." The prooftext for this definition they located in John 4:24, "*Pneuma ho theos*." The word *pneuma* means air, breath, wind. *Pneuma* is that which rustles leaves on trees; *pneuma* is that which when taken into the lungs makes the body live. *Pneuma* cannot be seen, but it can be felt. *Pneuma* is the cool breeze one occasionally feels on one's face on an otherwise still hot day. God is a *pneuma*, a vitalizer.

The god concept is one of the members of that list of terms for mythic being which we noted above. Probably few of us can identify all those names of mythic being. Yet we all use the term "god," and think we know what it means. None of us would use dryad-talk to refer to living oak trees, but we use god-talk. We use the word "god" functionally. Of course we don't say in chemistry that 2 HCl plus Zn plus god yields H_2 plus $ZnCl_2$, and we don't say, "Aspirin plus god cures headache," but we use god-talk about cosmic origins or cosmic endings, or human origins and human endings, or matters of morals and religion. And when we use the god-concept we find that we bring in many of the primitive notions which caused us to employ dryads, dragons, mermaids, trolls, and all the rest on that list. Just why the word "god" has been given preferential treatment is hard to say. But it has been so treated both in the East and in the West. Feelings of fear and awe, of love and piety, have so encrusted the word that many people found the "death of God" movement of the 1960's shocking. Many of us are astonished when we hear terms like "religious atheism." As soon as we get over the shock we can begin to examine seriously whether the god-concept has served us well. Has it created more problems than it has solved? Is there a better way of saying what we want to say when we talk about god? I think there is—at least there is an alternative way.

John Wisdom in a penetrating and delightful essay entitled "Gods" tells a story about two people who returned to examine a garden which they had long neglected. They found a few plants surprisingly vigorous among the weeds. One surmised that a gardener had been coming occasionally and tending the plants, but the neighbors said they had seen no gardener. One of the two rejected completely the hypothesis that a gardener had been coming to the garden, but the other insisted that an invisible gardener had been coming. Wisdom concludes the story with these words: "What is the difference between them? The one says 'A gardener comes unseen and unheard. He is manifested only in his works with which we are all familiar;' the other says 'There is no gardener' and with this difference in what they say about the gardener goes a difference in how they feel towards the garden, in spite of the fact that neither expects anything of it which the other does not expect."[5] Of course, Wisdom is talking about god. He says two things: (1) the one who uses god-talk feels differently about the world, and (2) they both expect the same things to happen in the world. I accept the first, but I deny the second. It seems to me that the person who selects the term "god" from that list of mythical entities uses that term to indicate an important assumption about the nature of reality.

When a modern man uses the term "god" he is symbolizing his assumption that the cosmic environment is one in which reality and value are integrated, that the higher one penetrates into reality the deeper one penetrates into value, that goodness and beauty are not subjective human assessments pinned on an indifferent world, that values are objective facts about the world, that values are discovered as well as created. If he uses god-talk, it is because he feels differently about the world than does the man who believes the world is the chance collision of atoms. God-talk is poetic talk, like "sunsets," "sunrises," and "stars in the sky." We need not give up god-talk for terms like "reality-value integration," nor need we speak only of visual perspectives of the sun created by earth rotations. But we ought to know what we are saying when we talk about god. Furthermore, because of the load of primitive connotations which cluster around the term, we probably ought to use it less often than we do. The chief merit of god-talk is that it clothes the reality-value integration in anthropomorphic, personal terms which resemble the way we talk about each other: God speaks, hears, walks, loves, blesses, hates, repents, forgets—even as we do. The chief problem in using god-talk is that we literalize when we ought to deliteralize. God-talk is taken as denotative of a being rather than as symbolic of the essence of being.

A Protestant theologian in this century has pointed the way we should go in thinking about the use of "God" in our language. This man was Paul Tillich. The word "God," he said, is a symbol, but is not a symbol for a thing. It "points to ultimate reality."[6] The words "God" and "existence," he added, ought to be definitely separated. "God does not exist. He is being-itself beyond essence and existence. Therefore, to argue that God exists is to deny him."[7] The symbol

"God," like all symbols, must be understood as a symbol. There are two ways of seeing through the symbolic character of symbols. One way is to fight against the objective, literalistic distortations of symbols, yet to continue to use the symbols, knowing that they are symbols. This is known as living with broken symbols. This is the way of religion. This is *bhakti mārga*. Religion is primarily an ecstatic experience. It requires the symbolic power of artistic and poetic forms. The other way of seeing through the symbolic character of symbols is to remove mythic symbols as vehicles of religious expression and to substitute the language of science, morality, and philosophy. Tillich rejected this because he said "it would silence the experience of the holy."[8] This is *jñāna mārga*, the way of knowledge.

Paul Tillich performed a noble service for religion in the West in his call for a reinterpretation of the word "God" within Christianity. "God," he said, is the "religious word for what is called the ground of being."[9] But it was a pity that by keeping his mind firmly on the Christian tradition he argued for what others in different religious and philosophical traditions had reached centuries before him. It is such a waste to repeat the discoveries of others. A few years before his death I asked Tillich in a private conversation if his conception of the ground of being was similar to the doctrine of Saguṇa Brahman as interpreted by Śaṅkara. He was excited by the question, and answered, "Yes, but don't forget Parmenides. My ideas are like his, too." During the last two years of his life he worked with Mircea Eliade in a seminar on comparative studies in the history of religions. Tillich was the speaker at a banquet to celebrate the conclusion of the seminar. In his address he said somewhat wistfully that if he had had the benefit of the seminar before writing his systematic theology, it would have been different. Two weeks later he was dead. We can only speculate how his theology would have been different.

Perhaps in the seminar Tillich discovered that in many cultural traditions there is both god-talk and talk beyond god-talk. God-talk uses the warm, human symbols which are music to the emotions and the will. But the user of god-talk must reserve a modicum of critical faculties, realizing even while using god-talk that there is reality transcending the god of his talk. The Hebrews caught glimpses of this when they said "the Lord is the greatest of all gods."[10] A few Christians were aware of this, e.g. Eckhart distinguished *Gott* (God) and *Gottheit* (Godhead). But we must look to the East for the most illuminating instances of talk beyond god-talk. I refer to *Ṛta* in the *Vedas*, Tao in Taoism, Li in Confucianism, Chi in Neo-Confucianism, Ādi-Buddha in Tibetan Buddhism, Ālaya-vijñāna in Yogācāra, Sūnyata in Mādhyamika, and above all to Brahman in the *Upaniṣads*, particularly as interpreted by Śaṅkara. In the *Upaniṣads* one finds the innocent looking word *iva* (as it were) used occasionally. For example, in *Bṛhad-Āraṇyaka Upaniṣad* 2. 4. 14. and 4. 5. 15, "For where there is a duality, *iva*, there one sees another." This, I think, is an early recognition of what Tillich was later to call "broken myths." From passages like these, Śaṅkara received clues for his doctrine of *māyā*. And because of this doctrine, Śaṅkara, who in his *jñāna mārga* recognized only one Real, the Brahman, in whom was integral existence (*sat*), consciousness (*chit*), and value (*ānanda*), also found a place for *bhakti* to an *iṣṭa-devatā* (chosen deity). What greater devotion could be found than in the prayers attributed to Śaṅkara! "Forgive me, O Śiva, my three great sins. I came on a pilgrimage to Kāśī forgetting that you are omnipresent; in thinking about you, I forget that you are beyond thought; in prayer to you I forget that you are beyond words." "O Lord, even after realizing that there is no real difference between the individual soul and Brahman I beg to state that I am yours and not that you are mine. The wave belongs to the ocean, not the ocean to the wave."[11] *Swāmi* Nikhilananda has speculated that the prayers and hymns of Śaṅkara were composed by him as concessions to his weaker followers.[12] I do not agree with the *Swāmi.* I hold there is a place for god-talk as well as a place for the talk that is beyond god-talk. There is a time and place for prosaic non-mythological attempts to state what is involved in the assumption of the integration of reality and value, and there is a time and place for poetic mythological symbolization of the faith in the integration of reality and value. An astronomer should enjoy a sunset, although he knows it is not a *sunset*; and an artist who enjoys a sunset needs to remind himself occasionally that it is an *iva* sunset! Both god-talk and talk beyond god-talk are needed, but we must be fully appraised that when we use the symbol "god" we are using a term from the preternatural-mythical language of primitive man, a symbol which denoted an entity, a being. It still does for many, even when we write the initial letter upper case. While it is possible to give new meanings to an ancient symbol, it is difficult to slough off all its former denotations and connotations. Insofar as the words "Allah," "Kṛṣṇa," "Father," "God," etc. belong in the language of human hopes, imaginations, fears, loves, and inspirations these symbols have powerful pragmatic and poetic usefulness. They can enrich our lives, especially by establishing an I-Thou relationship with our widest environment. But when we want to signify precisely the reality-value integration, the symbol "god" is dangerously misleading. To talk of god is to use language that has "something of a performative character." But I contend that in god-talk we are not making God of that which "ontologically was already God." Rather god-talk can be a method of creating a psychological environment to make more obvious to us that our knowledge creations and our value creations are responses to the absolute integration of *sat*, *chit*, and *ānanda*.[13] The danger in using god-talk is that for many it still carries its ancient designations, and thus it repeats the error of primitive man by making god an idol or thing. Those on the other hand who can use god-talk fully aware of its strangeness and those who can express the reality-value integration in ways beyond god-talk exhibit an important dimension of what it means to be truly human.

NOTES

1. In this paper I shall use "god" when referring to divinities generally and "God" when referring to a specific god in a specific culture.
2. R. G. Collingwood, *Speculum Mentis*. Oxford: The Clarendon Press, 1923, p. 136.
3. N. H. G. Robinson, "The Logic of Religious Language" in *Talk of God*. Royal Institute of Philosophy Lectures, Vol. II, 1967-1968. New York: St. Martin's Press, 1969, p. 2.
4. *Ibid.*
5. John Wisdom, "Gods" in *Proceedings of the Aristotelian Society*, New Series. Vol. 45. London: Harrison and Sons, 1945, p. 192.
6. Paul Tillich, *Systematic Theology*, Vol. II. Chicago: The University of Chicago Press, 1957, p. 94.

7. Paul Tillich, *Systematic Theology*, Vol. I. Chicago: The University of Chicago Press, 1951, p. 205.
8. *Systematic Theology*, Vol. II, p. 152.
9. *Systematic Theology*, Vol. I, p. 156.
10. Exodus 18:11. New English Bible.
11. Sarvepalli Radhakrishnan, *The Brahma Sūtra*. London: George Allen and Unwin, 1960, pp. 37-38.
12. *Swāmi* Nikhilananda, *Self-knowledge*. Mylapore, Madras: Sri Ramakrishna Math, 1947, p. xiv.
13. *Satchitānanda* (being-awareness-bliss) is the composite term most appropriate for designating the nature of the Brahman.

—14—

FIVE FORMS OF GOD-TALK AND THEIR PERVERSIONS

The analysis of religious language is one of the most promising studies of religious thought. One fruit of the analysis is a classification of modes of talking about God which makes more sense than traditional concepts. There are other schemata than the one herein suggested, but the following five forms of God-talk and their perversions constitute a clarification of theology.

The first step in applying the results of language analysis to theology is to note the meaning of *theos-logos*. Logos means knowledge, but more than this it means a knowledge that can be put into words. So *theos-logos* means a knowing about God that can be stated. When theology comes to the border of the unstateable, it ceases to be *logos*. Whitehead once said that the purpose of philosophy is to rationalize mysticism. Perhaps the same may be said of theology, but philosophy and theology must not hesitate to identify as intellectual nonsense the unspeakable profundities of the mystic. If it cannot be said, it cannot be theology. *Theos* means god, but the Greek term has a predicative force. The ancient Greeks did not assert the reality of a god and then say, "This god is love" or "God is love." Rather they used *theos* adjectivally: not "God is love" but "Love is divine." *Theos* connoted the value of a thing or an act. Thus Euripides wrote that to meet one's friends again after a long absence from home is a god, and Pliny said, "For mortals to aid mortals—this is god." Theology is not to be regarded as knowledge about a being called a god but as verbalization about those things which most matter.

The second step is to note that there are two basic kinds of language: sign and symbol. The language of signs is the language of literal statements. Signs represent objects. Signs are pointers; they stand outside their referents. They are arbitrary in the sense that another sign can function as well as the one selected. Traffic signs are a good example. Anyone who has driven a car in Europe has mastered the international highway signs and has discovered that they work admirably as directors of traffic. The language of symbols is the language of terms which enter into the meaning of that which they represent. Symbols are part of the totality of a meaning complex. The cross as symbol in Christianity is more than a sign of the crucifixion. Symbols are the raw data of mythologies. They point to a referent, but they also enrich the referent. They function analogically, metaphorically, and pictorially as well as denotatively. The statements formed of symbols may not be true but they are meaningful. Thus the symbolic statement "My love is a red, red rose" is far more valuationally meaningful than the sign statement "My love is female, brunette, 130 pounds, and 36-24-36," but both statements do point to "my love."

There are five ways to talk, write, and think about the central religious object, or we can say there are five ways to do religion. There are five ways to talk about God in the Greek sense of *theos-logos*. The five are:

1. Sign language of the principle of being
2. Symbolic language of a being
3. Symbolic language of a personal being
4. Symbolic language of a historical being
5. Soteriological language

Each of these legitimate forms of God-talk is subject to perversion. The three symbolic forms are perverted when they are literalized, i.e., when metaphors, analogies, symbols, and myths are treated as literal reports of events and things. The nonsymbolic are perverted when they are treated symbolically, i.e., when the principle of being becomes identified with a symbolic being and when the mystic violates his pattern of soteriological motivation and falls into symbolization. I wish to clarify briefly both the legitimate and the illegitimate forms of God-talk. My debt to Paul Tillich is obvious.

Sign Language of the Principle of Being

According to Tillich the statement "God is being-itself" is "a nonsymbolic statement," "the most abstract and completely unsymbolic statement which is possible [about God]," a statement which "does not point beyond itself," and a statement which "means what it says directly and properly." Moreover, it is the only nonsymbolic statement about God: "nothing else can be said about God as God which is not symbolic."[1] Unfortunately, Tillich had a way of shifting from theology to philosophy and from philosophy to theology. He often made theological assumptions when he philosophized and philosophical assumptions when he theologized. Perhaps this was inevitable for one who lived and thought "on the boundary." But it created confusions for Tillich and his interpreters, and at no point is the confusion more serious than in the central statement "God is being-itself." God, he informs us elsewhere, is a symbol. "The fundamental symbol of our ultimate concern is God."[2] "In each of our attempts to open up a religious symbol with the help of an existential analysis, we open up implicitly the basic and all-embracing symbol of religion, namely the symbol of God."[3] The statement "God is being-itself" is an ontological, i.e., philosophical, statement, but the subject of the statement is the "all-embracing symbol of religion," God. What sort of sense is it to state that "the religious symbol God is being-itself" is a nonsymbolic statement? Tillich mixed his universes of discourse inexcusably. What he wanted to say was that God is a religious symbol for being-itself. If he wished to refer nonsymbolically to being-itself, he ought to have eschewed the term "God" and used metaphysical concepts such as Absolute, Form of the Good, Nirguṇa Brahman, Satchitānanda, Tao, T'ai Chi, and Ālaya-vijñāna.

In his concept of being-itself, or the ground of being, or God beyond God (which should have been "God" beyond God) Tillich restored to Christian thought a sign which Augustine had created and which had been lost. According to Augustine truth is the foundation of all arguments to establish the reality of God, and truth is grounded in being. Therefore, being or existence is the pure actuality which makes truth possible. This is being-itself (*esse ipsum*), and it first appears in the intellect as the ground of all truth. It is by reason of such grounding that the religious symbol God is established. In being-itself is the integration of truth-itself (*verum ipsum*) and good-itself (*bonum ipsum*). Being is the single matrix of the true and the good. The total environment is a unity from which emerges all truth and value and to which at last all will return. In Augustinian language the City of Man comes from and returns to the City of God. The sign language of the principle of being is ontological God-talk whose subject is being-*ness*, not *a* being. It transcends worship, poetry, and symbol. Anselm was the chief architect of the perverted form of the sign language of the principle of being. This great churchman transformed the principle of primary being (*primum esse*) into a universal being (*ens realissimum*). Thus Augustine's being, the ground of all truth, became a great and wonderful being—"a something than which nothing greater can be conceived." Being-itself was demoted to the status of a being. The term *primum esse* became a label for this being. But no being, however great, can be the ground of being or the integration of reality and value. It was this perversion which Tillich sought to repudiate, but Tillich found to his amazement and disgust that his own ontological sign language was sometimes perverted into the symbolic language of worship. Clergymen have been known to pray "May the Ground of Being bless and keep you." But the ground of being no more blesses than triangularity has three sides nor equinity eats hay!

Symbolic Language of a Being

Aquinas agreed with Augustine—"God is not only His own essence . . . but also His own being."[4] He also agreed with Anselm—"God and other things."[5] He affirmed that God's essence is existence, yet he wanted to establish the existence of God. Sometimes he sought consolation in the *via negativa*: " . . . we know only what God is not, namely, that God is called living because He does not belong to the genus of lifeless things."[6] Aquinas was clearest in his discussion of the nature of God when he was thinking in the context of language analysis. He borrowed heavily from the Aristotelian distinction between naming univocally and naming equivocally, i.e., between things having a common name and definition and things having a common name but not a common definition. Aristotle's example of the former was that of calling both a man and an ox an animal; his example of the latter was that of calling both a man and a drawing of a man an animal.

Aquinas held that nothing is predicated of God the creator and the things of His creation: "Now nothing is predicated of God and creatures as though they were in the same order, but, rather, according to priority and posteriority. For all things are predicated of God essentially. For God is called being as being entity itself, and He is called good as being goodness itself. But in other things predications are made by participation, as Socrates is said to be a man, not because he is humanity itself, but because he possesses humanity. It is impossible, therefore, that anything be predicated univocally of God and other things."[7] Aquinas' agreement with Augustine that God is being-itself is unfortunately muddled in this passage by linguistically implying that God is both being and a being. Although Aquinas rejected univocal predication of God and man, he could not accept a completely equivocal predication. This would be the way of disorder, irrationalism, and agnosticism. Moreover, this would make the Incarnation a completely impossible doctrine. So he offered as a linguistic form between univocation and equivocation the symbolic form known as analogy. God is good and a man is good, but God is good in the sense of goodness and a man is good in the sense of participating in goodness. Human good is an analogue of divine goodness, i.e., human good is what divine goodness is under the limitations of space and time. Man's existence is what divine existence means when it is some where, at some time, limited by other existing beings, and threatened by nonexistence. God's being may be inferred by reasoning analogously from the existence of man. "God is a being" does not mean that God is a being as man is a being, but rather the sentence affirms in an analogical symbol how God can be conceived from the perspective of man's existence.

Tillich is much clearer than Aquinas at this point. According to him "Everything has the power to become a symbol for the 'ground of being'." God is one of these symbols. Any being can be a symbol for the ground of being. That includes man, animals, plants—anything. Each being expresses the ground of being in its own special way, continues Tillich, because each being "is not merely a 'thing' but a part of the universal life which, at no point, is completely deprived of freedom, of that freedom which in the personal life comes to its own."[8] Hinduism expresses this in its concept of *iṣṭa devatā* (chosen deity), which might be described as the right to select one's own worship symbol.

Two serious problems arise from the symbolic language of a being. One is the temptation to be more specific as to what sort of being God is. Whereas Anselm was satisfied to leave the nature of God as a being or a something, the Westminster divines decided that God is a spirit—a spirit distinguished from other spirits by being "infinite, eternal, unchangeable, in His wisdom, being, power, holiness, justice, goodness, and truth." The other problem is that of the existence of God. Tillich was incensed by the problems we make for ourselves when we start with the question of the existence of God: "But we must not start with the question of the being of God, which, if discussed in terms of the existence or non-existence of God, is in itself a lapse into a disastrous literalism."[9] "It would be a great victory for Christian apologetics if the words 'God' and 'existence' were very definitely separated . . . God does not exist. He is being-itself beyond essence and existence. Therefore, to argue that God exists is to deny him."[10] Yet the truth is that people have become so accustomed to thinking of God as a being rather than as being that, according to Tillich, "If today you say God is Being, it sounds almost blasphemous."[11] The word "God" has become so widely used to designate a supreme being that it might be a good plan to stop using the word for a generation. Perhaps then it could be re-introduced as a symbol for the ground of being.

Symbolic Language of a Personal Being

This is the language of worship, i.e., the language which expresses the worth of the referent. This is the language of I-Thou. God is addressed as Shepherd, King, Counselor, Guide, Comrade, Friend, Father, etc. Tillich as one who lived on the boundary between worship and reason could say in adjacent paragraphs "The symbol 'personal God' is absolutely fundamental because an existential relation is a person-to-person relation" and " 'Personal God' is a confusing symbol."[12] In his essays collected under the title *The Protestant Era* he says that personality is "the most necessary symbol for God" and also that it is a dangerous symbol.[13] The necessity is in the fact that man cannot become fully concerned about anything except as a person related to that which is not less than a person. The absolute ground of all being must be the ground of persons as beings. "Personal God" is a symbol for the ground of being and value, but trouble begins when the symbol becomes a sign for a personal God, i.e., when it means that God is a person. Tillich says of this symbol, "It means that God is the ground of everything personal and that he carries within himself the ontological power of personality. He is not a person, but he is not less than personal."[14] Tillich reminds us that in classical theology *persona* and *prosopon* were used for the three hypostases of God, not for God himself. Again how much less confusing Tillich would have been had he worn the philosopher's cap while writing these words. Then he would have told us that being-itself cannot exclude the ground of personality from its essence; that, whereas a being may be a person, being-*ness* can have only person-*ness*.

The perversion of the symbol "Personal God" to a sign of God as a person is very recent, says Tillich: "God became a 'person' only in the nineteenth century, in connection with the Kantian separation of nature ruled by physical law from personality ruled by moral law."[15] Tillich may be correct with respect to Christianity, but the personalizing of the forces of nature is one of man's earliest forms of religion. This perverted form elicited strong rejections from Tillich: "The protest of atheism against such a highest person is correct."[16] He argued that when God becomes a person alongside other persons, God ceases to be the supporting and transcending center of every personal life. "When God became a person, man's personality was driven into neurotic disintegration."[17] What Tillich had in mind is that while the symbol "Personal God" is essential for worship purposes, it becomes dangerous when taken literally. The ground of being is reduced to a cosmic person whom man can influence, persuade, direct, and even dominate. God is used. Religion becomes magic. Prayer becomes conversation: "If it [prayer] is brought down to the level of a conversation between two beings, it is blasphemous and ridiculous."[18]

Symbolic Language of a Historical Person

The Incarnation is the heart of Christianity, but the interpretations of the Incarnation can only be described as efforts to explain the Incarnation to a Greek and Roman world. Arianism, Apollinarianism, Ebionism, Docetism, Montanism, Gnosticism, Monarchianism, and the theories of the atonement are evidences of the struggle to make sense of the Christ. A pattern was set. The Gospel stories instead of being regarded as symbols to win the hearts and lives of people became signs, descriptions, and records of actual events. The life of Jesus became a once-for-all event, thus losing its appeal as a dramatic spectacle of the eternal redemptive aspects of reality and becoming instead another sacrifice to appease the gods. An effort was made to build Christianity on one event, one act of God. But as Harvey Cox has said, " . . . the act of God in Jesus Christ offers slim pickings for those in hope of clues for the erection of some final system."[19] Christians in their concern for history turned the Christ into Jesus. Ronald Gregor Smith in 1955 accused the Christian church of "honouring not the incarnate Word in the bleeding helplessness of utter service, but an emasculated Jesus, the Jesus of the Ersatz gold halo and the tawdry pietism of decadent Jesusology."[20] These ringing words are needed even more today with the curious appearance of Jesus Freaks with their simplistic Biblicalisms, fundamentalisms, and glorifications of the person Jesus. This new breed of the pious ought to re-read Bonhoeffer, especially his assurances to his friends: "Don't worry. I shan't come out of here a *homo religiosus*! On the contrary my suspicion and horror of religiosity are greater than ever."[21] I have stressed the perversion of this third form of symbolism because it is so well known. The historical person Jesus bar Joseph may also be regarded as a symbol of the integration of reality and value. In him the power of salvation, the power of the New Being, was expressed. He reminds us that regeneration does not operate in a post-mortem state in heaven but in finite and earthly forms. Christology, as opposed to Jesusology, connotes the ending of estrangement and the restoring of wholeness. The Christ is not the instrument of the restoring but its symbol. He is with us and for us. The life, teachings, and death of Jesus the Christ remind us that the ground of being is also the ground of value, that love is a built-in feature of the universe. The goodness, beauty, and truth which we cherish are discovered facts of our total environment. We in pursuit of the good, the beautiful, and the true enter into the Christ event and become Christs to one another. Jesus the Christ is a symbol of the perfection we find, anticipate, and help create. Christians must recognize that the historical Jesus is not the only symbol of the redemptive aspects of the cosmos.

Soteriological Language

The fifth form of God-talk is the language of the mystic. The mystical experience is an intuitive, unitive experience which words may suggest but never state. Bergson once said the mystical experience is the golden coin for which we never cease making small change. Dance, music, *koans*, gestures, and other noncognitive forms also fail to express the experience. Yet the mystic continues to talk. The perversion is in assuming that the talk of the mystic is cognitive. But the verbalizations of mystics are neither signs nor symbols. Rather they are part of the effort of the mystic to arouse us to our own mystical experiences. His language is soteriological rather than factual or expressional. He talks to stimulate hearers to experiences of their own. His language is motivational, not descriptive. No truth is communicated. He speaks "truly" only when his words successfully stimulate others to actions which yield their own enlightenment. The Buddha's "Flower Sermon" in which he said nothing but aroused one monk to *satori* was one of his "truest" communications. Eckhart wrote in his "Talks of Instruction," "Let each keep his own way and absorb into it the good features of other ways and thus include in his own the merits of all. . . . You may, however, say of the Lord Jesus Christ, that his way was always the highest and that we ought to follow him in it. That may be true, but our Lord should be followed reasonably and not by details. . . . We are always to follow him in our own way."[22] The God-talk of the mystic is that strange form of talk which woos but does not express, entices but does not lead, arouses but gives no directions. To treat the God-talk of the mystic as theology is to pervert it and to destroy its special usefulness.

We shall move into happier days in religion when we agree there are five legitimate forms of God-talk: the sign language of being-itself; the three symbolic languages of a being, a personal being, and a historical being; and the nonsign, nonsymbolic language of the mystic. The sign language of the principle of being is home base. After excursions into symbolic forms or into soteriological patterns for purposes of worship and/or propagation of the Christian religion we can return to the sign language of the principle of being and "tell it like it is." "I believe in God" becomes "I believe in the integration of reality and value." "God redeems the world" becomes "Healing, integrating, preserving, and loving are objective aspects of being." "Christ is Savior" becomes "Jesus was one who witnessed and manifested the eternal redemptive aspects of the total environment." When we recognize the plural possibilities of God-talk we may cease canonizing victors and excommunicating losers in theological disputes. Perhaps we can never create the ideal form of God-talk, but we must talk, for not to think and speak about primary reality and ultimate values is to be less than human. The unexamined life is not fit for man.

NOTES

1. Paul Tillich, *Systematic Theology*, Vol. I. Chicago: The University of Chicago Press, 1951, pp. 238-239.
2. Paul Tillich, *The Dynamics of Faith*. New York: Harper and Brothers, 1957, p. 45.
3. Paul Tillich, "Existential Analysis and Religious Symbols" in *Contemporary Problems in Religion*. Edited by Harold A. Basilius. Detroit: Wayne State University Press, 1956, p. 54.
4. Thomas Aquinas, *Summa Theologica*, Question 3, Article 4. Anton C. Pegis (editor), *Basic Writings of Saint Thomas Aquinas*, Vol. I. New York: Random House, 1945, p. 30.
5. *On the Truth of the Catholic Faith. Summa Contra Gentiles, Book One: God.* Translated by Anton C. Pegis. Garden City, N.Y.: Doubleday and Co., 1955, p. 143.
6. *Ibid.*, p. 147.

7. *Ibid.*, p. 145.
8. Paul Tillich, *The Protestant Era*. Third impression. Chicago: The University of Chicago Press, 1960, p. 123.
9. "Existential Analysis and Religious Symbols," p. 45.
10. *Systematic Theology*, Vol. I, p. 205.
11. *The Protestant Era*, p. 63.
12. *Systematic Theology*, Vol. I, pp. 244, 245.
13. *The Protestant Era*, pp. 62, 119.
14. *Systematic Theology*, Vol. I, p. 245.
15. *Ibid.*
16. *Ibid.*
17. *The Protestant Era*, p. 63.
18. *Systematic Theology*, Vol. I, p. 127.
19. Harvey Cox, *The Secular City*. New York: The Macmillan Co., 1965, p. 258.
20. Ronald Gregor Smith, *The New Man*. London: SCM Press Ltd., 1956, p. 100.
21. Dietrich Bonhoeffer, *Letters and Papers from Prison*. Translated by Reginald H. Fuller. New York: The Macmillan Company., 1953, p. 95.
22. Raymond Bernard Blakney, *Meister Eckhart*. New York: Harper and Brothers, 1941, p. 24.

—15—

*THE LANGUAGE OF MYSTICISM**

Ever since Leuba pointed out that most definitions of religion emphasize either cognition, or affection, or volition,[1] those who define religion have attempted to make their definitions broad enough to include all three facets of religion, for example, Patterson defines religion as "the *belief* in a harmony between what is judged to be the highest part of our natures and the total environment, together with the *emotions* to which the belief gives rise and the type of *conduct* motivated by this belief and these emotions."[2] Another way to avoid a limited definition of religion is to define personal religious experience rather than religion, for example, Whitehead defines religion as "what the individual does with his solitariness."[3] This has the advantage of connoting religion as a way of life,[4] although it omits the social dimension of religion. When religion is conceived in the context of the life of the individual, emphasis is usually placed on the mystical experience. Thus James says at the opening of his two lectures on mysticism in his *The Varieties of Religious Experience*, "One may say truly, I think, that personal religious experience has its root and center in mystical states of consciousness."[5] Pratt distinguishes four "typical aspects of religion" or "temperamental kinds of religion"[6] (traditional, rational, mystical, and practical) and argues for the centrality of mysticism in religion: "And while it would indeed be

* This essay appears in *The Monist*, Vol. 47, No. 3 (Spring 1963), pp. 417-443. Reprinted by kind permission of the editor.

untrue to assert that only the mystical are genuinely religious, it is safe to say that all intensely religious people have at least a touch of mysticism."[7] Underhill agrees, "No deeply religious man is without a touch of mysticism; and no mystic can be other than religious, in the psychological if not in the theological sense of the word."[8] Some modern Christian theologians who are anxious to establish the uniqueness of Biblical religion deny that Christianity is a religious mysticism. For example, Wright claims "There is an objectivity about Biblical faith which cannot be expressed in the language of inner experience. For this reason Biblical religion cannot be classified among great mysticisms of the world."[9] Niebuhr also says, "Mysticism always regards the final depth of human consciousness as in some sense identical with the eternal order, and believes that men may know God if they penetrate deeply enough into the mystery of their own being. But on the other hand the transcendent God of Biblical faith makes Himself known in the finite and historical world."[10] The position of Tillich (another living Christian theologian) is more ecumenical: Tillich, after defining the religious mystical experience as "an immediate experience of something ultimate in value and being of which one can become intuitively aware,"[11] states that all religions contain both a mystical experience and a rational interpretation, and adds, "Christian theology is no exception. It does the same thing, but it does it in a way which implies the claim that it is *the* theology. The basis of this claim is the Christian doctrine that the Logos became flesh, that the principle of the divine self-revelation has become manifest in the event 'Jesus as the Christ.' "[12] I am assuming in this paper that mysticism as defined above by Tillich is an essential component of any religion and therefore that a study of a problem peculiar to religious mysticism is a study of a problem of all religions.

The problem to which this paper is directed is the universal feeling of religious mystics that they cannot express their mystical experiences nor the insights received in their mystical experiences in language. One of the most interesting examples of this phenomenon is that of St. Thomas Aquinas, who in December, 1273, after having a mystical experience while saying Mass, left unfinished the third part of the *Summa Theologica,* remarking to his secretary, "All that I have written seems to me like so much straw compared with what I have seen and with what has been revealed to me."[13] Many other mystics, unlike St. Thomas, do not choose to remain silent about their mystical experiences, although most warn that they are unable to convey in language the full reality and value of their mystical experiences. There have also been many non-mystics who have written on mysticism.[14] W. T. Stace, after an earlier attack on religion,[15] has joined the ranks of those non-mystics who are sympathetic toward mysticism. His volume, *Mysticism and Philosophy,* is an excellent contribution to the critical studies of mysticism. Stace writes "as a philosopher, and not as a mystic."[16] He classifies himself as an empiricist and an analyst, and confesses that "as an empiricist I do not hold that all experience must necessarily be reducible to sense experience. And as an analyst I do not hold that analysis is the sole business of philosophy."[17] The sixth chapter of this book is on mysticism and language; it contains a classification of the theories of the nature of the language of mysticism and Stace's suggestions towards a new theory.

"One of the best-known facts about mystics" writes Stace in the opening sentence of chapter six "is that they feel that language is inadequate, or even wholly useless, as a means of communicating their experiences or their insights to others."[18] Stace is correct in isolating this feature of mysticism, although he does not seem to give it the centrality assigned to it by others. For example, James believes that incommunicableness is "the keynote of all mysticism."[19] Mystics in diverse times, places, and cultures have insisted on the incommunicability of the mystical vision. The eleventh-century Sufi, Al-Ghazzali, writes, "During this solitary state things were revealed to me which it is impossible either to describe or to point out."[20] The sixteenth-century Spanish Carmelite, St. John of the Cross, says that the soul "finds no terms, no means, no comparison whereby to render the sublimity of the wisdom and the delicacy of the spiritual feeling with which she is filled . . . He (the mystic) can understand it, use and enjoy it, but he cannot apply a name to it, nor communicate any idea of it, even though all the time it be a mere thing of sense."[21] According to the Buddhist scripture, the *Laṅkāvatāra Sūtra*, "But neither words nor sentences can exactly express meanings,[22] for words are only sweet sounds that are arbitrarily chosen to represent things."[23] The *Tao Teh King* reports, "The Reason that can be reasoned is not the eternal Reason. The name that can be named is not the eternal Name . . . One who knows does not talk. One who talks does not know."[24] And Aurobindo, the twentieth-century philosophical mystic of India, writes, "The truth of the spirit is a truth of being and consciousness and not a truth of thought: mental ideas can only represent or formulate some facet, some mind-translated principle or power of it or enumerate its aspects, but to know it one has to grow into it and be it; without that growing and being there can be no true spiritual knowledge."[25]

Far more serious than Stace's failure to note the *centrality* of incommunicableness in mysticism is his assumption that mystics *seek to communicate* their experiences and insights. Stace seems to believe that mystics desire to communicate, try language for this purpose, discover that language does not communicate their experiences and insights, and conclude that language is inadequate. The assumption that when mystics use language they use it "as a means of communicating their experiences or insights to others"[26] underlies Stace's criticism of the three theories of "the alleged ineffability of mystical experience"[27] which he selects for analysis: (1) *The Emotion Theory*. Mystics cannot communicate mystical experiences or insights because mystical experiences are emotional experiences and emotions cannot be verbalized. Stace's criticism: Mystical experiences are more than emotional experiences: it is the vision itself, not the emotion, which cannot be communicated. (2) *The Spiritual Blindness Theory*. Mystics cannot communicate mystical experiences or insights if the communicatee has not had a mystical experience. Stace's criticism: This is no explanation, for it applies to almost every kind of experience, for example, a seeing person cannot explain light to a person born blind. (This author cannot understand why the incommunicability of both sense experiences and mystical experiences cannot be accounted for by a single theory.) (3) *The Symbolic Language Theory*.[28] Mystics cannot communicate mystical experiences or insights because mystical experiences cannot be understood by the intellect, and hence are unverbalizable. Stace's criticism: if the experiences are really unconceptualizable, then absolutely nothing can be stated either negatively or metaphorically, yet the mystics do use negatives and metaphors.

After rejecting all three theories that have been proposed to account for the alleged ineffability of mystical experiences, Stace offers his own "suggestions toward a new theory."[29] Stace somehow feels that a satisfactory theory is one based on making a distinction between language used *during* the mystical experience and language used *afterwards* to describe the mystical experience. This is without doubt an important distinction, but it is not a "new theory" as Stace himself admits in his quotation from Plotinus[30]—and it certainly does not answer all the problems of verbalization to call attention to the fact that the mystical experience is one of undifferentiated unity, whereas verbalization requires differentiated multiplicity. After Stace's criticism of the existing theories, one had hoped for something more original and penetrating than this well-known distinction between the subject-object unification of the mystical state and the subject-object differentiation of the conceptual-verbal state.

Stace pulls no punches in his criticism of mystics and interpreters of mysticism. He accuses those who support the emotion theory of being either "comparatively ignorant of the writings of the mystics" or "lacking in insight and sensitivity."[31] In another place he makes the same charge against both those who hold the emotion theory and those who hold the spiritual blindness theory.[32] He accuses the mystic of "irresponsible utterance"[33] and of being "a poor logician, a poor philosopher, and a poor analyst."[34] The mystic who says no language can express his experience, says Stace, "does not understand the root of his own trouble with language. He only vaguely feels that something must be wrong with what he says and is perplexed by this."[35] If I may attack Stace with a modification of his own words, I claim that there is something wrong with what Stace says about language and mysticism, but unfortunately I cannot discover that he is very perplexed about what he says!

My criticism of Stace's treatment of the language of mysticism is that he frames his analysis of the ineffability of mysticism within the context of communication. Not only does he state his problem to be the analysis of the feeling of mystics that "language is inadequate, or even wholly useless, as a means of *communicating* their experiences or their insights to others,"[36] but also he presents his own solution in terms of the mystic's effort "in *communicating* at least some part of the truth about his experience,"[37] and at the close of his argument he reminds the reader that when the mystic "returns from the world of the One, he wishes to *communicate* in words to other men what he remembers of his experience."[38] Stace admits that a mystical experience, "*during* the experience, is wholly unconceptualizable and therefore wholly unspeakable,"[39] and he recognizes that the mystic so regards his own mystical experience. Having made such a recognition about the mystic's behavior, is Stace fair to the mystic in assuming that when the mystic verbalizes he is attempting to *communicate* his own mystical experiences and insights? Stace is accusing the mystic of foolishly trying to communicate that which the mystic knows to be incommunicable. Stace thinks that the mystic is a poor logician who in communicating his insights contradicts his assertion that mystical insights are ineffable. This is a possibility. Another possibility is that Stace misconstrues what the mystic is doing when he speaks. I believe that Stace is mistaken in assuming that the mystic is *communicating* when he is verbalizing.

In one passage Stace says, "Language has been moulded by the intellect as a tool for its special purposes."[40] This, I believe, is the closest Stace comes to discovering the thread which would have led him out of the confines of his labyrinthine emphasis on only one of the uses of language. Language may be used to arouse emotions, to create images, or to motivate responses as well as to communicate information. I take seriously the statements of mystics that they cannot communicate their experiences and insights; therefore when the mystics speak, I conclude that rather than contradicting by their practice what they hold in theory, they are using language in a non-communicative fashion. The mystics speak to motivate, to stimulate, to arouse others to seek their own enlightenments through their own mystical experiences. The mystics do not attempt to convey some information, and then discover that they are unable. They do not desire to convey their own experiences and insights. One of the commonest claims of mystics is that each man must work out his own salvation.[41] One man's mystical experience will no more enlighten another man than one man's eating will nourish another man's body. The verbalizing mystic, in the terminology of the Hindu, is a *guru*, that is, he is an enlightened man who is primarily concerned about the salvation of his pupil, as distinguished from a *paṇḍit* who is a clever man primarily concerned about the education of his pupil. The distinction between *guru* and *paṇḍit* is a sharp one in India. The *guru* is a spiritual guide and teacher, a second father more venerated than a natural father. A *guru* is reluctant to take on the tutelage of a young man, for according to Hindu belief the *guru* assumes the *karma* of his pupil. In some parts of India the *guru* is worshipped as a deity; the Vallabhāchāris are the most extreme in this respect. The *paṇḍit* is a sage, perhaps an academic teacher, whose interests are frequently divided between concern for the progress of his pupils and concern for the fees he receives for his instruction. The mystic in his speaking acts as a *guru*, not as a *paṇḍit*.

Stace says in the section in which he presents his own solution to the language problem of mysticism,

> We have to begin by pointing to something which is very obvious, namely, that whatever the difficulty may be which the mystic feels, he does in fact normally overcome it. He says that he is speechless, but words break out from his lips. He does actually describe his remembered experiences, and his descriptions are often highly successful and effective. The only alternative to admitting this would be to say that his statements are either meaningless or false. For either he does succeed in communicating at least some *part* of the truth about his experience, or his words are no better than a sound of escaping steam. If he does successfully communicate the truth about a part of his remembered experience, however small that part may be, then he must have given a true description of that part of his experience. And in that case he must be mistaken when he supposes that no language can ever apply to remembered mystical experience.[42]

But is the only alternative to admitting that the mystic is successful and effective in his description of his mystical experience to say that his statements are either meaningless or false? Or perhaps in order not to become entangled in Stace's own trap, I should put the question in this fashion: Is there not the possibility that the mystic's statements about his experience may be neither factually true nor factually false, yet they may be rich with non-factual meaning? The statements of the mystic may have a great deal of emotional, pictorial, and motivational meaning. The literature of mysticism is full of incidents of mystics who used the right words at the right time to the right person and thus supplied the nudge which brought another into his own mystical experience. The mystic does not verbalize in order to convey some information to another, but to arouse another to achieve liberation for himself. The mystic "in communicating at least some *part* of the truth about his experience" does not necessarily attempt to give "a true description of that part of his experience." The mystic's "communication" is sometimes completely without verbalization, as was, for example, the Flower Sermon of the Buddha in which he merely stood before the monks and held a flower for all to see. The language of the mystic is motivational, not descriptive. No information is conveyed. The only truth in the "communication" is the existential truth aroused within the pupil. For the mystic the only truth worth having is "saving truth"—the truth that leads to enlightenment. A "true" mystical "communication" is not the correct description of an experience; it is the successful motivation of another to the realization of his own mystical experience. Truth in mysticism is a form of pragmatic truth. If a mystic through his statements woos another to discover his own salvation in his own way, then the mystic may be said to have spoken truly. The way of salvation is unique to each individual. This is a universal theme of mystics. Meister Eckhart, the thirteenth-century Christian mystic, says in his "Talks of Instruction," "Let each keep his own way and absorb into it the good features of other ways and thus include in his own the merits of all . . . You may, however, say of the Lord Jesus Christ, that his way was always the highest and that we ought to follow him in it. That may be true, but our Lord should be followed reasonably and not by details . . . We are always to follow him in our own way."[43] The *Bhagavad Gītā* invites the Hindu to select any one of the four yogas (works, thought, meditation, devotion) and to stay with it, since all roads lead to the top of the mountain. Why should a mystic try to communicate his way of liberation when each man must find his own?

Some of the best examples of the mystic's use of words to bring another direct enlightenment rather than to communicate experiences and insights are found in Zen Buddhism. In Zen hundreds of stories, conversations, poems, questions, and directives called *koans* have been preserved since the eleventh century and are used today in Zen monasteries as a mental shock treatment to knock the disciple off the track of his usual line of thinking. Here is a small sample selected and adapted from the writings of D. T. Suzuki:

> What is the sound of one hand clapping?
>
> When you have a staff, I will give you one; when you have no staff, I will take it away from you.
>
> A monk asked, "When the body crumbles all to pieces and returns to dust, there eternally abides one thing. Of this I have been told, but where does this one thing abide?"
>
> The master replied, "It is windy again this morning."
>
> A monk asked, "What is the fundamental teaching of the Buddha?" The master answered, "There is enough breeze in this fan to keep me cool."
>
> A monk asked his master to give him a Zen theme. Thereupon the master gave him a hearty blow.
>
> A master used to carry a short stick which he would hold before an assembly of monks, and say, "If you call this a stick, you affirm; if you call it not a stick, you negate. Beyond affirmation and negation what would you call it?"

These koans are given to unenlightened monks to "solve" in their meditations. They are means both for arousing and for testing the mystical experiences and insights of Zen monks. They do not communicate experiences nor insights.

Stace's error in interpreting the language of mysticism as an effort of the mystic to communicate his experiences and insights is part of a broader misunderstanding, namely, his supposition that mysticism is philosophy. In his first chapter he states that mysticism is "a component in philosophy."[44] He plans in a later book to "discuss the actual influence of mysticism on the great philosophers of the past."[45] Stace is correct in assuming that mysticism has influenced philosophy, but he is misleading, if not wrong, in treating mysticism as metaphysics or philosophy and in subjecting it to the criticism appropriate to philosophy. This is not an uncommon error. Pepper treats mysticism as a metaphysical system, although an "inadequate" one, in *World Hypotheses.*[46] Both Pratt and Otto have warned against this treatment. Pratt says, "It is a mistaken view which regards the expressions of the mystics and of those who have been inspired by them as *philosophy*, and which attempts to judge them accordingly. Rather they should be taken as a kind of earnest poetry."[47] Otto in the second chapter of Part A of his book, *Mysticism, East and West*—the title of this chapter is "Not Metaphysics but a Doctrine of Salvation"—writes,

> All affirmations and arguments in proof of the absolute unity, the complete simplicity, and the perfect identity of the soul with God, all the evidence and declamation against multiplicity, separateness, division and manifoldness—however much they may sound like rational ontology—are for both of them (that is, for Eckhart and Sankara) only ultimately significant because they are 'saving.'[48]

The compelling interest of Eckhart and Śaṅkara, whom Otto selects as the representative mystics of the West and the East, is according to Otto "not a scientific interest in the ultimate . . . but . . . both are guided by their interest in something which lies outside scientific or metaphysical speculation. This idea measured by these or any other rational standards must appear utterly fantastic and completely 'irrational'; it is the idea of 'salus,' of salvation, of śreyas, of Heil, and of how this is to be won."[49] The Being sought by Eckhart and Śaṅkara is a saving actuality. Both the *Sat* of Hinduism and the *Esse* of Christian mysticism connote the true and the good. Stace, on the other hand, noting that "mystics themselves philosophize;"[50] argues

> In doing so they descend to the intellectual plane and therefore cannot expect to escape from intellectual criticism and analysis. They cannot invade the philosopher's field and at the same time refuse to the philosopher any right to discuss their philosophical assertions . . . Mystics also do not even stop short at asserting general but isolated philosophical propositions of this kind. At least in the Orient they have gone further and constructed complete philosophical systems based on their mystical experiences. It is clear that in so doing they give a right to all other philosophers to examine and evaluate their systems.[51]

Stace in regarding mysticism as a philosophy, rather than as a soteriology, mistakes mysticism as being chiefly concerned about the correct understanding of the nature of reality. He does not see that the chief concern of the mystic is the salvation of man. This mistake is made more likely when the mystic holds, as he often does, that self-realization includes as an ingredient a specific view of the world. Metaphysics within mysticism is a *means* to salvation and not an end in itself. The mystic is not motivated by undiluted love of learning for its own sake; he seeks his own liberation from disintegration, sin, angst, and nihility, and insofar as he is able he suggests to others how they too might be saved. Metaphysics may be part of the instrumentality of salvation; it is not salvation itself. The mystic seeks to discover meaning, not metaphysical reality as such. Buddhist mystics often say that words and sentences are rafts to be abandoned upon reaching the other shore of the river. Otto says of Śaṅkara,

> His interest is not to correct a dosha, a mistake, that has befallen the Brahman; it is not an objective correction of the nature of Being. His true teaching as he sets it forth with great emphasis and earnestness in the introductory chapter of his principal book, is offered for this purpose: 'that none should injure *his own* blessedness, and fall into evil.' His teaching is for the purpose of salvation, not for the salvation of the Brahman, but for man who has need of saving.[52]

If the mystic is primarily a soteriologist and not a metaphysician, anyone who attacks the mystic as one who makes false or inconsistent statements does not hit a vulnerable spot. If false or paradoxical statements are successful in assisting another to his own salvation, why should the mystic *qua* mystic be concerned about their truth or validity? A philosopher who tried to make scientific or metaphysical sense out of Jonathan Edward's definition of nothing ("That of which sleeping rocks do dream.") would merely make himself look silly. Pascal made a verbal record of a mystical experience he had on the evening of November 23, 1654. The record which begins

> FIRE
> God of Abraham, God of Isaac, God of Jacob,
> not of Philosophers and Scholars.
> Certitude, Certitude. Sentiment. Joy. Peace.
> God of Jesus Christ,
> My God and your God.
> Thy God will be my God.
> Forgetfulness of the world and of all save God.
> He is found only by the ways taught in the Gospel.
> Greatness of the human soul.
> Righteous Father, the world hath not known Thee;
> but I have known Thee.
> Joy, Joy, Joy, tears of Joy.[53]

and which continues in this vein is certainly not a philosophical writing. Sometimes a mystic states either directly or indirectly that his object is not to convey information but to arouse the sleeping soul. For example, Eckhart[54] closes his sermon, "*Beati pauperes spiritu*," with these words: "If anyone does not understand this discourse, let him not worry about that, for if he does not find this truth in himself he cannot understand what I have said—for it is a discovered truth which comes immediately from the heart of God."[55] In other words, only he who has had the experience and has gained the insight can understand, since the discourse is on "discovered truth," that is, a truth which comes immediately from God and cannot be communicated by language. Sometimes a mystic shows his recognition of the incommunicability of mystical truths in curious ways. Eckhart closed another sermon in this fashion: "If anyone has understood this sermon, I wish him well! If no one had come to listen, I should have had to preach it to the offering box."[56] This is similar to St. Augustine's reply to the question about the nature of eternal life: "You had better ask eternal life itself and hear it." A Zen koan puts it this way: Hiju Yesho was asked by a monk, "What is the Buddha?" Yesho answered, "The cat is climbing up the post." The monk confessed his inability to understand the master. Yesho advised, "You ask the post."[57]

Thus far I have attempted to establish that the mystic uses language to motivate others to their own enlightenment through their own mystical experiences rather than to announce metaphysical truths. Now I turn to the problem of determining the characteristics of the language which the mystic uses in his soterial activity. I shall call attention to five characteristics of the language of mysticism.

In the first place, the language of mysticism is an emotional language. The scientist attempts to eliminate all connotative elements from his language, but the mystic rejoices in the connotative elements. The inner revelations are not to be subjected to the test of external authorities, nor objective measurements, nor even reason itself. The mystic holds that mystical insights bring with them their own convincing authority.[58] The elimination of the volitional, emotional, and pictorial elements would remove the rich diversity of mysticism. The mystic regards socially shareable, linguistically expressable, and quantitatively measurable statements as inferior to mystical insights. Anyone who has watched a committee reduce the creative idea of one man to the common denominator of the opinions and prejudices of the members of the committee can sympathize with the mystic's repugnance for public truths. The mystic agrees with Nietzsche: "But to eliminate will altogether, to unhinge—provided this were possible—each and every emotion—what? would not this mean to *castrate* the intellect."[59] According to Pepper the emotional basis of mysticism—the "root metaphor"—is the emotion of love.[60] Probably most mystics would agree. Romantic love sprang up in the West by adapting mystical love to the relationship between the sexes, as Bergson says, "When critics reproach mysticism with expressing itself in the same terms as passionate love, they forget that it was love which began by plagiarizing mysticism, borrowing from it its fervour, its raptures, its ecstasies: in using the language of a passion it had transfigured, mysticism has only resumed possession of its own."[61]

Secondly, the mystic in order to avoid making a verbal description of something words do not describe commonly uses negatives. Particularly when referring to the Ultimate Object of a mystical experience, the mystic avoids the use of a word which would tend to limit the Ultimate. To say that the Ultimate is this is to deny that it is that. So the mystic attempts to avoid all limitations by using only negatives. Dionysius the Areopagite, who probably lived in the fifth century, describes the Absolute in these words:

> The cause of all things is neither soul nor intellect; nor has it imagination, opinion, or reason, or intelligence; nor is it reason or intelligence; nor is it spoken or thought. It is neither number, nor order, nor magnitude, nor littleness, nor equality, nor inequality, nor similarity, nor dissimilarity. It neither stands, nor moves, nor rests. . . . It is neither essence, nor eternity, nor time. Even intellectual contact does not belong to it. It is neither science nor truth. It is not even royalty or wisdom; not one; not unity; not divinity or goodness; not even spirit as we know it.[62]

Śaṅkara says that the only "adequate" characterization of the Brahman is "*Neti, neti*" ("Inadequate, inadequate"). The monistic form of the Vedānta philosophy associated with Śaṅkara is known as the Advaita (non-dual). Eckhart negates God in this fashion: "How, then, shall I love him? Love him as he is, a not-god, a not-ghost, apersonal, formless."[63] In another passage Eckhart in attempting to clarify the negations of mysticism seems to confuse the issue and unintentionally makes the negations almost meaningless: "The One is a negation of negations. Every creature contains a negation: one denies that it is the other. An angel denies that it is any other creature; but God contains the denial of denials. He is that One who denies of every *other* that it is anything except himself."[64] But if God "contains the denial of denials," then God is not only "a negation of negations," but also "a negation of negations of negations," and "a negation of negations of negations of negations," etc. *ad infinitum*! Eckhart in trying to avoid limiting the Object of mystical experience seems to reduce the Object to an absolute nothing—or is this also negated, so that the mystic arrives full circle at Absolute Fullness?

Thirdly, the language of mysticism is often a language of paradoxes. Many of the koans of the Zen Buddhist are paradoxes. One of the best known is Fudaishi's:

> Empty-handed I go and yet the spade is in my hands;
> I walk on foot, and yet on the back of an ox I am riding:
> When I pass over the bridge,
> Lo, the water floweth not, but the bridge doth flow.[65]

Eckhart says in one of his sermons, "Therefore, no man can see God except he be blind, nor know him except through ignorance, nor understand him except through folly."[66] Stace in chapter five of *Mysticism and Philosophy* examines and refutes four theories that attempt to get rid of the paradoxes in the "logic" of mysticism and then argues for his own position which is that the paradoxes are "flat logical contradictions."[67] His argument is that the laws of logic (that is, identity, non-contradiction, and excluded middle) are "the necessary rules for thinking of or dealing with a *multiplicity* of separate items"[68] in the world of everyday experience, but that since the world of mystical experience is a world in which there is no multiplicity, the laws of logic cannot be applied there. His argument rests on the Aristotelian assumption that the laws of logic are not pure laws of thought but are expressions of the nature of the reality of ordinary experience. It seems to me that a critic of mysticism rather than agreeing that "in the One there are no separate items to be kept distinct, and therefore logic has no meaning for it,"[69] might argue that the mystic's use of paradoxes is a way in which the mystic protests as a radical positivist against all rationalistic epistemologies. The mystic is one who insists that the red color he sees when he looks at a red apple is the "real" red color and that this red is not the same red described as electromagnetic waves .00007 of a centimeter long. This is the distinction Northrop makes in *The Meeting of East and West* between "concepts by postulation" and "concepts by intuition." The mystic uses paradoxes because for him the human tongue is not an adequate organ for expressing the deepest truths of human experience. He agrees with Bridgman, "The more one thinks about it the more unlike do the structures of language and experience appear . . . not only is it impossible to get all the aspects of experience into language, but language does not afford a unique method of reporting any isolated aspects of experience . . . language as language is divorced from the activity which is the basal property of all our experience."[70] The paradoxes of mysticism are not foreign to the most unmystical person; anyone who has experienced the ambivalence of loving and hating the same person has had a direct experience of paradox.

A fourth characteristic of the language of mysticism and another way in which the mystic protests against rationalistic philosophies goes even beyond paradoxes. It is the way of ignorance! According to St. Paul "the foolishness of God is wiser than men."[71] "God despises ideas," says Dionysius. Eckhart holds that ideas cannot take one to God: "The moment you get [one of your own] ideas, God fades out and the Godhead too. It is when the idea is gone that God gets in."[72] In another sermon Eckhart says, "Thus it is true that you cannot know God by means of any creature science nor by means of your own wisdom. If you are to know God divinely, your own knowledge must become as pure ignorance, in which you forget yourself and every other creature."[73] Hence the language of mysticism is not the language of knowledge but the language of non-knowledge, of ignorance. The psychological state which corresponds to ignorance is known in Taoism and Zen as *wuhsin* (no mind). Eckhart calls it "a state of pure nothingness."[74] The point the mystic is trying to convey in his praise of ignorance is the condemnation of the habit of allowing the conceptualization of experience to displace experience. A man is asked a question by the very fact of his existence, says the mystic, but the answer cannot be given in concepts. Man is, and he knows that he is, and in his knowing he is both more and less than what he is. He can transcend his existence by knowing, and thus more than exist; but if he lives only in his knowing, he less than exists. In the words of the psychoanalyst, Fromm,

> There is no better example that can be cited for men who are dead to the question posed by existence than we ourselves, living in the twentieth century. We try to evade the question by concern with property, prestige, power, production, fun, and ultimately, by trying to forget that we—that I—exist. No matter how much he *thinks* of God or goes to church, or how much he believes in religious ideas, if he, the whole man, is deaf to the question of existence, if he does not have an answer to it, he is marking time, and he lives and dies like one of the million things he produces.[75]

The mystic's way of finding the answer through ignorance has been strikingly presented in a Zen story: A university professor once came to Nan-in, a Zen master, to inquire about Zen. Nan-in served tea. He poured his visitor's cup full, and then kept on pouring. The professor watched the overflow until he no longer could restrain himself. "It is overfull. No more will go in," he said. Nan-in said, "Like this cup, you are full of your own opinions and speculations. How can I show you Zen unless you first empty your cup?"[76] Words and ideas are symbols of reality; they are not reality. "The man who stops with the enjoyment of a symbol never comes to the inward truth," says Eckhart.[77] Therefore, Eckhart advises silence: "It is in the stillness, in the silence, that the word of God is to be heard. There is no better avenue of approach to this Word than through stillness, through silence."[78] Mystics of every land and time have practised silence as one of the means of enlightenment. The mystical ecstasy lies beyond symbolization. The mystic no longer thinks of God—he *is* God.

Finally, the mystic attempts to reveal the integrated point of view which characterizes all mystical experiences. Mystical unity transcends both the I-It and I-Thou relationships. The mystic amends Kant's philosophy by asserting that the thing-in-itself is not an object but a subject which has assimilated objectivity. It is impossible to express linguistically the mystical One since ordinary language, like logic, implies multiplicity. Therefore the mystic who does not wish to be silent speaks from "a higher point of view" which Chuang-tzu, the Taoist mystic, calls "the Fast of the Mind" and "Sitting in Forgetfulness." In the words of Chuang-tzu, "Heaven and Earth came into being with me together, and with me, all things are one."[79] The mystical unity is suggested by the use of language which subjectifies the object and objectifies the subject. The non-mystic, on the other hand, objectifies the object. He seeks the "real" world, that is, the world outside himself. He assumes he can stand off from this world and know it. Language is a symptom of the non-mystical process of objectifying the object. It presupposes the other-than selfness of the referent of the word. Language both results from objectification and leads to objectification. It implies a knower and a known, a subject and an object. The non-mystic reifies and externalizes the word. His reason tends to turn everything into an object. This is the Platonic fallacy: universals are made into objects transcending all particulars. This fallacy was what brought about the Aristotelian rebellion in the Platonic Academy. Aristotle claimed that by objectifying the constructions of the mind Plato had created a world of pseudo-reality. The goal of mysticism is victory over objectification of the object. For the mystic objectification is exteriorization, the alienation of spirit from itself. This was the horror Pascal felt when confronted by the endlessness of space. Objectification is above all depersonalization. Hence for the mystic the world becomes a naught; God becomes a not-god; and all that is not-self becomes *māyā*. These are not evidences of illusionism, as some have charged. These are linguistic attempts of the mystic to break down the subject-object dichotomy, to suggest that the object world is one with the immediate reality of the Self, that Brahman is *Ātman*. But if the mystic were to leave the matter at this point, the accusation of being solipsistic might be relevant. However, the mystic not only uses a language which subjectifies the object, but also he uses a language which objectifies the subject. This aspect of mysticism is often missed by critics. The objectification of the subject appears in subtle ways in the writings of mysticism. For example, Eckhart begins one sermon by referring to himself in the third person: "Meister Eckhart once said, when he stood up to preach . . ."[80] Even more striking is a poem of

Chao-pien, a government official of the Sung dynasty, in which the poet recalls a satori experience. Note the shift from first person singular before the experience to the impersonal tone after the experience.

> Devoid of thought, I sat quietly by the desk in my official
> room,
> With my fountain-mind undisturbed. as serene as water;
> A sudden clash of thunder, the mind-doors burst open,
> And lo, there sitteth the old man in all his homeliness.[81]

If one asks the mystic, "Do not the subjectification of the object and the objectification of the subject cancel each other?", the mystic will probably reply, "Of course! 'Nothing in all creation is so like God as stillness.'[82] 'Only listen to the voice of pines and cedars when no wind stirs!' "[83]

NOTES

1. J. H. Leuba, *A Psychological Study of Religion*. New York: The Macmillan Co., 1912, Appendix.
2. Robert Leet Patterson, *An Introduction to the Philosophy of Religion*. New York: Henry Holt and Co., 1958, p. 31. Italics are mine.
3. Alfred North Whitehead, *Religion in the Making*. New York: The Macmillan Co., 1926, p. 16.
4. According to Charles Sanders Peirce ". . . it is absurd to say that religion is a mere belief. You might as well call society a belief, or civilization a belief. Religion is a life, and can be identified with a belief only provided that belief be a living belief—a thing to be lived rather than said or thought." *Collected Papers of Charles Sanders Peirce*, Vol. VI. Edited by Charles Hartshorne and Paul Weiss. Cambridge: Harvard University Press, 1935, p. 306. John E. Smith places another emphasis on personal religious experience: " . . . there is one fact which the history of religion makes clear and that is the indispensability of direct experience as a ground for belief in God." *Reason and God*. New Haven and London: Yale University Press, 1961, p. 179.
5. William James, *The Varieties of Religious Experience*. New York: Random House, The Modern Library, 1936, p. 370. First published in 1902.
6. J. B. Pratt, *The Religious Consciousness*. New York: The Macmillan Co., 1920, p. 14.
7. *Ibid.*, p. 18.
8. Evelyn Underhill, *Mysticism*. New York: E. P. Dutton and Co., 1914, p. 70.
9. G. Ernest Wright, *God Who Acts*. London: SCM Press, 1952, p. 23.
10. Reinhold Niebuhr, *The Nature and Destiny of Man*, Vol. I. New York: Charles Scribner's Sons, 1941, p. 126.
11. Paul Tillich, *Systematic Theology*, Vol. I. Chicago: University of Chicago Press, 1951, p. 9.

12. *Ibid.*, p. 16.
13. F. C. Copleston, *Aquinas*. London: Pelican Books, 1955, p. 10.
14. While there are many kinds of mysticism, in this paper the word "mysticism" always means religious mysticism.
15. W. T. Stace, "Man Against Darkness," *Atlantic Monthly*, September 1948, pp. 53-58.
16. W. T. Stace, *Mysticism and Philosophy*. Philadelphia and New York: J. B. Lippincott Co., 1960, p. 6.
17. *Ibid.*, p. 6.
18. *Ibid.*, p. 277.
19. James, *op. cit.*, p. 396.
20. *Ibid.*, p. 395.
21. *Ibid.*, p. 398.
22. The meanings referred to are those grasped within mystical experiences.
23. Dwight Goddard, *A Buddhist Bible*. New York: E. P. Dutton and Co., 1938, p. 286.
24. Paul Carus (translator). *The Canon of Reason and Virtue*. LaSalle, Illinois: Open Court Publishing Co., 1927, pp. 73, 112.
25. Aurobindo, *The Life Divine*. New York: The Greystone Press, 1949, p. 789.
26. *Mysticism and Philosophy*, p. 277.
27. *Ibid.*, pp. 280-294.
28. Stace subdivides this theory into "The Dionysian Theory" and "The Metaphor Theory." He says " . . . in the Dionysian theory the relation between symbolization and symbol is *causal*, whereas the metaphor theory implies a relation of *resemblance*." *Ibid.*, p. 292.
29. *Ibid.*, pp. 295-306.
30. "Plotinus makes the right distinction, and in fact briefly states what I believe to be the correct solution. 'In this apprehension,' he says, 'we have neither power nor time to say anything about it. Afterwards we can reason about it.' In other words we cannot speak of it when we have it, but we can afterwards. We have only to elaborate their theory in full." *Ibid.*, p. 297.
31. *Ibid.*, p. 283.
32. *Ibid.*, p. 295.
33. *Ibid.*, p. 279.
34. *Ibid.*, p. 306.
35. *Ibid.*
36. *Ibid.*, p. 277. Italics are mine.
37. *Ibid.*, p. 298. Italics are mine.
38. *Ibid.*, p. 305. Italics are mine.
39. *Ibid.*, p. 297.
40. *Ibid.*, p. 296.
41. These were the last words of the Buddha.
42. *Mysticism and Philosophy*, p. 298.
43. Raymond Bernard Blakney, *Meister Eckhart*. New York: Harper and Brothers, Torchbook edition, 1957, p. 24.
44. *Mysticism and Philosophy*, p. 13.
45. *Ibid.*, p. 17.
46. Stephen C. Pepper, *World Hypotheses*. Berkeley: University of California Press, 1942, pp. 127-137. Pepper says regarding mysticism, "As *the* philosophy of unity and love, it is the most destructive of all world theories in cognition and

finally destroys itself by the very intensity of its desire for unity and peace." p. 127.

47. Pratt, *op. cit.*, p. 468.
48. Rudolf Otto, *Mysticism, East and West*. New York: The Macmillan Co., 1932, p. 17.
49. *Ibid.*, pp. 16-17.
50. *Mysticism and Philosophy*, p. 21.
51. *Ibid.*, p. 22. Note that the expression "all other philosophers" indicates again that Stace thinks mysticism is a philosophy.
52. Otto, *op. cit.*, pp. 83-84.
53. Eugene William Lyman, *The Meaning and Truth of Religion*. New York: Charles Scribner's Sons, 1933, p. 109.
54. Eckhart is obviously Stace's favorite among the mystics. He says that Eckhart is one of "the more philosophical Christian mystics." (p. 66); he praises him as one of those "who usually keep their emotions well under control" (p. 53); and he refers to him far more often than to any other mystic (See Index, p. 346).
55. Blakney, *op. cit.*, p. 232.
56. *Ibid.*, p. 226.
57. William Barrett, *Zen Buddhism*. Garden City, New York: Doubleday and Co., Anchor Books, 1956, p. 248.
58. Robert Barclay, a seventeenth-century Scottish Quaker, writes, "Moreover, these divine inward revelations, which we make absolutely necessary for the building up of true faith, neither do nor can ever contradict the outward testimony of the scriptures, or right and sound reason. Yet from hence it will not follow, that these divine revelations are to be subjected to the test, either of the outward testimony of the scriptures, or of the natural reason of man, as to a more noble or certain rule and touchstone; for this divine revelation and inward illumination, is that which is certain and clear of itself, forcing, by its own evidence and clearness, the well-disposed understanding to assent, irresistibly moving the same thereunto, even as the common principles of natural truths do move and incline the mind to a natural assent." *An Apology for the True Christian Divinity, being an Explanation and Vindication of the Principles and Doctrines of the People called Quakers*. Philadelphia: Friends' Book-Store, no date, p. 28. First published in 1675.
59. Alexander Tille (editor), *The Works of Friedrich Nietzsche*, Vol. X. *A Genealogy of Morals*. Translated by William A. Hausemann. New York: The Macmillan Co., 1897, p. 164.
60. Pepper, *op. cit.*, p. 133.
61. Henri Bergson, *The Two Sources of Morality and Religion*. Garden City, New York: Doubleday and Co., Anchor Books, 1954, p. 42. Translated by R. Ashley Audra and Cloudesley Brereton. First published in 1932.
62. James, *op. cit.*, pp. 407-408.
63. Blakney, *op. cit.*, p. 248.
64. *Ibid.*, p. 247.
65. Barrett, *op. cit.*, p. 115.
66. Blakney, *op. cit.*, p. 200.
67. *Mysticism and Philosophy*, p. 253.
68. *Ibid.*, p. 270.
69. *Ibid.*, p. 271.
70. P. W. Bridgman, *The Nature of Physical Theory*. Princeton: Princeton University Press, 1936, pp. 22-24.

71. I Corinthians 1:25.
72. Blakney, *op. cit.*, p. 127.
73. *Ibid.*, p. 119.
74. *Ibid.*, p. 121.
75. D. T. Suzuki, Erick Fromm, and Richard De Martino, *Zen Buddhism and Psychoanalysis*. New York: Harper and Brothers, 1960, p. 92.
76. Paul Reps, *Zen Flesh, Zen Bones*. Garden City, New York: Doubleday and Co., Anchor Books, 1961, p. 5.
77. Blakney, *op. cit.*, p. 197.
78. *Ibid.*, p. 107.
79. Yu-lan Fung, *A History of Chinese Philosophy: The Period of the Philosophers*. Peiping: Henri Vetch, 1937, p. 244.
80. Blakney, *op. cit.*, p. 136.
81. D. T. Suzuki, *Essays in Zen Buddhism, Second Series*. London: Rider and Co., 1950, p. 32.
82. Blakney, *op. cit.*, p. 243. A fragment from Eckhart.
83. Reps, *op. cit.*, p. 46. A poem by Ryonen, a nineteenth-century Buddhist nun.

—16—

*THE SILENCE OF THE BUDDHA**

The sixth century B.C. marks the beginning of an intellectual renaissance in India. Radhakrishnan has said of this period, "There are many indications to show that it was an age keenly alive to intellectual interest, a period of immense philosophic activity and many-sided development. . . . It was an age full of strange anomalies and contrasts. With the intellectual fervour and moral seriousness were also found united a lack of mental balance and restraint of passion. . . . When the surging energies of life assert their rights, it is not unnatural that many yield to unbridled imagination."[1] Another authority on Indian philosophy has written, "Speculation was almost rampant in the period just preceding the time of the Buddha and an excessive discussion of theoretical questions was leading to anarchy of thought."[2]

One restraining influence in this period of speculation was Siddhārtha Gautama, the Buddha, who by counsel and example discouraged abstract theorizing. When asked to express his view on a number of metaphysical problems, he remained silent. Thus, there came to be in Buddhism a group of problems which are known as the *avyākṛtavastūni*—the undetermined, or unelucidated, or unprofitable questions. The most comprehensive list of forbidden speculations is found in the *Brahma Jāla Sutta* of the *Dīgha Nikāya*. Here are listed sixty-two ways in which "recluses

* This essay appears in *Philosophy East and West*, Vol. IV, No. 2 (July, 1954), pp. 125-140. Reprinted by kind permission of the Journals Manager of The University Press of Hawaii.

and Brahmans . . . reconstruct the past and arrange the future." The Buddha says they "are entrapped in the net of these sixty-two modes; this way and that they plunge about, but they are in it; this way and that they flounder, but they are included in it, caught in it."[3] Buddhists are warned to avoid the net altogether.

Only ten of the questions raised in the *Brahma Jāla Sutta* appear in the Lesser Māluñkyāputta Sermon which is *Sutta* 63 of the *Majjhima Nikāya*, yet these are especially important, for with some alterations they constitute the *avyākṛtavastūni*. The *Sutta* opens as follows:

> Thus have I heard. On a certain occasion The Blessed One was dwelling at Sāvatthi in Jetavana monastery in Anāthapiṇḍika's Park. Now it happened to the venerable Māluñkyāputta, being in seclusion and plunged in meditation, that a consideration presented itself to his mind as follows: "These theories which The Blessed One has left unelucidated, has set aside and rejected,—that the world is eternal, that the world is not eternal, that the world is finite, that the world is infinite, that the soul and the body are identical, that the soul is one thing and the body another, that the saint exists after death, that the saint does not exist after death, that the saint both exists and does not exist after death, that the saint neither exists nor does not exist after death,—these The Blessed One does not elucidate to me. And the fact that The Blessed One does not elucidate them to me does not please me nor suit me. Therefore I will draw near to The Blessed One and inquire of him concerning this matter."[4]

Māluñkyāputta adds that if the Buddha will solve these problems he will lead the religious life under him; but if the Buddha will not solve them, he will abandon religious training and return to the lower life of a layman. By adding the pairs, eternal-non-eternal and infinite-finite, which are found in other lists of the *avyākṛtavastūni*, we have fourteen questions to which no reply is given:[5]

1. Is the universe eternal?[6]
2. Is the universe non-eternal?
3. Is the universe at one and the same time eternal and non-eternal?
4. Is the universe neither eternal nor non-eternal?
5. Is the universe infinite?[7]
6. Is the universe finite?
7. Is the universe at one and the same time infinite and finite?
8. Is the universe neither infinite nor finite?
9. Are the vital principle (*jīva*) and the body identical?
10. Are the vital principle and the body non-identical?
11. Does the Tathāgata[8] survive death?
12. Does the Tathāgata not survive death?

13. Does the Tathāgata both survive death and not survive death?
14. Does the Tathāgata neither survive death nor not survive death?

Questions about the origin and end of the cosmos, about the relationship of soul and body, and about human immortality are questions which positivists from Comte to Carnap would reject as insoluble by scientific methods, as unverifiable, as super-empirical, as metaphysical, as meaningless.

There are many other incidents in the life and teachings of Gautama in which he avoids metaphysical speculation. On one occasion he engages in delicate ridicule of the gods.[9] A monk goes to each of the gods and asks, "Where do the four great elements—earth, water, fire, and wind—cease, leaving no trace behind?" But the gods do not know. Finally, the monk asks the question of the Great Brahmā. Brahmā does not answer until he has led the monk aside. Then he explains, "These gods, the retinue of Brahmā, hold me, brother, to be such that there is nothing I cannot see, nothing I have not understood, nothing I have not realized. Therefore I gave no answer in their presence." Then he, too, confesses his ignorance and suggests that the monk put his question to the Buddha. When the question finally reaches the Buddha, the Buddha informs the monk that he asks the wrong sort of question. Again, in a number of passages in the Pāli texts the Buddha refuses to give information as to the workings of *karma*.[10] In the *Sāmañña Phala Sutta*, King Ajātasattu asks the Buddha what are the fruits of the life of the religious recluse. The Buddha's answer is that the recluse is treated with respect and reverence; he enjoys freedom from the hindrances of household life; he develops compassion and kindness for all creatures; he is content; he attains self-possession, etc. In other words, the returns of the religious life are all terrestrial in character. Finally, there is the record that the last words of the Buddha were not on immortality or annihilation, as might have been expected; instead, they were advice to his disciples to work out their own salvation with diligence: "Decay is inherent in all component things! Work out your salvation with diligence!"[11]

Gautama's avoidance of these metaphysical subtleties has been called "the silence of the Buddha." His silence has been as fruitful as his utterances in the production of philosophies and theologies.

Sometimes it is far more interesting to conjecture what a prophet might have meant if he had spoken than to listen to what he actually said. In this paper, however, we are concerned with the more prosaic question: Why was the Buddha silent on these metaphysical issues? There are several possible answers:

1. *He accepted the current views.* One reason the Buddha did not answer the questions about the termination of the universe, the extent of the universe, the relation of soul and body, and the state of the saint after death may have been that he accepted the conclusions of the Brahmanism of his day. He had nothing new to offer. Many students of Buddhism have pointed out that the Buddha did not break away from the religious and philosophical thought of his culture. E. G. A. Holmes contends,

> The teachings of Buddha can in no wise be dissociated from the master current of ancient Indian thought. The dominant philosophy of ancient India was a spiritual idealism of a singularly pure and exalted type, which found its truest expression in those Vedic treatises known as the Upanishads. The great teacher is always a reformer as well as an innovator; and his work is, in part at least, an attempt to return to a high level which had been won and then lost. Whether Buddha did or did not lead men back (by a path of his own) from the comparatively low levels of ceremonialism and asceticism to the sublimely high level of thought and aspiration which had been reached in the Upanishads is, perhaps, an open question. But that he had been deeply influenced by the ideas of the ancient seers can scarcely be doubted; and the serious and sympathetic study of their teaching should therefore be the first stage in the attempt to lift the veil of his silence and interpret his unformulated creed.[12]

Coomaraswamy observes, "the more profound our study, the more difficult it becomes to distinguish Buddhism from Brahmanism."[13] Keith thinks that the Buddha and the early disciples believed in the existence of the gods. This conviction, according to Keith, must be held "in the absence of a single hint to the contrary in the texts of early Buddhism, and in face of the belief of pious Buddhists throughout the ages."[14] Radhakrishnan writes, "Early Buddhism is not an absolutely original doctrine. . . . Buddha himself admits that the *dharma* which he has discovered by an effort of self-culture is the ancient way, the Aryan path, the eternal *dharma.* Buddha is not so much creating a new *dharma* as rediscovering an old norm. To develop his theory Buddha had only to rid the *Upaniṣads* of their inconsistent compromises with Vedic polytheism and religion, set aside the transcendental aspect as being indemonstrable to thought and unnecessary to morals, and emphasize the ethical universalism of the *Upaniṣads*. Early Buddhism, we venture to hazard a conjecture, is only a re-statement of the thought of the *Upaniṣads* from a new standpoint."[15] Even the Pāli scholar T. W. Rhys Davids admits, "Gautama was born, and brought up, and lived, and died a Hindu. . . . There was not much in the metaphysics and psychology of Gautama which cannot be found in one or another of the orthodox systems, and a great deal of his morality could be matched from earlier or later Hindu books."[16]

While it is obvious that the Buddha cannot be understood save in his Hindu background, one cannot but feel that some critics have deprived the Buddha of the uniqueness commonly associated with his doctrine. Takakusu goes to the opposite extreme in his emphasis on the originality of the Buddha. He makes the Buddha stand alone—much too alone. "It is difficult to determine how such a man as the Buddha, who is so different from the other philosophers and religious men of India, could have appeared there, for he denied entirely the traditional gods, religious beliefs, institutions and customs."[17] While Takakusu's generalization may seem to be too broad, since the Buddha took for granted such basic doctrines as rebirth, *karma*, and *nirvāṇa*, consider the fact that, whereas in the *Upaniṣads* ultimate reality (*Brahman*) is characterized by being (*sat*), thought (*chit*), and joy (*ānanda*), in original Buddhism these attributes are displaced by impermanence (*anitya*), ignorance (*avidyā*), and suffering (*duḥkha*).

2. *He rejected the current views.* Perhaps the Buddha's silence was a formal denial of the views of Brahmanism. On at least one occasion he was silent because he rejected the current views. According to the *Saṁyutta Nikāya*, a wandering monk, Vacchagotta, once asked the Buddha if there was an ego (*ātman*, *āttā*). When Gautama made no reply, the monk asked, "How then . . . is there not the ego?" But to this also Gautama gave no response. When Vacchagotta had left the company, Ānanda asked Gautama why he had not answered the questions put to him by the monk. Gautama replied, "If I . . . had answered: 'the ego is,' then that, Ānanda, would have confirmed the doctrine of the Samanas and

Brahmanas who believe in permanence. If I . . . had answered: 'the ego is not,' then that, Ānanda, would have confirmed the doctrine of the Samanas and Brahmanas, who believe in annihilation."[18] The obvious interpretation of this conversation is that the Buddha did not agree with the Samanas and the Brahmanas; he believed that any answer to Vacchagotta's questions would give an impression contrary to his convictions. Oldenberg finds more than this in the incident. He writes, "We see: the person who has framed this dialogue, has in his thought very nearly approached the consequence, which leads to the negation of the ego. It may almost be said, that, though probably he did not wish to express this consequence with overt consciousness, yet he has in fact expressed it. . . . Through the shirking of the question as to the existence or non-existence of the ego, is heard the answer, to which the premises of the Buddhist teaching tended: The ego is not. Or, what is equivalent: The Nirvana is annihilation."[19] Oldenberg may here be charged with reading into the document an idea which became a fundamental one in the later development of Buddhism. Keith in his discussion of this passage warns that even if we feel the idea is hinted at, the author is teaching the doctrine of non-ego, "it is perfectly obvious that we have no right to go beyond the plain assertion of the text as to the doctrine of the Buddha."[20]

Yet Oldenberg's position may be supported by appeal to other Pāli texts in which the assertion of the non-existence of the ego is indisputable, e.g., in the *Visuddhi Magga* we find the following: "the words 'living entity' and 'ego' are but a mode of expression for the presence of the five attachment groups,[21] but when we come to examine the elements of being one by one, we discover that in the absolute sense there is no living entity there to form a basis for such figments as 'I am,' or 'I'; in other words, that in the absolute sense there is only name and form."[22] Again, in the *Saṁyutta Nikāya* the priest Yamaka, who held the view that "on the dissolution of the body the priest who has lost all depravity is annihilated, perishes, and does not exist after death," has his heresy corrected by the venerable Sāriputta, who reveals to him that according to the teachings of the Buddha there is no ego to be annihilated.[23]

La Vallée Poussin says that the record of Gautama's refusal to discuss metaphysical topics is a technique by which he denied the existence of the ego, God, and the *Tathāgata* and is the view which must be taken by modern Buddhists, but it need not be taken by scientific-minded students of Buddhist religion and philosophy.[24] And Geden is of the opinion that, although the Buddha consistently refused to teach about the supernatural, the "inference . . . that he intended to imply personal disbelief in the supernatural and in the existence of God, and to urge or enjoin this upon his disciples, is certainly mistaken."[25]

My conclusion is that neither of these first two reasons for the Buddha's silence is adequate, although this opinion may be explained by the inevitable difficulties a modern Westerner has in trying to understand the dialectics of ancient Eastern minds. It is patent, at least to the disinterested student, that the teachings of the Buddha were in part a continuation of and in part a revolt against Brahmanism.

3. *He had no views of his own.* A third possible solution to the problem as to why Gautama gave no answers to the *avyrākṛtavastūni* is that he had no answers to give. He could not accept the Upaniṣadic solutions; he could not offer alternatives. He was agnostic. Agnosticism is a word of many meanings. For our purposes only two general meanings need to be distinguished. One may be agnostic in the sense that one believes that the mind of man is congenitally unable to arrive at a cognitive grasp of the real world; or one may be agnostic in the sense that one believes that the real world is of such a nature that it forever lies beyond the cognitive grasp of the human mind. Perhaps these should be described as two emphases in agnosticism rather than as two types of agnosticism. Some agnostics emphasize the inadequacy of the mind and its operations, e.g., Hume and Kant; others emphasize the unknowable character of the world, e.g., Herbert Spencer. In Buddhism both emphases are found. The limited capacity of the human mind is implied in the Buddha's reply when he was asked to reconcile *anātman* and *karma*, "Shall one who is under the dominion of desire think to go beyond the mind of the master?"[26] The unknowability of ultimate reality is stressed in Mādhyamika and Zen.[27] But such passages cannot be interpreted as suggesting that the Buddha mind was agnostic in any sense.

We should note that the doctrine that Gautama had no views of his own on these metaphysical questions, that he was ignorant, is *possible* only in Hīnayāna Buddhism, although it is never so stated. In the Pāli texts he is portrayed generally as a teacher, considerate, kindly, fatherly. Even though he was said to have changed his heritage by reason of his enlightenment, he still remained subject to the physical limitations of all flesh: he became weary, he hungered and thirsted, he died as the result of food poisoning. In the Sanskrit texts, on the other hand, the Buddha is a celestial, transcendental figure. He is worshipped by animals, men, demons, *bodhisattvas* and other *buddhas*. He speaks not as a man who has found salvation and who willingly shares what he has discovered, but as a supernatural being who condescends to reveal some of his truth to man. The earthly Gautama is a Docetic messianic incarnation of the Eternal Buddha. The Vetulyakas believe that the Buddha dwelt in the Tuṣita heaven while a magic form acted out a life on earth. Some Mahāyānists describe the earthly life of the Buddha as a "skillful device" (*upāya-kausālya*) to lead creatures in the Buddha way. The *Suvarna Prabhā Sūtra* teaches that the Buddha did not die; he gave the appearance of death for the sake of sentient beings.[28] Suzuki says that "the Buddha in the Mahāyāna scriptures is not an ordinary human being walking in a sensuous world; he is altogether dissimilar to that son of Suddhodana, who resigned the royal life, wandered in the wilderness, and after six years' profound meditation and penance discovered the Fourfold Noble Truth and the Twelve Chains of Dependence; and we cannot but think that the Mahāyāna Buddha is the fictitious creation of an intensely poetic mind."[29] Much of the confusion as to the nature of the Buddha would be avoided if it were always clear whether references were being made to the Hīnayāna Buddha or to the Mahāyāna Buddha.

Keith is one of the few students of Buddhism who explains the silence of the Buddha on the grounds that the Buddha did not have answers to certain fair and reasonable questions put to him. Keith writes, "To deny that the teaching of the Buddha himself stopped at this attitude of agnosticism appears contrary to every sound principle of criticism. It is true that it has been suggested that it is impossible to conceive that the master would be contented with offering nothing more positive in the way of a hope for the future, but this is obviously to beg the question. [Keith has been discussing the nature of *nirvāṇa*.] By leaving the matter unexplained the Buddha allowed men to frame their own conceptions of the future of the enlightened man after death. . . . It has, however, been urged that we cannot suppose that so able a thinker as the Buddha was without personal convictions on such a vital issue, even though he may have deemed on good grounds that it was neither advantageous nor necessary to explain his opinions to his disciples. Here again we are confronted with bare possibilities; it is quite legitimate to hold that the Buddha was a genuine agnostic, that he had studied the various systems of ideas prevalent in his day without deriving any greater satisfaction from them than any of us to-day do from the study of modern systems, and that he had no reasoned or other conviction on the matter. From the general poverty of philosophical constructive power exhibited by such parts of the system as appear essentially Buddha's, one is inclined to prefer this explanation."[30] On the other hand, Poussin says that the agnostic position has nothing to support it other than a few texts and "the sympathy of several European scholars."[31] And Radhakrishnan advises, "To believe that Buddha himself did not know the truths and covered up his confusion and non-knowledge by silence, is hardly consistent with his claim to have attained enlightenment or *bodhi*."[32]

None of the texts which may be interpreted as implying agnosticism present the Buddha as saying, "I do not know." Rather, they affirm that the information requested is not necessary for salvation;[33] or that men hold a variety of opinions on the issue in question;[34] or that men have only a limited view of the world. For example, in the *Udāna*, Gautama tells the story of a king who, wishing to stop a long discussion in his court, called in all the blind men of the city and asked them to describe an elephant. The blind men were soon quarreling among themselves because they could not agree as to the physical characteristics of an elephant. The king observed:

> In such points Brahmans and recluses stick
> Wrangling on them, they violently discuss—
> Poor folk! they see but one side of the shield.[35]

Thus, one ought to maintain an attitude of intellectual indecision until evidence sufficient for a well-founded opinion has been acquired. One ought to see both sides of the shield—and all parts of the elephant. We must not fail to note, however, that the Buddha is not speaking directly here about his own knowledge or lack of knowledge. Buddhists insist that the Buddha was the one who saw all sides.

The conclusion that the Buddha was all-knowing is a much more defensible conclusion to be drawn from the texts of the Buddhists than the conclusion that the Buddha was agnostic. He is the Enlightened One, the one possessing perfect enlightenment (*bodhi*). Not only is he said to be omniscient (*sarvajña*) in the sense that he possessed all the knowledge one needs for salvation, but he is also said to be universally omniscient (*sarvākārajñatva*), that is, he knew everything past, present and future. Poussin says that the only work he knows which denies that the Buddha was universally omniscient is that of the *Brahmin* Kumārila, in which the author admits that the Buddha did not know the number of the insects![36]

Thomas holds that Gautama may be said to be an agnostic "in excluding from investigation certain definite problems which were useless to the practical aim of the seeker after freedom from pain."[37] But merely refraining from investigating problems on the ground of their failure to contribute to a practical end does not make one an agnostic.

4. *He would not tell his own views.* Gautama's silence may be accounted for by the hypothesis that, while he had solutions for all speculative problems, he did not reveal them because he believed men would not understand them. It would be better to let men work out their own answers than to give them doctrines which they would corrupt. Like St. Paul he gave milk to babes and reserved the solid nourishment for the spiritually mature. In other words, the Buddha had an esoteric doctrine besides the exoteric doctrine of the Fourfold Noble Truth and the Twelvefold Wheel of Causation. Several passages from the Pāli scriptures lend themselves to this interpretation. One is this story from the *Saṁyutta Nikāya*: "At one time the Lord dwelt at Kosambi in the sisu-grove. Then the Lord took a few sisu leaves in his hand and addressed the monks: 'What do you think, monks, which are the more, the few sisu leaves I have taken in my hand, or those that are in the sisu-

grove?' 'Small in number, Lord, and few are the leaves that the Lord has taken in his hand: those are far more that are in the sisu-grove.' 'Even so, monks, that is much more which I have realized and have not declared to you; and but little have I declared.' "[38] In the Mahāyāna scriptures may be found passages such as the following which support the theory of an esoteric doctrine: "My original vows are fulfilled, the Dharma (or Truth) I have attained is too deep for the understanding. A Buddha alone is able to understand what is in the mind of another Buddha."[39] Radhakrishnan is one of the modern interpreters who accepts the esoteric doctrine theory. He concludes that the "hypothesis remains that Buddha knew all about the ultimate problems, but did not announce them to the multitudes who came to him for fear that he might disturb their minds. This view seems to us to be the most satisfactory."[40]

The theory of an esoteric doctrine easily explains the conversation between Gautama and Vacchagotta. Gautama, according to this theory, had answers to Vacchagotta's questions about the existence of the ego, but, knowing that the impetuous and bargaining monk was not ready to grasp his full doctrine, he gave no answer to the questions. But the theory of an esoteric doctrine can be refuted by quoting the Buddha himself: "I have preached the truth without making any distinction between exoteric and esoteric doctrines, for in respect of the truths, Ānanda, the Tathāgata has no such thing as the closed fist of a teacher who keeps something back."[41] In *The Questions of King Milinda*, one of the twenty-five virtues of a good teacher is: "He should be zealous, he should teach nothing partially, keep nothing secret, and hold nothing back."[42] In the same writings the Buddha is quoted as having said, "The Dhamma and the Vinaya proclaimed by the Tathāgata shine forth when they are displayed, and not when they are concealed."[43] Davids in footnotes to the above two passages writes: "So that, in the author's opinion, there is no 'Esoteric Doctrine' in true Buddhism";[44] and "The fact is that there never has been any such thing as esoteric teaching in Buddhism, and that the modern so-called esoteric Buddhism is neither esoteric nor Buddhism."[45] In a literature as large as the Buddhist scriptures it is not surprising that conflicting statements can be found on many issues.[46] La Vallée Poussin is the author of the following discouraging observation: "*Cependant, prenons-y garde, si on peut parfois affirmer quelque chose du Bouddhisme, il est rare qu'on ne puisse affirmer et demontrer le contraire.*"[47] ("Yet let us take care, if one is sometimes able to affirm anything at all of Buddhism, it is seldom that one is not able to affirm and to prove the contrary.") Here is a fertile field for a second Abelard to write another *Sic et Non*. The esoteric doctrine has not proved to be a fully satisfactory explanation of early Buddhism's avoidance of metaphysics.

5. *He could not tell his own views.* A fifth reason for the unwillingness of Gautama to answer metaphysical questions is found in the inadequacies of language. Some questions put to him carried implications which he could not accept. To answer them would have confirmed the implications. They were weighted questions like the well-known logic textbook illustrations: "Have you stopped beating your mother-in-law?"; "Has your home town sold its horse yet?" In the Vacchagotta incident mentioned above, Gautama told Ānanda that whether he had answered Vacchagotta's questions in the affirmative or in the negative he would have confirmed the doctrine of a substantial self. Therefore, silence was the proper answer to the questions.[48]

There are other instances in which Gautama corrected a question, so he could answer it. In the parable which forms a part of the *Kevaddha Sutta* a man asks the gods, "Where do the elements pass away?" But Gautama changed the question to "Where do the elements find no footing?" Then he answered it. He changed the question, so that it became an epistemological rather than a metaphysical question. And in the framework of an idealistic epistemology the answer is obvious: the existence of the elements depends upon intellection; intellection has ceased in "the intellect of arahatship"; therefore, in the mind of the *arahat* the elements find no footing. Again, in the *Mahāvagga*, when Sīha, a disciple of the Nigantha sect, asks the Buddha if he teaches the doctrine of annihilation after death, the Buddha's answer involved a rephrasing of the question, for he answered, "I proclaim, Sīha, the annihilation of lust."[49] At another time we are told explicitly that the Buddha was unable to answer certain questions because they had a frame of reference which made an answer impossible for him. I refer to the occasion in which King Pasenda asked the nun

Khemā why the Buddha had not revealed whether the Enlightened One exists after death. The nun replied that the question assumes that the existence of the Buddha can be measured in terms of the physical, but this is not the case: "these predicates of the corporeal form are abolished in the Perfect One, their root is severed, they are hewn away like a palm-tree, and laid aside, so that they cannot germinate in the future. Released, O great king, is the Perfect One from this, that his being should be gauged by the measure of the corporeal world: he is deep, immeasurable, unfathomable as the great ocean. 'The Perfect One exists after death,' this is not apposite; 'the Perfect One does not exist after death,' this also is not apposite; 'the Perfect One at once exists and does not exist after death,' this also is not apposite; 'the Perfect One neither does nor does not exist after death,' this also is not apposite."[50] Thus, in typically labored fashion we are informed that existence is not a predicate which can be applied to the being who has entered into the state of *parinirvāṇa*. Existence becomes a meaningless word when used in this context.

Gautama, like all religious reformers, faced the problem of pouring the new wine of his teachings into old bottles, the verbal patterns which were familiar to those to whom he preached. Mahāyānists believe that some of his doctrines would not fit the language patterns of his day. According to the Zen school his doctrine will not fit the language patterns of any day. The Mahāyāna texts warn over and over again against the dangers that lurk in the use of words. They are fingers which point to the moon. One must beware lest one concentrate on the word and miss the reality to which the word points. "But neither words nor sentences can exactly express meanings, for words are only sweet sounds that are arbitrarily chosen to represent things, they are not the things themselves, which in turn are only manifestations of mind."[51] Zen masters, beginning with Bodhidharma, are fully convinced of the insufficiency of human language to express the fundamental nature of reality. Even to say "I do not know" is inadequate, since a confession of not knowing implies a measure of knowledge. Silence is the best expression of reality. "What I think may be stated thus: That which is in all beings wordless, speechless, shows no signs, is not possible of cognisance, and is above all questioning and answering."[52] Man should live in reality, not discourse about it. But this silence is not the silence of the misologist; it is the silence of a "higher affirmation."

6. *He would not be distracted from his main purpose.* We noted at the opening of this paper *Sutta* 63 of the *Majjhima Nikāya*, in which is found an important listing of the undetermined questions. After Māluñkyāputta had put his questions to the Buddha with the threat that unless they were answered he would desert the order, the Buddha gives one of his most elaborate refusals to answer speculative questions. He reminds Māluñkyāputta that he had never promised to give such teachings to his followers, nor had Māluñkyāputta set this as a condition of his becoming a disciple. Furthermore, adds the Buddha, to set up such a condition for joining or remaining in the order would be acting as foolishly as a wounded man who refused to have a poisoned arrow removed from his body until he learned the caste of the man who shot the arrow. "The religious life . . . ," continues the Buddha, "does not depend on the dogma that the world is eternal; nor does the religious life . . . depend on the dogma that the world is not eternal. Whether the dogma obtain . . . that the world is eternal, or that the world is not eternal, there still remain birth, old age, death, sorrow, lamentation, misery, grief, and despair, for the extinction of which in the present life I am prescribing." The Buddha then reiterates the other issues on which Māluñkyāputta is seeking information, viz., the finitude or infinitude of the world, the identity of soul and body, and the existential status of the saint after death. The consideration of these problems, he contends, is not profitable, and does not touch the fundamentals of religion. "And what, Māluñkyāputta, have I elucidated? Misery . . . the origin of misery . . . the cessation of misery . . . and the path leading to the cessation of misery have I elucidated. And why . . . have I elucidated this? Because . . . this does profit, has to do with the fundamentals of religion, and tends to aversion, absence of passion, cessation, quiescence, knowledge, supreme wisdom, and Nirvāṇa."[53] The Buddha's reply is a pragmatic reply. He is a religious teacher, not a philosopher. He has come to show men how to overcome the sufferings inevitably involved in living. Anything which does not contribute to that end is extraneous.

Similar responses are found in other *suttas*. For example, in the *Pāsādika Sutta* the Buddha tells Cunda that when men ask why the Buddha has not revealed whether a Tathāgata exists after death, they are to be told: "Because, brother, it is not conducive to good, nor to true doctrine, nor to the fundamentals of religion, nor to unworldliness, nor to passionlessness, nor to tranquillity, nor to peace, nor to insight, nor to enlightenment, nor to Nibbāna. Therefore, it is not revealed by the Exalted One."[54] And in the *Saṁyutta Nikāya* the Buddha, admitting that there is much that he knows which he has not revealed, explains, "And why, monks have I not declared it? Because it is not profitable, does not belong to the beginning of the religious life, and does not tend to revulsion, absence of passion, cessation, calm, higher knowledge, enlightenment, Nirvāṇa. Therefore have I not declared it."[55] A slightly different answer is given in the *Kevaddha Sutta*. Kevaddha, a young householder, asks the Buddha to perform, or to have one of his monks perform, a miracle in the town of Nālandā. In his reply the Buddha says nothing about his disbelief in miracles. Instead, he says that he abhors the practice of miracles: "It is because I perceive danger in the practice of mystic wonders, that I loath, and abhor, and am ashamed thereof."[56] Then he adds that if Kevaddha really wants to see a miracle he ought to study the self-training of a monk.

If one must choose only one of the six hypotheses as the reason Gautama the Buddha avoided speculative questions, the pragmatic hypothesis seems to me to be the best explanation. The picture we get of the Buddha is that of a remarkably single-minded man. Speculation was not only useless but harmful, for it would sidetrack him from his main goal. He had no disinterested love for truth. He admitted that he had more truths which he might disclose, but he refrained and limited himself to the revelation of only those truths which he considered to be religiously significant. Truth was a value for him only when it was a means to man's release from suffering. For Gautama, all knowledge was ideology, that is, all knowledge was held and expressed for certain reasons. His *dharma* was revealed only because it contributed to man's salvation.

What do the *avyākṛtavastūni* reveal about Gautama himself? They reveal the greatness of Gautama the religionist. He saw clearly that religion is first and foremost a way of life. Religion need not have a fully developed philosophy. Many of its foundation stones may remain unexamined. The Buddha did not argue for the truth of his Fourfold Noble Truth. Men were expected to see its truth intuitively and to test it in the logic of *life*.

NOTES

1. S. Radhakrishnan, *Indian Philosophy*, Vol. I. London: George Allen and Unwin, 1927, p. 272.
2. M. Hiriyanna, *Outlines of Indian Philosophy*. London: George Allen and Unwin, 1932, p. 136.
3. T. W. Rhys Davids (translator), *Dialogues of the Buddha. Sacred Books of the Buddhists*, Vol. II. London: Oxford University Press, 1899, p. 54.
4. Henry Clarke Warren (translator), *Buddhism in Translations*. Harvard Oriental Series, Vol. III. Cambridge: Harvard University, 1896, p. 117.
5. Other lists of the *avyākṛtavastūni* may be found in the following works: *Majjhima Nikāya, Sutta* 72; *Pāsādika Sutta*; *Poṭṭapāda Sutta*; *Dharmasaṁgraha*.
6. I.e., without beginning.
7. Sanskrit authorities define "infinite" as having no end in time, whereas in Pāli it connotes having no end in space, e.g., in the *Brahma Jāla Sutta* "finite" according to the translation of T. W. Rhys Davids means "that a path could be traced round it."
8. Etymologically this term means "he who has gone (or come) thus."
9. *Kevaddha Sutta*. T. W. Rhys Davids (translator), *Sacred Books of the Buddhists*, Vol. II, pp. 280-284.
10. *Anguttara Nikāya* ii. 80; *Dīgha Nikāya* iii. 138; *Saṁyutta Nikāya* iii. 103.
11. *Mahā Parinibbāna Sutta* vi. 10. T. W. Rhys Davids (translator), *Buddhist Suttas. The Sacred Books of the East*, Vol. XI. Oxford: The Clarendon Press, 1881, p. 114.
12. E. G. A. Holmes, *The Creed of the Buddha*. New York: John Lane Co., 1908, p. x.
13. Ananda K. Coomaraswamy, *Hinduism and Buddhism*. New York: The Philosophical Library, 1943, p. 45.
14. A. Berriedale Keith, *Buddhist Philosophy in India and Ceylon*. London: Oxford University Press, 1923, p. 94. But doesn't the *Kevaddha Sutta* contain "a single hint to the contrary"?
15. Radhakrishnan, *op. cit.*, pp. 360, 361.
16. T. W. Rhys Davids, *Buddhism*. London: Society for Promoting Christian Knowledge, 1894, pp. 83, 84.
17. Junjirō Takakusu, *The Essentials of Buddhist Philosophy*. Honolulu: University of Hawaii, 1947, p. 20.
18. *Saṁyutta Nikāya*. Hermann Oldenberg, *Buddha: His Life, His Doctrine, His Order*. Translated by William Hoey. London: Williams and Norgate, 1882, pp. 272, 273.

19. *Ibid.*, p. 273.
20. Keith, *op. cit.*, p. 62.
21. According to Buddhism the individual being consists of a combination of five *skandhas* (groups), viz., *rūpa* (body, form), *vedanā* (sensation, feeling), *saṁjñā* (conception, thought), *saṁskāra* (action), and *vijñāna* (consciousness).
22. Warren, *op. cit.*, pp. 133, 134.
23. *Ibid.*, pp. 138-145. In time the doctrine of the non-ego became the orthodox view in Buddhism. Suzuki says, "What distinguishes Buddhism most characteristically and emphatically from all other religions is the doctrine of non-atman or non-ego." *Outlines of Mahāyāna Buddhism.* London: Luzac and Co., 1907, p. 32. Yet some Buddhists refuse to deny the reality of a self. They use the term *pudgala* (individual) which seems to serve for all practical purposes as a self. L. de la Valée Poussin surmises that the word *pudgala* is used rather than the word *ātman* to avoid the suspicion of heresy. See the article by Poussin entitled "Agnosticism (Buddhist)" in James Hastings, editor, *Encyclopedia of Religion and Ethics.* New York: Charles Scribners' Sons, 1928, Vol. I, pp. 220-225. See also Keith, *op. cit.*, p. 81.
24. Poussin, *op. cit.*, p. 225.
25. Alfred Shenington Geden in his article "God (Buddhist)" in James Hastings, Editor, *Encyclopedia of Religion and Ethics*, Vol. VI, p. 270.
26. *Saṁyutta Nikāya* iii. 103. Keith, *op. cit.*, p. 78.
27. See Troy Organ, "Reason and Experience in Mahāyāna Buddhism," *The Journal of Bible and Religion*, Vol. XX, No. 2 (April, 1952), pp. .77-83.
28. See Keith, *op. cit.*, pp. 221, 271, 272. Also Suzuki, *op. cit.*, pp. 242-256.
29. Suzuki, *op. cit.*, p. 245.
30. Keith, *op. cit.*, pp. 62, 63.
31. Poussin, *op. cit.*, p. 224.
32. S. Radhakrishnan, "The Teaching of the Buddha by Speech and Silence," *The Hibbert Journal*, Vol. 32, No. 3 (April, 1934), p. 353.
33. See section 6 below.
34. *Saṁyutta Nikāya* v. 437; *Dīgha Nikāya* i. 179.
35. Quoted from the *Udāna* by T. W. Rhys Davids (translator), *Sacred Books of the Buddhists*, Vol. II, p. 188.
36. Poussin, *op. cit.*, p. 223. How this doctrine of full omniscience can be reconciled with the Buddha's obviously false prediction that his teachings would last but five hundred years I cannot imagine. E.g., "Not a long time, Ānanda, will holy living remain preserved; five hundred years, Ānanda, will the Doctrine of the truth abide." Oldenberg, *op. cit.*, p. 387. Text not given.
37. Edward J. Thomas, *The Life of Buddha as Legend and History.* London: Kegan Paul, Trench, Trübner and Co., 1927, p. 202.
38. *Saṁyutta Nikāya* v. 437. Edward J. Thomas, *Early Buddhist Scriptures.* London: Kegan Paul, Trench, Trübner and Co., 1935, pp. 117, 118.
39. *Sūtra on the Cause and Effect in the Past and Present.* Quoted by D. T. Suzuki in *Essays in Zen Buddhism, First Series.* London: Rider and Co., 1927, p. 47, footnote 1.
40. *Indian Philosophy*, Vol. I, p. 466. See also Oldenberg, *op. cit.*, p. 273.
41. *Mahā Parinibbāna Sutta, Dīgha Nikāya* ii. 100. T. W. and C. A. F. Rhys Davids (translators), *Dialogues of the Buddha*, Part II. *Sacred Books of the Buddhists*, Vol. III. London: Oxford University Press, 1910, p. 107.
42. T. W. Rhys Davids (translator), *The Questions of King Milinda* iv. 1. 8. *The Sacred Books of the East,* Vol. 35. Oxford: The Clarendon Press, 1890, p. 142.

43. *The Questions of King Milinda* iv. 4. 4. *Ibid.*, p. 264.
44. *Ibid.*, p. 142, footnote 3.
45. *Ibid.*, p. 268, footnote 3 (footnote begins on p. 267).
46. According to Dwight Goddard there are over one thousand titles in the Buddhist scriptures. He adds, "In the Sung Dynasty about 972 A.D. a Chinese version of these scriptures was published consisting of 1521 works in more than 5000 volumes covering 130,000 pages." Dwight Goddard, *A Buddhist Bible.* New York: E. P. Dutton and Co., 1952, p. v. When one considers the difficulty Christianity has had with the problem of establishing consistency among the sixty-six books of its Bible, the problem of consistency in the Buddhist scriptures seems ridiculously impossible. There are other factors which have made for diversity in the Buddhist scriptures, e.g., there have been no councils to determine the canonicity of the books (although there was at least one council to determine the orthodox doctrine of Buddhism), and—most confusing of all—the Buddhist have an open canon. New works are constantly being added. Furthermore, the figure of the Buddha in the later scriptures is a vehicle for other men's words and ideas.
47. L. de la Vallée Poussin, *Bouddhisme.* Paris: Gabriel Beauchesne and Co., 1909, p. 139.
48. In some schools of Mahāyāna Buddhism silence is regarded as the only fitting manner in which to describe ultimate reality. D. T. Suzuki has written, "Bodhi-Dharma . . . was fully convinced of the insufficiency of the human tongue to express the highest truth which is revealed only intuitively to the religious consciousness." And again Suzuki writes, "Another interesting utterance by a Chinese Buddhist, who, earnestly pondering over the absoluteness of Suchness for several years, understood it one day all of a sudden, is: 'The very instant you say it is something (or a nothing), you miss the mark.' " *Outlines of Mahāyāna Buddhism*, p. 105 and p. 105, footnote 1.
49. *Mahāvagga* vi. 31. 7. T. W. Rhys Davids and Hermann Oldenberg (translators), *Vinaya Texts*, Part II. *The Sacred Books of the East*, Vol. 17. Oxford: The Clarendon Press, 1882, p. 112.
50. *Saṁyutta Nikāya.* Oldenberg, *op. cit.*, p. 286.
51. *Laṅkāvatāra Sūtra.* Goddard, *op. cit.*, p. 286.
52. *Vimalakīrti Sūtra.* Quoted by D. T. Suzuki in *Outlines of Mahāyāna Buddhism*, p. 107.
53. *Majjhima Nikāya.* Warren, *op. cit.*, pp. 118-122.
54. *Pāsādika Sutta, Dīgha Nikāya* iii. 136. T. W. and C. A. F. Rhys Davids (translators). *Dialogues of the Buddha*, Part III. *Sacred Books of the Buddhists*, Vol. IV. London: Oxford University Press, 1921, p. 128.
55. *Saṁyutta Nikāya* v. 437. Thomas, *Early Buddhist Scriptures*, p. 118.
56. *Kevaddha Sutta*, Rhys Davids, *op. cit.* p. 278.

—17—

*CAUSALITY: INDIAN AND GREEK**

Comparative philosophy is filled with pitfalls. One of the most common is the lexiocographic fallacy. This results from the facile temptation to compare the philosophies of two or more cultures by examining their treatment of what is thought to be a shared concept with the same denotation and connotation. For example, a Christian who seeks to compare the Hindu and the Greek conceptions of God might collect passages from classical Indian literature in which the term *deva* appears and passages from classical Greek literature in which the term *theos* appears, since *deva* and *theos* are both translated "god." But this ignores the fact that *deva* as "giver" has been used by the Indians for the sun which gives light, for the father who gives life, and for the guest who gives pleasure, and that *theos* as "everlasting" has been used by the Greeks to denote the Olympians, the joy of meeting friends after a long absence, and humane acts to fellow creatures.

Our topic is causality. The Sanskrit term is *kārya-kartva*; the Greek term is *aition*. The root for the Sanskrit is *kāra* (making, producing, fashioning). *Aition* comes from the courts of law; it means culpability, responsibility, charge, accusation, blame. "To hold guilty," "to accuse of a thing," "to impute the fault to one," and "to acquit of fault" are Greek expressions using *aition*. In time it came to mean ground, origin, occasion, and cause in non-

* This essay appears in *Philosophy East and West. Essays in Honour of Dr. T. M. P. Mahadevan*. Edited by H. D. Lewis. Bombay: Blackie & Son (India)Limited, 1974, pp. 48-67. Reprinted by kind permission of the Managing Director.

legal senses. At once a difference in connotation appears: the Sanskrit word for cause comes from an action word, a word denoting the process of making; the Greek word for cause comes from a possession word, a word denoting what is one's own, what one must identify as belonging to one's life and works. Further analysis reveals more striking differences. From *kāra* comes *kārya* (that which is made, produced, fashioned, i.e., the effect) and also *kāraṇa* (that which makes, produces, fashions, i.e., the cause), and, when referring to the abstraction "causality," the term used is *kārya-kartva* (effect-cause). Greeks never referred to the causal relationship as the effect-cause relationship; they always called it the cause-effect relationship. Greeks, because they took a chronological view, called it cause-effect; Indians, because they took an ontological view, called it effect-cause. Perhaps even the title of this paper exhibits Western bias, but words like "effectuality" or "result-ness" are too contrived. The paradigmatic causal question for Greeks was: What are the conditions sufficient for bringing into existence a specifically desired effect? The paradigmatic causal question for Indians was: Given this effect, what are the entities without which this would not be?[1] But both would agree that an effect is a non-self-sufficient event or object. An effect cannot be accounted for by appealing only to itself. A cause is that which must be appealed to in order for the non-self-sufficient event or object to be, so the cause is that without which the effect would not be. The terms "cause" and "effect" designate mutually implicative aspects of things.

The problem I propose to examine in this paper is the relationship between cause and effect in the classical philosophies of India and Greece, and the program is to compare four main theories in the two philosophical traditions.

When one sets out to compare a philosophical concept from Indian tradition with its counterpart in a Western tradition, it is a good rule of practical wisdom to look to the Indian for a classification of the various possibilities of interpretation of the concept. For some reason the Indian philosophers were adept at classification. This virtue of clear thinking was not always a virtue in critical thinking, since often they seemed to have regarded classification as sufficient. "In India to penetrate a subject more deeply is to classify it further."[2] The criterion for classification of cause-effect theories used by Indian philosophers is the ontic status of the relata. Two questions are asked: (1) Are the relata real? (2) Is the effect a mode of the cause? On the basis of answers given to these two questions a fourfold classification was offered, and by combining the words *sat* (real), *asat* (unreal), and *vāda* (theory) with the words *kārya* (effect) and *kāraṇa* (cause) the four classes of causal theories can be precisely stated:

1. *asatkāraṇavāda.* The theory which denies that the cause is real and which affirms that the effect is real.
2. *asatkāryavāda.* The theory which denies that the effect is in the cause.
3. *satkāryavāda.* The theory which affirms that the effect is in the cause.
4. *satkāranavāda.* The theory which affirms that the cause is real and which denies that the effect is real.

In other words, two answers are given to each question:

1. Are the relata real?
   The cause is not, but the effect is. (*asatkāraṇavāda*)
   The cause is, but the effect is not. (*satkāraṇavāda*)
2. Is the effect a mode of the cause?
   No. (*asatkāryavāda*)
   Yes. (*satkāryavāda*)

Asatkāraṇavāda

The non-pre-existent-cause theory holds that a non-real cause yields a real effect. Contrary to what one might expect from this flat statement, *asatkāraṇavāda* is not an affirmation that one can get something from nothing, although it is an affirmation that one can get something from no thing. The cause, in other words, is not an identifiable entity. Buddhism holds this theory. The Buddhist view of the world in its inception in the sixth century B.C. was a polemic against substance. Hence, causality for the Buddhists could not be a relation between a substantial cause and a substantial effect. But as radical empiricists the Buddhists could not deny the realities of their experience, and they could not believe that the realities were self-sufficient and self-sustaining, so they were forced to affirm a causal relationship even though they could not affirm the reality of an identifiable cause. An interesting consequence of this was that the Buddhists were forced to eschew all cosmogonies lest they find themselves in the uncomfortable position of admitting the necessity of a First Cause.

The substance view of things is a sectional view, a slice of a movement. It is a static view which assumes that there is a stability and a fixity identifiable as independent units. But the world aggregate does not continue the same for any two moments. Everything is *saṁtāna* (flux). Reality must be thought of as a stream of water or a self-producing and self-consuming flame. Everything is on fire, said the Buddha. A "thing" is a series (*vīthī*) of happenings. Ceaseless movement is the reality; constancy is the illusion. There is change but no substratum of change; action but no agent. The doctrine of momentariness (*kṣanikavāda*) is only a doctrine of Hindu philosophers who could not comprehend what Buddhism was trying to say and who offered this doctrine to express in substance-language that which cannot be expressed in any language. In this connection it is well to remember that the Buddha is said to have made a list of fourteen questions which could not be answered in words, and also that on one occasion he delivered the "Flower Sermon," a sermon without words.

The Buddhist theory of causality is the central teaching of the Buddha. Kamalasila said, "Among all the jewels of Buddhist philosophy its theory of Causation is the chief jewel."[3] According to Buddhism the world is completely causal. All things depend upon causes. There are no breaks in the workings of *karma*. But each cause is contingent upon other causes. There is no *sui generis* cause, no permanent cause, no first cause. The word "cause" is misleading. "Causal efficiency" (*artha-kriyā-kārita*) in the sense of Y whose being is contingent both upon the being of X and also upon Z whose being is contingent upon the being of Y. In other words, Y's "being" is a becoming from X and to Z. "To exist" in Buddhism means to exercise the capacity to be "effect" and to be "cause." The real is the process of cause-effect (or effect-cause) relating. To be real is to participate in the chain of causing-effecting. Existence is change itself. Reality as the total process might be identified as coming-into-being-and-passing-into-non-being, except that no *thing* comes into being and no *thing* passes into non-being! "Production" and "annihilation" are but words to remind us that change, motion, flux is the real. Every event is both effect and cause. All are conditions (*saṃskṛta*), i.e., everything is a combination and a concurrence of conditions. *Saṃskṛta* means literally "only where this is, there that is."

The Buddhists in typical Indian fashion began with an event whose reality is not self-sufficient. It is an effect. To account for its coming-into-being they offered the theory of dependent origination (*pratītya-samutpāda*), which means literally "because of that occurring, this occurs." *Pratītya-samutpāda* has had a variety of translations: "The Wheel of Dependent Origination," "The Cycle of Causation and Becoming," "Co-ordinated Co-production," and "Combined Dependent Origination." When the theory is considered in the context of man's existential predicament, terms such as "The Wheel of Life," "The Circle of Birth and Death," and "The Wheel of Bondage" are used. An insight into the twelve divisions (*nidānas*) of the conditioned nature of co-production is regarded by Buddhists as the ultimate understanding prior to full enlightenment. Buddhologists, while not desiring to detract from the worth of the Wheel in the *sādhana* of practicing Buddhists, regard it as a patchwork system made up of many formulae. The twelve *nidānas* (divisions, stages, links, or spokes) are—beginning as is customary with *avidyā*—Ignorance, Will to live (*sankhāra*), Sub-conscious mind (*viññāna*), Name-Form (*nāma-rūpa*), Six organs of sense, Contact, Perception, Desire (*tanhā*), Cleaving (*upādāna*), Existence (*bhava*), Birth, and Death. The *nidānas* are to be read in the order given, which is usually indicated as clockwise on the wheel. Each *nidāna* is both cause and effect, but its effect-nature is differently conceived from its cause-nature. In its effect-nature it is conceived as the result of the co-production of the other *nidānas*, but in its cause-nature it is conceived as co-productive. That is, the *nidānas* as causes are not separate entities which can be examined by themselves. A thing never produces anything alone. Causation is always a set of co-factors. A cause is a cause only in a contextual arrangement of events. This means that the word "cause" is a misnomer in Buddhism; there are no "causes," there is only causation. Cause is *asat* (non-existent). In terms of the Twelve-divisioned Wheel of Becoming, if one selects a spoke, say Desire, and asks for its cause, the answer is not to be in terms of the immediately preceding spoke, viz., perception, but in terms of the other eleven spokes of the Wheel. Thus the entire wheel is causal in the production of each effect. A formula often used by the Buddhists was "Nothing single comes from single; from a totality everything arises." The universe is so interconnected that an effect is nothing over and above the presence of the totality of causation at any given moment. Each event is a universal event! An event can therefore be understood only in its gestalt. Its reality and meaning depend upon the total environment of which it is a part, and also upon the conditions under which it is being considered. Buddhists would do well to cease using the word "cause" and to speak instead of the multiple conditions necessary for an event, since all the *nidānas* of the Wheel of Dependent Origination operate as a unit. Junjiro Takakusu writes, "It is clear that the Causation Theory of Buddhism is not like the theory of causality of classical physical science which is a fixed theory. In Buddhism every stage [*nidāna*] is a cause when viewed from its effect; when viewed from the antecedent cause, it is an effect. It may be also said that there is a cause in the effect, and an effect in the cause. There is nothing fixed in this theory."[4] This is partly true but misleading. Takakusu's statement suggests a transformation theory of causality, when he ought to call attention to the fact that "cause" is a term useful in Buddhism only when it denotes the dependence of each *nidāna* upon the other *nidānas*. Or perhaps "cause" can be used to denote the entire cycle of Dependent Origination as the cause of *duḥkha*. Taking this as a cue, one can state Buddhism in one cause-effect proposition: "Because of the activity of ignorance leading to will-to-action, of will-to-action leading to consciousness, of consciousness leading to psycho-physical existence, of psycho-physical existence leading to the six organs of sense, of the six organs of sense leading to contact, of contact leading to perception, of perception leading to desire, of desire leading to craving, of craving leading to becoming, of becoming leading to birth, and of birth leading to death, *duḥkha* results; and with the cessation of these activities *duḥkha* ceases to be a result."

This analysis of Buddhism, I should add, is of Adhidharma Buddhism. Later modifications were added when Buddhists through the concept of "Ideation Store" (*Ālaya-vijñāna*) tried to explain the origin of activity and through "Thus-ness" (*Tathatā*) tried to explain the origin of Ideation Store.

Buddhism's parallel among the Greeks is the philosophy of Heraclitus. He, like the Buddha, was fascinated by fire: "This world order always was and is and will be an everliving fire." He also believed that all things were in process: "All things come into being through opposition, and all are in flux like a river." "You cannot step twice into the same river." Heraclitus was the voice of protest and challenge in the fifth century in the Hellenic world. He rejected the notion of fixity in the world of reality: to be is to change; and he challenged the notion of fixity in the world of thought: to know is to know from a position. For him the old order was death, but, unlike the Buddha, he had no message for those who would live in the new order. For him also the flux was orderly. His *Logos* is remarkedly like the ancient Indian *Ṛta.* Change followed a pattern even as the *nidānas* in the Cycle of Dependent Origination.

The feature of the thought of Heraclitus which caused his contemporaries to shake their heads, first in amazement, and then in exasperation, and finally earned for Heraclitus the nickname "The Obscure," was his belief in the identity of opposites. "Sea water is the most pure and the most polluted of water; drinkable and healthful for fishes, but undrinkable and unhealthful for men." The same object may have different consequences for different beings. "Disease makes health pleasant and good." Of course, we do appreciate value when it is contrasted with disvalue. "The path traced by the pen is straight and crooked." Perhaps that is the case from the points of view of gross observation and careful inspection. "In a circle, beginning and end are the same." That causes no problem since there is no "beginning" or "end" in a circle. Perhaps his most shocking saying was "God is day-night, winter-summer, war-peace, satiety-hunger." We are able only to conjecture what he meant, but I submit that he meant that there is a point of view which does not depend upon contrast. Most of our perceptions and understandings are in, through, and because of contrast. We see white when there is also non-white, good only in contrast with evil, and beauty in the context of the ugly. Heraclitus was trying to seduce us into understanding things as they are, not as they are contrasted. Ordinarily when we see an object of beauty, we see it as non-ugly, but from a higher perspective—the view of God?—contrast is not required because the "contrast" is part of the harmony. For God the "opposites" are united. A beautiful object is not non-ugly; it is beautiful-ugly. The saying most useful for our purposes here is "The way up and the way down are the same." "Up" is the direction of the growth of plants, the direction of the sun, the giver of light and life, and the way to the Olympians; "down" is the direction of the death and decay of plants, the way to Hades and the Shades of Death. Yet they are the same! Creation and destruction! What are they but two ways of viewing the same event. A "thing" is the processing-up and the processing-down. "Cause" and "effect" are the turning points in the process. The total process is circular, and in the circle the "beginning" and the "end" are the same. If we but listen to the *Logos*, said Heraclitus, we shall acknowledge "that all things are one." To single out the "cause" of events—even the cause of the world event—is to fall into the common error of making distinctions where there are none. Nature loves to hide, but if we look we can find the hidden harmony of opposed tensions, the agreement of unlikes, and the fairest of all harmonies. But alas, said Heraclitus, this is more than we can hope for, since it is not the nature of man to be intelligent—that belongs only to God! To the divine all things are beautiful and good and just; only humans find things ugly, bad, and unjust.

We cannot trust that the one hundred and thirty sayings of Heraclitus that have survived are his, or that they fairly represent the thinking of the man, but there is enough in them to indicate that this crochety misanthrope from ancient Ionia was, like the Buddha, trying to express a process view of the world in which, while one can recognize in the experiences of the immediate moment a lack of self-sufficiency which merits the term "effect," one cannot in a dynamic, changing world hope to identify the "cause."

Asatkāryavāda

The non-pre-existent-effect theory holds that the effect does not exist in the material cause. Cause and effect are two different substances. The cause must cease to be in order for the effect to be. The effect-substance does not have any reality before the process known as creation, evolution, growth, making, etc. It was never a mode of the cause-substance. An effect is the counter-entity of its own prior non-existence. This was the theory of the Nyāya-Vaiśeṣika philosophers.

According to these philosophers a cause has three necessary characteristics: (1) *Pūrvaṛtti* (antecedence). The cause must always precede the effect. (2) *Niyatapūrvavṛtti* (invariability). The cause and effect must be so related that qualitative and quantitative differences in the cause will be paralleled with the same differences in the effect. (3) *Ananyathāsiddha* (necessity). The relation between cause and effect must be such that the latter unconditionally follows the former.

The Nyāya-Vaiśeṣika philosophers held that the cause is needed to produce the effect, but there is no transfer of anything, although unlike the Buddhists they held that in causality there must be a change of things. Rather there is such a power inherent in the atoms that a new substance with new characteristics comes into being. The atoms of clay, stick, wheel, and water are such that when brought together in certain relationships a pot is produced. The powers in the clay, water, stick, etc., are able to destroy the cause and produce a new being (*ārambha*). Therefore the theory is called *ārambhavāda*, i.e., the coming into being of that which did not exist before, the creation of a novelty.

The *asatkāryavāda* theory has many weaknesses, and its supporters were constantly attempting to patch it to make it more plausible. The chief problem was that of maintaining that cause and effect are separate substances and yet are necessarily related. If they are entirely separate, how can they inhere? Wherein is the continuity? And if they inhere, how can they be separate? One line of defense was to distinguish between material cause and operative cause, and to point out that there is a difference in the separation of material cause and effect and of operative cause and effect. The material cause of the pot is the clay; the operative causes are the potter, the wheel, the process of turning the wheel, etc. There is an "inherence" between clay and pot which one does not find between potter, wheel, process of turning, etc., and the pot. In the words of the *Padārthadharmasaṁgraha*, a Vaiśeṣika work of the fourth century A.D., "Inherence is the relationship between things that are inseparably connected, and which stand to each other in the relation of the container and the contained,—the relationship, namely, that serves as the ground of the notion that 'such and such a thing subsists in this.' That is to say, the relationship named 'inherence' is that from which proceeds the notion that 'this subsists in this,'—with regard to substances, qualities, actions, universals, and individualities, *that appear in the form of causes and effects*, as well as those that do not appear as causes and effects, which are inseparably connected." (IX. 157. Italics are mine.) This explanation of "inherence" almost gives up the position, but it is easy to see why the author felt the need of showing that although cause and effect are separate, they must inhere. Substances in the cause-effect relationship may be separate, but they are not as "separate" as things not in a cause-effect relationship. But degrees of separateness is a strange notion. Two things either are or are not separate. How can they be more or less separate?

To account for the separation of cause and effect the later members of this school introduced the category of *abhāva* (negation or non-existence). It was a unique *padārtha* (category) in that, unlike all the other categories, it was relative rather than absolute, or, to be more accurate, three of the four kinds of *abhāvas* were relative. The absolute *abhāva* was *atyantābhāva* (impossible non-existence), e.g., the child of a barren mother. The three relative *abhāvas* were: (1) *anyonyābhāva*, the non-existence of a thing as another thing which is different from it, e.g., a clay pot is not a wooden spoon. (2) *prāgabhāva*, the non-existence of a thing before its production, e.g., the non-existence of a pot before it is made. (3) *prabhvaṁsabhava*, the non-existence of a thing after its destruction, e.g., the non-existence of a pot after it has been smashed. The last two kinds of non-existence are relevant to the understanding of the *asatkāryavāda* theory of causality. The effect is in a state of *prābabhāva* with respect to the cause before the process of production, and the cause is in a state of *prabhvaṁsabhāva* with respect to the effect after the process of production. Unfortunately this explanation of "separation" fares no better under analysis than the explanation of "inherence," for both *prāgabhāva* and *prab-*

hvaṁsabhāva are said to be forms of non-existence, yet in the quotation given above the cause-effect relationship is said to be one in which "such and such a thing subsists in this." Can a non-existent thing subsist? Somehow non-existence turns out to be a form of existence! The process by which this happened is not difficult to trace. If the statement "It is not blue" can be obverted into "It is non-blue," then why not obvert "It does not exist" into "It does non-exist"? The answer, as all logicians and most theologians know, is that existence is not an attribute. It is one thing to talk about a thing as not existing, but quite another to talk about a thing's non-existence.

It is interesting to note that the conceptions of antecedent non-existence and subsequent non-existence can be utilized to make defensible the theories of cosmic creation out of nothing and cosmic dissolution into nothing—theories which are fundamentally opposed to the usual Indian concept of beginninglessness and endlessness of cosmic cycles. This theory of causality is sometimes known as *ārambhavāda* (the doctrine of new creation) since it holds that new things can be added to those already in existence.

If the causal process is one in which the "cause" is eliminated and the "effect" appears, one might wonder how it can be called a "process." Relations as external as required by *asatkāryavāda* make causality into a form of legerdemain—now you see it, now you don't! A "cause" is Exhibit A, and an "effect" is Exhibit B, and they are put together by human minds who, noticing that A invariably precedes B, assume there is a necessity about A and B, and they call that necessity "causality." This is straight Humism, and this may be what the Nyāya-Vaiśeṣika philosophers were saying. If so, it is a pity they did not say it this way, rather than by introducing the notion of non-existence. The concept of negative facts is interesting, and may be required in some forms of philosophical argument, but it does not seem appropriate as an explanatory device in dealing with causality.

Asatkāraṇavāda and *asatkāryavāda* share in their "non-Hinduness." The concept of a creation out of nothing—of a genuine newness—is not consistent with the prevailing Hindu attitude that the universe is a self-adjusting continuum, that there must be at least as much reality in the source as in the result, that the world of our experience is an unfolding of an inexhaustible fullness. Whereas the Western man lusts for the new, the Hindu has an urge to console himself with a long tradition, a halcyon past, and an infinite matrix. The *śruti* syndrome of the orthodox Hindu is the desire to establish that his ideas and values are explicative of and correlative with what is explicit or implicit in the Vedic scriptures.

The Greek atomists Leucippus and Democritus did not discuss the concept of causality—at least we have no remains from their works which would indicate that they did—but from their thinking on the nature and behavior of atoms we can infer a theory of causality similar to that of the Nyāya-Vaiśeṣika philosophers. The fact that both these Indian and Greek philosophers happened to be atomists is immaterial for our purposes. We are only interested in what the Greeks did with their atomic theory insofar as it relates to causality. A Greek atom might be described as an infinitesimal Eleatic One. All atoms were said to have the same basic structure. The essential property of an atom is indicated in the word "atom" (indivisible). An atom was the theoretical terminus of the operation of division of any material body. It was a unit too small to be seen, yet it had size, shape, position, and arrangement. Weight seemed to be inferred from the notion of size. Some were angular, some concave, some convex, and some were said to have "hooks." They were the uncreated, indestructible, and unchangeable building blocks of the universe. Each atom was a plenum; it could take on no more of what it was. Their number was said to be innumerable—and presumably none could be added nor taken away.

All atoms possessed the inherent ability to move, and all atoms were continually exercising that capacity. Their motion was in the void. The void could only be described as the place of non-atoms, since the notion of empty space was foreign to the Greeks at this time. In other words, there was no notion of a space which could or could not be occupied by atoms. The atoms moved in the void, colliding, entangling, interlocking, clinging; and thus came into existence the gross bodies of this world. These bodies had qualities not found in atoms, such as hardness, softness, sweetness, bitterness, heat, cold, colour, etc. In other words, the secondary characteristics associated with gross bodies were not found in the primary bodies. In the words of Aetius: "Democritus says that colour does not exist in nature; for the elements—both the solids and the void—are without qualities." "Sweet exists by convention, bitter by convention, color by convention; but in reality atoms and void alone exist," said Sextus Empiricus.

According to Democritus and Leucippus the world of gross bodies with its colors, odors, tastes, and—presumably—sounds is the effect of atoms possessing only primary qualities. The effect is not in the cause. Therefore, this is a non-pre-existent-effect theory. Admittedly, the Greek atomists did not work out the theory. They may not even have thought of it as a theory of cause and effect. The problem of change and permanence, not of cause and effect, was paramount in their minds. They did not think of the atoms as ceasing to exist upon the formation of the gross bodies, so we must note that properties, not substances, fit the pattern of the Nyāya-Vaiśeṣika *asatkāryavāda*. This prepared the way for a reality-appearance theory of the world which was to be developed in the Greek world later by Plato and carried into Europe as "a series of footnotes to Plato."

Satkāryavāda

The third causal theory is the pre-existent-effect theory, the theory that before the effect appears as an independent entity it exists as a mode or potentiality in the cause. The cause is transformed or modified in the process into the effect. Therefore it is also called *pariṇāmanvāda* (the modification or change view of the cause). This is the view of the Sāṁkhya philosophers.

According to the Sāṁkhya philosophy the cause of all things in the phenomenal world is *prakṛti* (matter, nature, or object). *Prakṛti* is the generative source of all, a source which is never exhausted in its products. *Prakṛti* ceaselessly evolves under the stimulus of *puruṣa* (spirit or subject). *Prakṛti* is dynamic, self-efficient, and self-contained, but it is not self-sufficient since it acts only when catalyzed by the presence of *puruṣa*. The evolvements of *prakṛti* are real transformations, yet nothing really new comes into being, since the evolvents as effects pre-existed in *prakṛti*. Evolution is a self-becoming from the determinate matrix of all that is and all that is to be. Within the evolved world things are continually emerging from material causes, and are continually merging back into their material causes. The clay that became a pot because of the pot-potentiality of the clay will in time return to clay with its pot-potentiality. This, which the Sāṁkhya called secondary evolution, is an analogue of the primary evolution of *prakṛti* and its evolvents. Creation is manifestation of the effect, which before its manifestation was implicitly contained in the material cause, and destruction is return to the cause from which it was manifested. Causality is an unfolding of the unmanifested within the cause. It is a transformation—a real transformation—of *prakṛti* (*prakṛti-parināmavāda*). The effect is in the material cause in a latent form. The rationale of this view is offered in *Sāṁkhya Kārikā* 9: "The effect is existent; (1) because what is 'non-existent' cannot be produced; (2) because there is a definite relation of the cause with the effect; (3) because all is not possible; (4) because the efficient can do only that for which it is efficient; (5) because the effect is of the same essence as the cause." Perhaps the most important reason is the second in that it properly calls attention to the fact that causality is a *relation* and that relations must relate. This was the Sāṁkhya philosopher's criticism of *asatkāryavāda*. When the cause and the effect are thought to be two independent entities as in *asatkāryavāda* so that causality is the destruction of the cause, causality ceases to be a relation of relata and becomes a magic show in which all things are possible. But, said the Sāṁkhya philosophers, "all is not possible" and "the efficient can do only that for which it is efficient." So the effect must be "of the same essence as the cause," and what is "non-existent [in the cause] cannot be produced."

"Cause" and "effect" for the Sāṁkhya philosophers are names which do not denote specific independent entities but call attention to different forms of the same thing. The "effect" is the "cause" transformed. "Effect" is potentiality actualized. Milk-containing-curd-potentiality is the cause of curds. In the Jha translation of *Sāṁkhya Kārikā* 42 and 43 the words "cause" and "effect" appear in quotation marks. So the *satkāryavāda* is that the cause (which contains in a latent form the effect) is transformed into the effect (which is the latent effect now manifested and yet able to return again to the cause status).

The *satkāryavāda* was utilized by the Sāṁkhya philosophers in developing their dualistic interpretation of Upaniṣadic speculation, but for an analysis of this theory of causality we have to turn to Aristotle.

Greek philosophers prior to Aristotle were like Molière's *bourgeois gentilhomme* who rejoiced when he discovered that he had been speaking prose all his life without knowing it, for they had been using causal principles without recognizing them as such. Part of the greatness of Aristotle was his methodological sensitivity. His analysis of causality stands as one of the peaks of Western philosophy. According to Aristotle that which the philosopher passionately seeks is wisdom, and wisdom is the knowledge of the fundamental causes (*aitia*) and principles (*archai*). While all men by nature crave to know, the philosopher is unique in the sort of knowledge he seeks. The man of experience seeks practical knowledge, the knowledge *that* (*hoti*) such and such is the case; the man of craftsmanship seeks productive knowledge, the knowledge *how* (*pou*) it is that such and such is the case; the man of wisdom seeks theoretical knowledge, the knowledge *why* (*dioti*) it is that such and such is the case. All other forms of knowledge are more necessary than philosophical knowledge, but none is more important.

The term *aition* is ordinarily translated "cause," and so translated is open to many misunderstandings—and the plural *aitia* when translated "causes" is still more likely to be misinterpreted. Causality in Aristotle's analysis is not a list of four ingredients but a configuration of necessary conditions of natural processes and artificial productions. They are the theoretically divisible but actually indivisible aspects of the complete explanation of the existence of a substance. Aristotle, in other words, offers an analysis of causality rather than of cause or causes.

We do not know how Aristotle arrived at his doctrine of causality. He presents the causes as self-evident. He may have arrived at the doctrine by direct reflection on instances of natural processes and artistic productions, although he was aided by the works of his predecessors. In his review of Greek philosophy in the first book of the *Metaphysics* he indicates that the material cause was utilized by all his predecessors. The efficient or moving cause he finds in the doctrine of Love and Strife in Empedocles and in the doctrine of *Nous* in Anaxagoras. The formal cause he finds in the Platonic doctrine of Forms. The final cause, he says, "they assert to be a cause in a way, but not in this way, i.e., not in the way in which it is its nature to be a cause." (988 b 6) The final cause appears animistically among the early Greek philosophers, but according to Aristotle it was never treated as one of the conditions necessary for existence. It is one thing to say that the sun shines in order to make grass grow; it is quite a different thing to say that shining-to-make-grass-grow is a necessary ingredient in the being of the sun. While Aristotle finds intimations of the four aspects of causality in the work of the Greek philosophers prior to him, he notes that no one has recognized the causal syndrome as necessary for all change. Aristotle opened the first book of the *Metaphysics* with the observation that all men seek knowledge; the bulk of this book is an argument that the knowledge men seek is the knowledge of causes; and the conclusion is that the causes men seek are the causes Aristotle has analyzed: material, efficient, formal, and final. "But they seek these vaguely; and though in a sense they have all been described before, in a sense they have not been described at all. For the earliest philosophy is, on all subjects, like one who lisps, since it is young and in its beginnings."

In his discussion of causality Aristotle has two sorts of questions in mind: one is the static question, "What is it?" and the other is the dynamic question, "How did it come to be?" The answers he gives to the questions are the same, but the emphasis is different. For example, in answering a question like "What is a house?" Aristotle replies that a house is what it is made of, e.g., stone, wood, glass, etc. He calls this the material condition, the that out of which a thing comes to be. Secondly, a house is a plan or an arrangement, e.g., it is a four-sided structure with roof, floor, windows, doors, etc. This is the formal condition or the archetype. Thirdly, a house is what it is made for, e.g., a house is made as a place in which people can live. This is the final condition, the that for the sake of which a thing is. And finally, a house is the result of activity—the activity of carpenters, plumbers, masons, etc. This is the efficient, operative, or moving condition. The more significant question for Aristotle—and for our analysis of causality—is the dynamic question, "How did this house come into being?" The answers to this question, says Aristotle, are variations of the question, "Why?" The house comes into being because there was some material stuff, because there was a plan, because there was an end, and because there was a movement. The first two causes are the more passive; the latter two are the more active.

The danger in enumerating the causes of Aristotle is that of assuming that the causes are four items in a list of things necessary in order to make something. But the four causes are not things in themselves. They are abstractions in the context of processes, and the same thing is a different cause in different processes. For example, a fine straight fir board is a material cause in the context of house building, whereas it is a final cause in the activities of the sawmill.

The classification of causality into four necessary conditions is an arbitrary and artificial classification, as is evidenced by the fact that Aristotle also offers three-fold and two-fold classifications. The three-fold classification is indicated at the close of chapter 1 of the first book of the *Metaphysics*: "Clearly then wisdom is knowledge about certain principles (*archai*) and causes (*aitia*)." The three-fold classification is developed in *Physics* Book I, since this work is chiefly concerned with change, and the three-fold classification is predominantly an analysis of change. The three are the substratum, i.e., the unchanging identity which persists throughout change, the privation of form, and the possession of form. The "form" indicated here is the form with reference to a selected modification. Thus a block of marble before it has been sculptured into a statue is a block of marble deprived of form vis-à-vis the process of making a statue, and the block of marble after it has been sculptured into a statue is a block of marble possessed of form vis-à-vis the process of making a statue. Again the principles, as is also the case of the causes, are relative to the point of view of the observer. The block of marble is form-possessed from the point of view of the quarry worker but is form-deprived from the point of view of the sculptor. Aristotle says this in a curious passage in *Metaphysics* 1070 b 20: "One might say that there are three principles—the form, the privation, and the matter. But each of these is different for each class; e.g., in colour they are white, black, and surface, and in day and night they are light, darkness, and air."

At the opening of the *Physics* Aristotle intimates that he has three different ways of organizing the necessary conditions of change: "When the objects of an inquiry in any department have principles (*archai*), causes (*aitia*), or elements (*stoicheia*), it is through acquaintance with these that scientific knowledge is attained." "Elements" indicates the two-fold classification. The two-fold classification is stated also in *Physics* 198 a 23-25: "Now, the causes being four, it is the business of the physicist to know about them all, and if he refers his problems back to all of them, he will assign the 'why' in the way proper to his science—the matter, the form, the mover, 'that for the sake of which.' The last three often coincide." The two elements are matter and form. Matter is the determinable, that which takes on modification; form is the determinant, that which modifies the determinable. Matter is the potentiality for change; form is potentiality actualized. Or in terms of the Indian classification "matter" is the name for the pre-existent-effect, and "form" is the name for the existent-effect. A much more exact manner of stating this would be to indicate that in a primary substance, which is a matter-form complex, the form of the complex is the potentiality for becoming a new matter-form complex in which the form is the actualization of the potentiality. For example, an acorn is a primary substance—a case of informed matter. The form of the acorn with respect to the oak tree is potentiality. Under proper conditions oak tree potentiality undergoes a real transformation into oak tree actuality.

But whether Aristotle used a four-fold necessary conditions manner of interpretation, or a three-fold principles interpretation, or a two-fold elements interpretation, or a two-fold potentiality-actuality interpretation (a variation of the elements interpretation) he was always offering but variations of the pre-existent-effect theory. He had fewer problems than did the Sāṁkhya philosophers since he did not hold to the ontic separation of matter and form. Whereas the Sāṁkhya philosophers were motivated primarily by an effort to offer an alternative to Upaniṣadic monism and secondarily by an effort to account for change, Aristotle was motivated primarily by an effort to offer an alternative to the

Eleatic denial of change and secondarily by an effort to refute Eleatic monism.

Satkāraṇavāda

The fourth theory of causality is the pre-existent-cause theory. This is the theory of Śaṅkara's Advaita Vedānta. According to this theory there is but one Reality, but it is the "natural procedure" of man because of his ignorance of the real nature of the total environment to superimpose upon that Reality attributes which do not in fact belong to it. Prominent among these attributes is the notion of cause itself. Absolute Reality, i.e., Brahman, is the Real—and the only Real. The physical world, individual selves, and divine beings are regarded as the effects of the Brahman. These "effects," however, are but the illusory appearance or manifestation of Brahman. They are the superimpositions (*adhyāsas*) which our minds place upon Brahman. The Brahman as "cause" is real; the world as an "effect" is phenomenal (*māyā*). Hence this is called the *vivartavāda* (appearance theory), but to call it the appearance theory of *causality* is not correct, for a reality which does not have an effect has not met the criterion for being a cause. In one sense the "cause" of the world is not Brahman but man who superimposes the false attributes upon Brahman. The "effects" are the phenomenal superimpositions of *nāma-rūpa* (name-form) upon Brahman. Brahman, though unchanged, has the appearance of undergoing change. "Cause" and "effect" are non-different, non-dual (*advaita*), identical. Śaṅkara appealed to the observation in *Chāndogya Upaniṣad* 6. 1. 4 that a lump of clay may appear as pots, jugs, plates, etc. but in reality it is only clay. Again he argued that Brahman is the "cause" of the world in the same manner in which a rope is the "cause" of the "snake" a traveler sees in the road at twilight. So to say that Brahman is real is not to say that Brahman is a real *cause*. Brahman is Reality, and therefore insofar as there are any "effects" the cause of the effects must be Brahman. However the world is experienced, the foundation of the experience is Brahman. The most illusory experience and the most erroneous conclusion drawn from the experience are rooted and grounded in Absolute Reality. The one who makes the error and the error he makes cannot be outside the Brahman. Perhaps one can say that *by reason of* Brahman the world is experienced in its phenomenal state rather than *because of* Brahman the world is experienced in its phenomenal state.

Śaṅkara also tried to account for the world of superimpositions without implicating Brahman in error by describing the world as Brahman's creative activity. The world is the result of the Creator's joyous, free, spontaneous play (*līlā*). There is no purpose, no goal-seeking in the creation of the world. The creation and the Creator are both *māyā*, that is, the real seen from a point of view, and therefore both concepts must be demolished as one moves in thought out into wider and wider circles to attempt to grasp the nature of the Brahman. Philosophizing in Advaita Vedāntism consists of forming theories which are always inadequate, since Brahman as Absolute Reality is beyond all theories, beyond all points of view. Only through the negation of all thought (*neti, neti*—not this, not that), only through non-thought, can one be said to understand Brahman! Non-understanding is the highest form of "understanding!"

Satkāraṇavāda as a theory of causality is a confession that the Reality (*Sat*) which is known as Brahman is the "cause" for all our experience of the world of "effects." In our ignorance we assume the "effects" to be real, and we infer the nature of the "cause" from the "effects," whereas in truth the "effects" is Reality seen under the limitations of *nāma-rūpa*. When the individual realizes the Brahman and comprehends the manner in which Brahman is manifested to senses and minds, he transcends causality in that he now understands that causality itself is a superimposition.

Satkāraṇavāda among the Greeks is found in the philosophy of Plato. Plato, like Śaṅkara, arrived at a theory of Reality which lay beyond language and concepts, and which was the source of all existence, all knowledge, and all value. Plato, unlike Aristotle, exhibited rather than examined his theory of causality. Philosophizing on philosophy was not his forte.

In the *Seventh Epistle* Plato defended himself against his former pupil, Dionysius, who had written a book which the author claimed to be about "the first and highest principles of Nature" as taught by Plato. Plato wrote the letter in anger. In the first place, the book itself was sheer drivel, reflecting badly the quality and substance of Plato's teaching. Secondly, Dionysius had attempted to state a teaching which Plato had explained to him but once. But beyond this, the important teaching Dionysius thought he had expounded, the most serious of Plato's studies, could not be put in written form: "There does not exist, nor will ever exist, any treatise of mine dealing therewith. For it does not at all admit of verbal expression like other studies." This *upaniṣad*, continued Plato, cannot be fully stated in writing or in speeches to the public. If it could, Plato himself would have done it, for "what nobler action could I have performed in my life than that of writing what is of great benefit to mankind and bringing forth to the light for all men the nature of reality?" But this teaching can be understood only when "as a result of continued application to the subject itself and communion therewith, it is brought to birth in the soul on a sudden, as light that is kindled by a leaping spark."

Plato next outlined his method of teaching this fundamental truth about reality. One begins pedagogically with the three instruments of apprehension: names, definitions, and verbal and sensual illustrations. By such the student is led to a subjective apprehension of the object of instruction which has various degrees indicated by such terms as "true opinion," "knowledge," and "rational understanding." This, which Plato called "the fourth," has its abode in the rational soul. The four intellectual approaches lead by discursive reasoning to what Plato called "the somewhat" (*poion ti*), "the particular property" (*to poion ti*), and "the knowable" (*gnoston*). This is what language denotes. Language represents the attributes of an object, that which both authors and readers suppose to be the being of an object. But that which the rational soul seeks is not attribute but essence. The four instruments present what the soul is not seeking, although in its ignorance the soul often thinks it has gotten to the object of its quest. Śaṅkara would have said that *avidyā* or *māyā* is not seen for what it is by the unenlightened man. Those who listen and those who read, said Plato, forget that the instruments of name, definition, illustration, and knowledge are defective as disclosures of reality. This is why "anyone who is seriously studying high matters will be the last to write about them and thus expose his thought to the envy and criticism of men. No book contains the best the rational soul has to offer. A man's best thoughts . . . are stored away with the fairest of his possessions. And if he has committed these serious thoughts to writing, it is because men, not the gods, 'have taken his wits away.' "

The "first and highest principles of nature"—which Plato called "the fifth," "the what" (*ti*), "the real essence" (*to on*), and "the truly real" (*alēthōs on*)—may be disclosed to the individual but they cannot be learned nor taught by argument or reason. The disclosure is an illumination (*eklampsis*). This illumination is not a mystical insight revealed from an external or divine source. It is a consequent of the pupil's efforts in the sense that the efforts are propaedeutic rather than causal. Moreover, it comes only to those who have an affinity with the object. "In short, neither quickness of learning nor a good memory can make a man see when his nature is not akin to the object, for this knowledge never takes root in an alien nature; so that no man who is not naturally inclined and akin to justice and all other forms of excellence, even though he may be quick at learning and remembering this and that and other things, nor any man who, though akin to justice, is slow at learning and forgetful, will ever attain the truth that is attainable about virtue." Only the wise and the good will find Truth and Goodness.

The *Seventh Epistle* deals only with the problem of becoming aware of the Reality which is the source of all reals and all values; it does not even hint at the nature of that Reality. This we find in *The Republic*, Book 6, where Socrates converses with Glaucon and Adeimantos about the nature and training of the philosophical rulers of the Ideal State. They agree that the rulers must love knowledge, possess good memories, and be quick-witted. The rulers must also have steady characters, be trustworthy, not easily moved by fear, and able to endure "the hardest of studies." "And what do you mean by 'the hardest of studies'?" asks Glaucon. Socrates replies that he means the studies which "would show all clearly." When pressed still more, Socrates says he is talking about "the perfect ideal of goodness" (*hē tou agathou idea*). When Socrates is asked to discourse on this, he backs off on the grounds that his "present impulse is not strong enough," and suggests a discourse on "the offspring of the good" with a promise to discourse on "the parent" at another time—a promise, which of course, he never fulfills because, as noted in the *Seventh Epistle*, it cannot be talked about.

In his efforts to speak the unspeakable, Socrates offers the analogy of the sun. The sun provides the power of growth and nutrition so that growing creatures come into being, although the sun is not itself a growing creature; the sun makes objects visible by supplying the power of sight to the eye and also the light which makes the objects visible to the eye. So there is that which makes all things exist although It cannot be said to exist, which makes all things knowable although It is not known, and which makes all things beautiful although It transcends beautiful objects. "Then that which provides their truth to the things known, and gives the power of knowing to the knower, you must say is the idea or principle of the good, and you must conceive it as being the cause of understanding and of truth in so far as known; and thus while knowledge and truth as we know them are both beautiful, you will be right in thinking that it is something different, something still more beautiful than these." "The Good," continues Socrates, "is not a thing which actually exists. It is beyond existence. It transcends existence in rank and power." The Good is the source of all existing, but It does not exist; the Good is the source of all knowing, but It is not known nor knower; the Good is the source of all beauty and goodness, but It is not beautiful nor good. The Good is the inexpressible source of all reality, all truth, and all value. All things that exist, that are known, and that possess value originate from the Good. The Good as beyond being is the source of existing things, as beyond knowing is the source of knowledge, and as beyond value is the source of all values. It is the Cause—the *Kāraṇa* that is *Satchitānanda*.

In his Myth of the Cave Plato expanded on the doctrine of the Good. The life of man, he said, is a life in a cave, "the prisonhouse of sensation." Ontologically, this is the world of becoming rather than of being, of appearance rather than of reality; epistemologically, it is the world of opinion rather than knowledge. The cave is a dim reflection of Reality beyond the cave. Were someone to break his chains and experience the Reality transcending just, beautiful, and good things, he could return to the cave to explain to the prisoners that their "realities" are only shadows and echoes. Although Plato was not hopeful that the voice of the one who had seen the Good would be well received, his conviction was that evils among men will not cease until wisdom and power are united: "Until philosophers are kings, or the kings and princes of this world have the spirit and power of philosophy, and political greatness and wisdom meet in one, and those commoner natures who pursue either to the exclusion of the other are compelled to stand aside, cities will never have rest from their evils,—no, nor the human race, as I believe,—and then only will our State have a possibility of life and behold the light of day."[5] Perhaps we might add that one step in that desired direction is for philosophers East and West to study each other that our minds may yet be of one accord.

NOTES

1. I state this in the negative because I agree with Hajime Nakamura that Indians have a preference for the negative. See his *Ways of Thinking of Eastern Peoples: India-China-Tibet-Japan*. Honolulu: East-West Center Press, 1964, pp. 52-59.
2. Louis Renou, *Religions of Ancient India*. London: Athlone Press, 1953, p. 72.
3. Quoted by F. Th. Stcherbatsky, *Buddhist Logic*, Vol. I. New York: Dover Publications, 1962, p. 119.
4. *The Essentials of Buddhist Philosophy*. Honolulu: University of Hawaii Press, 1947, p. 33.
5. *The Republic* 473 E. Jowett translation.

—18—

*RADHAKRISHNAN AND TELEOLOGY**

Charles Hartshorne in his contribution to the Radhakrishnan volume in The Library of Living Philosophers reports that while he discovers Radhakrishnan rejects two types of idealism—which Hartshorne identifies as panpsychism and subjectivism—he is "not able to discern any third possibility for idealism."[1] Radhakrishnan in his reply to Hartshorne says, "I thought I had made my position clear," and he offers as a third possibility a statement from his book, *An Idealist View of Life*.[2] I agree with Radhakrishnan that he does present in this volume a third type of idealism, but I çannot agree that the presentation is clear. I wish to begin this essay on Radhakrishnan by attempting to restate the distinctions which he makes in *An Idealist View of Life* of three types of idealism.

According to Radhakrishnan the three types of idealism emerge from three approaches philosophers take toward their subject matter: the epistemological, the ontological, and the axiological. The idealism which grows out of the epistemological approach may be called subjective idealism, mentalism, or subjectivism. The idealism which grows out of the ontological approach may be called objective idealism or spiritualism; this type may appear either in pluralistic forms such as panpsychism or personalism, or in monistic or absolutistic forms. The idealism which grows out of the axiological approach is the type which may most appropriately be called ideal-ism; the other two should properly be called idea-isms. However, the broader use of the term has been fixed,

* Reprinted from *Dr. S. Radhakrishnan Souvenir Volume*. Edited by B. L. Atreya and J. P. Atreya. Moradabad, India: Darshana Printers, 1964, pp. 323-330.

so the three may be designated as three types of idealism: subjective, objective, and valuational.

Subjective idealism emphasizes the subjective aspect of the knowing relationship. "Whatever is real in the universe is such stuff as ideas are made of. . . . An 'idea' is taken as a particular mental image peculiar to each individual."[3] A thing is "a particular image." The danger peculiar to this type of idealism is solipsism, that is, the elimination of any sharable realities.

Objective idealism emphasizes the spiritual character of reality. In this form of idealism also, whatever is real in the universe is such stuff as ideas are made of, but here an idea is "a quality of the existent which is sharable by other existents and knowable by other minds." The world "extends beyond the given datum" which is presented to individual minds. "Mind is immanent in all cognitive experience as an active process which gives objective form to knowledge. It does not stand in a transcendent relation to an extraneous object which it passively contemplates." A thing is "a general relation." The danger peculiar to this type of idealism is illusionism, that is, the elimination of all material reality.

Valuational idealism emphasizes the worth of things rather than the knowability of things or the nature of things; indeed in this type of idealism a thing is a "meaning" or a "purpose." An idea in valuational idealism is an "operative creative force," "the principle involved" in a thing, and the "purpose" of the being of a thing. This metaphysical system is an idealism because it finds the world to be teleological: "The world is intelligible only as a system of ends." An idealist of this type is one who holds that the universe is purposive. The rejections of this idealism mark it off from the subjective and objective types: "Such a view has little to do with the problem whether a thing is only a particular image or a general relation. The question of the independence of the knower and the known is hardly relevant to it. Nor is it committed to the doctrine that the world is made of mind, an infinite mind or a society of minds. Idealism in the sense indicated concerns the ultimate nature of reality, whatever may be its relationship to the knowing mind. It is an answer to the problem of the idea, the meaning or the purpose of it all. It has nothing in common with the view that makes reality an irrational blind striving or an irremediably miserable blunder. It finds life significant and purposeful. It endows men with a destiny that is not limited to the sensible world." The danger peculiar to this type of idealism is utopianism, that is, the elimination of "an ultimate connection of value and reality."[4]

The reason for much of the confusion regarding Radhakrishnan's idealism is that whereas idealists—at least in the West—have generally regarded the core of idealism to be either the mind-dependent nature of reality or the internality of relations, Radhakrishnan holds that he who interprets ideas as ideals or values is an idealist.[5] An idealist in Radhakrishnan's understanding of the term asks, "What's the idea?" (i.e., what is the purpose of its being or its acting?) rather than "Is reality idea-like?" or "Does reality depend on minds?" Radhakrishnan reveals his own type of idealism—and confuses the Western philosopher—by including S. Alexander among the idealists[6] and by confessing that "in a sense . . . all philosophy is idealistic."[7]

Bernard Phillips in his study of Radhakrishnan's critique of naturalism accurately identifies both the core and the weakness of Radhakrishnan's metaphysical system in a single sentence: "The basic claim is merely that the universe is not a blind process, but a teleological one, and that the course of evolution is not accidental, but in some way the expression of purpose."[8] The core is the teleological character—the world is "a system of ends"—and the weakness is the difficulty in identifying and explaining the purposiveness of the world. Once one grasps the teleological character of Radhakrishnan's idealism, many of the problems of his metaphysical system vanish—but others take their places: (1) What is the relation between teleology and causation? (2) In what manner is the universe teleological? These two problems I now propose to examine.

Teleology is a topic upon which most twentieth-century philosophers prefer to remain silent. It is more often assumed than established by the theist. In the words of Radhakrishnan, "The case for theism from the moral side is questioned. If we argue from our moral aspirations to their ultimate fulfilment, we assume as a premise what requires to be proved, viz., that the world is reasonable, that it is teleologically ordered and that it is the very proposition we wish to prove."[9] The scientist usually gives teleology no more consideration than an observation that it is a primitive anthropomorphism. Some have ridiculed the conception, e.g., Francis Bacon compared final causes to vestal virgins—"dedicated to God, and . . . barren"—and Nicolai Hartmann regarded the greatest achievement of modern thought to be the deliverance from "the nightmare of teleology." Whitehead is one of the few philosophers who has had the wit to reply in kind to those who ridicule teleology: "Scientists animated by the purpose of proving that they are purposeless constitute an interesting subject for study."[10]

Radhakrishnan is not opposed to scientific methodology. He believes that scientific knowledge can be trusted within limits, but he believes that the limits are defined too loosely by most scientists. Such knowledge is "inadequate, partial, fragmentary, but not false. . . . It is, however, an essential stage in the evolution of human consciousness."[11] The trouble arises when scientists assume that the physical world is a closed system in which everything is determined. The physical world, according to Radhakrishnan, has two striking features: continuity and change. Events have references both to the past and the future, and the "prospective reference" or the "creative advance into the future" may be anticipated, but it cannot be predicted. "No event is complete. It seeks for its completion in an undetermined future. Throughout the process of nature we have creativity, or the coming into being of the new which is not reducible to or reducible from the old. We cannot forecast the future on the basis of our knowledge of the present."[12] According to Radhakrishnan the universe is open-ended. Something new is always happening, and each innovation is unpredictable. Events have causal and creative aspects. Determinism as a methodology is especially inadequate in the area of living organisms and conscious processes. Radhakrishnan ridicules those who regard man as an "assembled organic machine ready to run" and thought as "talking with concealed musculature."[13] In particular, causality is unsatisfactory when dealing with living organisms since it is incapable of dealing with the controlling aims which are the essential feature of organisms. "Life is a dynamic equilibrium which tends to maintain itself."[14] But an "atom can neither mend itself nor reproduce itself."[15] An amoeba advances to food and retreats from acid. It selects the response it makes to stimuli. Litmus paper does not *choose* to react to acid. If materialism is the answer to the question "What is the ultimate stuff?", and if mechanism is the answer to the question "What is the relationship of parts within bodies?", then living bodies are very odd mechanisms. They are the only mechanisms which avoid their own destruction. A dog that dodges the rock thrown at it is not acting like the runaway car which slips down the hill and over the embankment. The self-repair which takes place in a living body in the healing of a wound is a very different sort of mechanical action from the self-destruction of the combustion engine which has lost an important bolt. To call entities that engage in self-repair and self-preservation "mechanisms" and also to call entities that do not engage in self-repair and self-preservation "mechanisms" does not seem to give much meaning to the word "mechanism." To call the former teleological objects at least points out that they are bodies in which the end of survival is a determining factor in their activities.

Science, claims Radhakrishnan, is "a system of second causes which cannot describe the world adequately, much less account for it."[16] The naturalist, insofar as he bases his metaphysical system on scientific determinism, confuses "a descriptive method for the creative cause."[17] Radhakrishnan accuses scientists of concluding that the world is non-teleological because they have used non-teleological methods to study the world. But methodology must not determine metaphysics; rather methodology should be determined by both the nature of the subject matter and the nature of the results which the scientist wishes to secure. Since the scientist wishes to get knowledge which is inter-subjectively verifiable, quantitatively measurable, and linguistically expressible, he selects methods of knowing which will give him these results. But when he contends that reality is exactly as he grasps it through his methods, he forgets that his methods were determined by the subject matter as well as by the sort of knowledge he seeks. For example, if one were handed a sealed box and asked to determine its contents without using visual sensations, one's method could not establish whether the contents were colored. Only a simpleton would declare that the contents are not colored because he cannot discover whether or not the contents are colored by using the agreed-upon methodology. Yet does not the scientist reject teleology because he is not able to handle such a subject matter with his scientific methods?

Ends are items which scientific causality cannot handle. And the world is "a system of ends." However, I think we should add to Radhakrishnan's treatment of teleology the observation that causality is not contradictory to teleology. Indeed, teleology implies causality in the sense that teleology is dependent upon causality. Causality is an asymmetrical or one-way relationship between two events. If A is the cause of B, then B cannot be the cause of A. Teleology is a type of symmetrical relationship. At least there is a sense in which events related teleologically may be reversible. The teleological relationship is best described as a means-end relationship, rather than a cause-effect relationship, but if there were no cause-effect relationships there could be no means-end relationships. Let us consider an example. We are standing on the corner of Fifth Street and Main Street of a city. We are trying to locate an address marked "Sixth and Main." Our end, i.e., reaching Sixth and Main, causes us to walk one block up Main Street until we have accomplished our end. Thus the end determines the means, and the means determines the end. Or more precisely, the end-in-view (the finding of the address) causes the means (walking up Main Street), and walking up Main Street causes us to realize the end-accomplished. Teleology may be defined as any means-end situation in which the end partially determines the means.

Let us now turn to the second question, "In what manner is the universe teleological?" In spite of Radhakrishnan's confidence that the world is "a system of ends," I do not find him very explicit as to what sort of ends there are in the universe. That is, are these ends of the whole or of the part? Are they immanent or transcendent? Are they purposive or non-purposive? Statements like the following reveal the teleological nature of his world view, but they are tantalizingly frustrating as clues to the nature of his teleology: "The physical world is not a futile play of senseless atoms engaged in a deadly conflict. . . . The earth and its contents prepared for life. . . . In spite of the little ups and downs of change, there seems to be a compelling drift towards better things. . . . There is a universal tendency discernible in every state from its origin to its present condition."[18] No wonder Phillips concludes that according to Radhakrishnan "the course of evolution is . . . *in some way* the expression of purpose."[19] The problem of course is to identify in exactly what way the development of the world is the expression of purpose.

A teleologically motivated process may be either of the whole, e.g., the Psalmist's conception of the universe as the handwork of Yahweh, or of the parts. The latter type of teleology may be of the parts within the individual, e.g., the process by which parts of an organism fight an infection, or of the individual, e.g., the process by which the salmon deserts the salt water of the ocean and returns to its freshwater spawning grounds.

A distinction can also be made between immanent teleology and transcendent teleology. In the former the end is internal to the process. Aristotle's teleology is clearly immanent. For him the end of each individual within a species is to actualize fully the potentiality of the species. The end of an acorn is to become all that an acorn is supposed to become, viz., a good specimen of oak tree. Teleology is transcendent when the end is external to the process. For example, the Calvinist says that the end of man is to glorify God—not to actualize the fullness of the form of man. When considering transcendent teleology of the whole, we have to make a further distinction, i.e., between an external agent which uses the world as means for the realization of its own ends, e.g., St. Augustine said God created the world in order to repopulate heaven after the revolt of Lucifer, and the world process as striving to an end which transcends the process itself, e.g., Tennyson's "one far-off divine event to which the whole creation moves."

A third distinction is that between purposive and non-purposive teleology. Teleology is purposive when the end is consciously chosen by a mind. A man picks up a hammer because he intends to drive a nail; he reads a book in order to learn about a certain subject. There are some philosophers who claim that the notion of a teleology which is not the purpose of any mind is unsatisfactory, but others recognize the possibility of an end which is not consciously chosen by a mind. Aristotle's teleology was non-purposive.

According to Aristotle the acorn does not consciously purpose to become an oak tree, yet the form of the oak tree does act as an end in the process by which acorns become oak trees.

When these dichotomous divisions are put together we have eight theoretically possible types of teleology:

1. Whole, immanent, purposive.
2. Whole, immanent, non-purposive.
3. Whole, transcendent, purposive.
4. Whole, transcendent, non-purposive.
5. Parts, immanent, purposive.
6. Parts, immanent, non-purposive.
7. Parts, transcendent, purposive.
8. Parts, transcendent, non-purposive.[20]

Which type of teleology does Radhakrishnan offer in his idealism? In his Hibbert Lectures of 1929, Radhakrishnan stated his belief in cosmic teleology and denied that the end of the cosmic process could be life: "Life, which is such a merely local and superficial peculiarity, cannot be the end of the universe, as some are inclined to believe. There must be a relevant relation between purpose and output, end and means. The stars in their courses are plainly about some other business."[21] In the volume in The Library of Living Philosophers he writes in the autobiographical introduction that the meaning of cosmic history is "to make all men prophets, to establish a kingdom of free spirits."[22] Spiritual freedom is both the "highest product" and the "hidden principle."[23] Spirit works in complementary opposition to matter. Matter is a relative non-being which when guided by Spirit has the potentiality of becoming revelatory of being. The work of the Spirit is not a purposing. In another connection Radhakrishnan says that the living organisms engage in self-repair, nutrition, and reproduction without intelligence, i.e., they engage in actions which when engaged in by humans are described as due to foresight. Radhakrishnan will not accept a vital force in his system.[24] He does refer to teleology of the parts, but he constantly comes back to the Upaniṣadic view of Spirit which is at work at all levels of existence.[25] The "prospective adaptations" of individual organisms are in the final analysis manifestations of Spirit. So we may conclude that Radhakrishnan's teleology is of the whole, and that it is non-purposive. Is it immanent or transcendent? The answer seems to be that it is neither or both! In his open-ended view of cosmic history the emphasis is on specific forms not yet realized. Spirit is both the *terminus a quo* and the *terminus ad quem*: "Spirit is working in matter that matter may serve the Spirit."[26] Yet the Spirit is not a fixed telos. What is of the Spirit is always in evolution: "The process of the world is not a mere unfolding of what is contained in the beginning. It is not a question of mere preformation. The end of the world is not contained in the beginning, such that God might retire from the process altogether."[27] Herein is the joy, the *ānanda*, of Radhakrishnan's professional philosophy and personal faith: the Spirit is at work in the world for the richer manifestation of Itself. Self-realization of the Spirit is the end of the cosmic evolution—and That thou art.

NOTES

1. "Radhakrishnan on Mind, Matter, and God" in *The Philosophy of Sarvepalli Radhakrishnan*. Edited by Paul Arthur Schilpp. New York: Tudor Publishing Company, 1952, p. 316. This book will be hereafter designated as PSR.
2. PSR, p. 795.
3. Sarvepalli Radhakrishnan, *The Idealist View of Life*. London: George Allen and Unwin Ltd., 1932, pp. 14, 13. This book will be hereafter designated as IVL. Quotations in the next two paragraphs are taken from pp. 13-15 of IVL unless otherwise indicated.
4. IVL, p. 16.
5. IVL, p. 17.
6. IVL, p. 16.
7. IVL, p. 16.
8. PSR, p. 138.
9. IVL, p. 27.
10. A. N. Whitehead, *The Function of Reason*. Princeton: Princeton University Press, 1929, p. 12.
11. PSR, p. 792.
12. IVL, p. 240.
13. IVL, pp. 28, 29.
14. IVL, p. 249.
15. IVL, p. 250.
16. IVL, p. 316.
17. PSR, p. 32.
18. IVL, p. 313.
19. PSR, p. 138. Italics are mine.
20. It is outside the scope of this paper to present and defend examples of each of

the eight types of teleology, but I think it is possible to illustrate each type by reference to historical philosophers, e.g., (1) Hegel, (2) Aristotle, (3) Epictetus, (4) S. Alexander, (5) Rāmānuja, (6) Aquinas with respect to individuals, (7) even in a Watsonian behaviorist, and (8) Driesch with respect to embryos.

21. IVL, pp. 23-24.
22. PSR, p. 30.
23. PSR, p. 31.
24. PSR, p. 28.
25. PSR, p. 31.
26. PSR, p. 31.
27. IVL, p. 339.

—19—

*THREE INTO FOUR IN HINDUISM**

Ernest Wood in one of his many books on *yoga* explains that the yogic candidate must progress from the muscular flexion known as *mahābandha* to the more complex physical exercise known as *mahāvedha*, and finally to the recitation of the mantric syllable *OM*, "remembering that the world and life are full of threes—it is a fundamental classification in turn with the characters of the three great Agencies, Gods, or Angels."[1] Wood had in mind the classification of the Vedic divinities into the terrestrial, the atmospheric, and the celestial. But in affirming that "the world and life are full of threes" Wood ignored a tendency within Hinduism to move from three to four. In fact, this movement has generally been unnoticed by Indologists. C. G. Jung in his fascinating study, "A Psychological Approach to the Trinity,"[2] argues that the conception of the Trinity in Christianity is deficient since it leaves out matter and evil: "There is no getting around the fact that if you allow substantiality to good, you must also allow it to evil. If evil has no substance, good must remain shadowy, for there is no substantial opponent for it to defend itself against, but only a shadow, a mere privation of the good."[3] Jung speculates that the doctrine of the Assumption of Mary may pave the way for a Quaternity in which matter has full metaphysical status. A divine Quaternity, he thinks, would force Christian theology to make adjustments in line with the ancient

* This essay appears in the *Ohio Journal of Religious Studies*, Vol. I, No. 2 (July, 1973), pp. 7-13. Reprinted by kind permission of the editor.

Hebrew tradition which placed the Evil One among "the sons of God," with the tendency of ancient Greek philosophy to follow thinking of a quaternary type, e.g., the four "elements," earth, air, fire, and water, and with his own interpretation of human psychology. But Jung missed the opportunity to support his thesis that Christianity ought to move from Trinity to Quaternity by pointing out that Hinduism has in many instances already undergone such a movement. The object of this paper is to call attention to this lacuna in the studies of Hinduism, and to suggest a few possible theories to account for the shifting from three to four within Hinduism.

The Sanskrit word for four—*kṛta*—connotes wholeness. In the ancient Indian dice game the number four was the winning throw. The number one (*kali*) was the losing throw. The great cosmic cycles (*yugas*) are four in number, and the best is the *Kṛta Yuga*, which is so named because it is four times as long as the worst of the *yugas*, the *Kali Yuga*. One of the marks of excellence of the *Kṛta Yuga* is that in it the life span of men is four hundred years.

The earliest Vedic priests were of three kinds: the *hotṛ* who tended the fire, the *adhvaryu* who used the ritual instruments, and the *udgātri* who sang the chants. Later there was added a fourth, the *brahmin* who supervised the entire sacrifice in order that the power of the rite might be maintained and protected. The *brahmin* became far more important than the other three because it was he who insured that the ceremony would accomplish the pragmatic purposes for which the patron subsidized the entire operation.

The earliest collections of hymns and prayers were three, the collections of *hotṛs*, *adhvaryus*, and *udgātris*, i.e., the *Ṛg*, the *Sāma*, and the *Yajur*. The *Muṇḍaka Upaniṣad* refers to "the triad of the Vedas."[4] Manu the Lawgiver referred to them as the *Trayī* (The Triad) and also as the *Trayī Vidyā* (The Triple Knowledge). He says they had been milked from fire, air, and sun. Pāṇini, the greatest grammarian of India, described the *Vedas* as three. Jaimimi in his *Mīmāṁsā Sūtras* ignores the *Atharva*. However, sacrificial priests began to use *mantras* not found in the *Trayī Vidyā*, and eventually these were given Vedic standing. Thus there came into being a fourth *Veda*, the *Atharva*. The Puruṣa Hymn (*Ṛg Veda* 10. 90) mentions the Vedas as three with no reference to the *Atharva*, unless verse 9 with its words "spells and charms" can be so regarded. The *Brāhmaṇas* of the *Ṛg* do not mention the *Atharva*. The same is true for the *Kātyāyana Brāhmaṇa* of the *White Yajur* and the *Lātyāyana Brāhmaṇa* of the *Sāma*. Even the seventh-century Chārvāka work, the *Tattvapaplavasiṁha*, says the *Vedas* are three. On the other hand the *Mahābhārata* and the *Purāṇas*, which are of course several centuries later in composition, often mention the *Vedas* as four. In the *Viṣṇu Purāṇa* we find the first passage in which the *hotṛ* is associated with the *Ṛg*, the *udgātri* with the *Sāma*, the *adhvaryu* with *Yajur*, and the *brahmin* with the *Atharva*. This is probably an effort to establish symmetry. The question of three or four Vedas is still debated. The problem involves more than an argument among scholars. What is at stake is a fundamental difference in the interpretation of Hinduism. The issue is Tantrism. Is it indigenous in Hinduism? If so, then the *Atharva* has Vedic standing. If Tantrism is an appurtenance, then the *Atharva* ought not to be listed as a fourth *saṁhita*.

The oldest commentary on the *Vedas*, the *Nirukta* by Yāska (c. 500 B.C.), states that the *devas* (deities) are divided into three classes according to position of their influence in the cosmos—the earth, atmosphere, and sky—but to this threefold division, says Yāska, a "Fourth" was added. This is the Brahman which is not a *deva* and which has no spatial location in the cosmos. Brahman is the Reality manifested in the *devas*. Yet Brahman changes the three to four. On one of the seals from the Harappa culture is the image of a three-faced anthropomorphic being in a yogic posture surrounded by animals. He is often called "Lord of the Animals," and he is assumed to be a prototype of Śiva. In time the creator god, Brahmā, had four faces.

Another interesting movement from three to four is seen in the shortest and most sacred of all *mantras*, the syllable *OM*. *OM* was at first composed of three phonemes, A, U, and M. Later, according to Hindu tradition, a fourth was added: the sound which is not heard! In the *Māṇḍūkya Upaniṣad* the *mantra* is said to consist of the letter A, the letter U, the letter M, and "the fourth"—"The fourth is that which has no elements, which cannot be spoken of, into which the world is resolved, benign, non-dual."[5] The adding of a plus factor in the form of a non-sensed reality is quite common in Hinduism, e.g., at Allahabad there is the confluence of three rivers, the Ganges, the Jumna, and the Sarasvatī—only the Sarasvatī is unseen.

Attention should also be called to four aspects of the life of the Hindu in which an original three has been expanded to four. The *āśramas* or stages of life were originally *Brahmacarya* (studentship), *Gṛhastha* (householdership), and *Vānaprastha* (retirement), but to these was added the *Sannyāsa*, the stage of concentrated attention to the attainment of liberation. The three Vedic modes of experience were waking, dreaming, and deep sleeping, and to these came to be added the *turīya* state, the experiencing in which experiencer and experienced are inseparable. Again according to the earliest conception of the human life in Hinduism the goods or goals are three: *kāma* (pleasure), *artha* (possessions), and *dharma* (duties and responsibilities). These were known as the *trivarga* (the threefold class). But after the hedonic period of early Vedism there came into prominence a fourth goal which transformed and transcended the others. This is *mokṣa*, the liberation and release from the bonds of the other three goals. The goals of the full life (*puruṣārtha*) were then known as the *chaturvarga* (the fourfold class). Also the first class structure or *varṇa* of Hindu society was three-fold: the preservers of sacred lore (*Brahmins*), the rulers and defenders of the state (*Kṣatriyas*), and the traders and agriculturalists (*Vaiśyas*). The fourth *varṇa*, the servants (*Śūdras*) was added after the other *varṇas* had been well established. Three of the *mārgas* are clearly old and well defined: *jñāna*, *bhakti*, and *karma*; the fourth *mārga*—*yoga*—seems to be a later addition, and one which is open to a variety of interpretations and emphases. The famous *Puruṣasūkta* of the *Ṛg Veda* (10. 90) divides the cosmos into four quarters of which one quarter is earth and three quarters are heaven:

> All creatures are (but) one-fourth of him,
> three-fourths eternal life in heaven.
> With three-fourths Puruṣa went up: one-
> fourth of him again was here.

The *Atharva Veda* says, "Three quarters of it [the universe] are set down in secret."[6]

There are curious three and four situations described in Hindu literature which may have no significance, e.g., in the *Ayur Veda* one of the cures for jaundice involves the tying of three yellow birds to a four-legged bed. Others are rich in symbolism. For example, one of the legends of the Āḷvārs, the South Indian singers of the love of Viṣṇu, recounts that Poygai, Bhutattar, and Pey took refuge from a heavy shower by crowding into the tiny corridor of a house. As they stood pressed together in the dark corridor they were aware of the presence of a Fourth. According to the *bhakti* interpretation of the legend, one Āḷvār perceived the divine through works, one through knowledge, and one through love, but only when all three ways come together is the Divine present.

What explanations can be offered for these movements from three to four? Why is three held to be of less worth than four? What does four add that three does not possess? In keeping with the preference for four, I shall offer four hypotheses to account for the introduction of a fourth to an original three! They are *expansion*, *transcendence*, *integration*, and *polarization*.

The first theory for the introduction of a fourth to an original three is that in this manner the meaning of the three is expanded. In some cases the fourth serves as a fulfillment of the three. The *brahmin* insures that the activity of *hotṛ*, *adhvaryu*, and *udgātri* will be efficacious. The Hindu in the *Sannyāsa* stage of life may be regarded as at last accomplishing that for which the other *āśramas* were preparations.

A second theory can be constructed on the hypothesis that the fourth is not intended to enrich or fulfill but to repudiate or transcend the three. *Mokṣa*, for example, is a turning away from *kāma*, *artha*, and *dharma*. Zimmer seems to have had such a theory in mind when he referred to *kāma*, *artha*, and *dharma* as "The Philosophies of Time" and *mokṣa* as "The Philosophies of Eternity."[7] *Turīya* as a mode of experience may also be interpreted as a rejecting and transcending of the other modes of experience. The infinity of reality may be demonstrated by calling attention that reality is always one more than what was thought to be final.

A third way to account for the movement from three to four is based on the integrative aspect of Hinduism.[8] The monistic tendencies of Hinduism were clearly established in the Vedas.

Some of these are the following: the classifying of the gods into familial groups, e.g., Maruts, Rudras, Aśvins, Vasus, Viśvas, and Viśvedevas (all the gods); the selecting of one god as absorbing the properties of other gods, i.e., kathenotheism or henotheism; the naming of a creator god who antedates all the other gods, e.g., Viśvakarman, Hiraṇyagarbha, Brahmaṇaspati, Prajāpati, and Kā; the identifying of a mother of all the gods, a *Deva-matṛ*, e.g., Aditi; and the naming of an abstract cosmic principle transcending the gods, e.g., *Ṛta* (the order of things), *Tat* (That), *Tat Ekam* (That One), *Sat* (Being), and *Vāc* (Speech or Sound). One of the aspects of the philosophy of Aurobindo which has caused him to be suspect among Indian philosophers, particularly among Advaita Vedāntins, is his claim that both involution (movement from the one to the many) and evolution (movement from the many to the one) are parts of the cosmic game (*līlā*). Yet according to Aurobindo "the divine life" culminates in the one-ing into *Satchitānanda*. Oneness, not manyness, is the *summum bonum* in Hinduism. The clue to this theory is in the connotation of *kṛta* (four) as "whole." To move from three to four is not to move from many to more but from many to one. The logic for this remarkable statement is that four offers the possibility of dialectical polarization not possible in three. The dimensions of this polarization in the examples cited above are yet to be worked out, but a case study can be developed from Aristotle and his predecessors.

Hellenic speculation long before the appearance of the first Milesian philosophers had arrived at the notion of the four "stuffs" of which reality is formed. Thales, Anaximander, Anaximenes, Heraclitus, and others, desiring to push this unsatisfactory theory of the four "stuffs" into a "unified field theory," speculated that the one from which all came into being had to be either one of the four "stuffs" or something else. But Aristotle argued that the solution to their problem, i.e., the problem of how to get unity out of plurality, had been tumbling at their feet and they had not discovered it. The elements they were seeking, he said, were not earth, air, fire, and water, but the opposites (*atikeimena*), i.e., hot-cold and wet-dry. Earth, air, fire, and water are the products of diametrical polarizations of the opposites, i.e., earth is dry-cold, air is wet-hot, water is wet-cold, and fire is dry-hot. Earth, air, fire, and water constitute the totality of our phenomenal world, and they are the result of the shifting along the polar axes of hot-cold and wet-dry. Everything that is is located on these dual necessary opposites. Nothing can be that is not of the dimensions of hot-cold and wet-dry. To state this in a slightly different way: a hot thing must be also a wet or a dry thing, a wet thing must also be a cold or a hot thing, a dry thing must also be a hot or a cold thing, and a cold thing must also be a wet or a dry thing. Hence, the unity which the pre-Socratics sought in earth, or air, or fire, or water, or something else, said Aristotle, is to be found in the four polarities of the two pairs of opposites. That unity is hot-cold-wet-dry.

The fourth theory I am offering—polarization—may be regarded as a form of integration, but it has such an important role in Indian thought that it should be treated as a separate theory. The polarities of Hinduism have not yet been sufficiently examined. Richard Lannoy in an interesting new study entitled *The Speaking Tree* writes, "One of the most pervasive Indian views is that the entire phenomenal world is a balance of opposing forces (binal opposition). This dual organization is as fundamental to the Indian outlook as cell and sex divisions are fundamental processes to the biologist. . . . in the daily life of caste society the commonest manifestation of opposition is that of purity and impurity. In traditional Indian thought the basic complementaries are form and flux, or order and disorder. In social institutions we have already encountered the disjunction of power and status, ascribed to king and priest respectively; the disjunction of pure Brahman and Untouchable menial; and finally, the unequal relation between one caste and another, in superiority and inferiority. Everything in the complex social structure of India reflects this dual organization."[9] Support for this theory can be made by appeal to Holi, the most ancient of all Hindu festivals. This is the season of the year in which the "twice-born" act like the "once-born." At Holi time regenerative flux and overt transgression, even orgiastic license, displaces ritualized order and pattern. Polarity is noted also in the Vedic cosmology of a world of *Sat* inhabited by the gods (*devas*) and a world of *Asat* inhabited by the anti-gods (*asuras*). There are also the polarities of *Ṛta* and *Anṛta* (order and chaos) and *sṛṣṭi* and *parlaya* (creation and dissolution Śaktis and Tantrics stress the polarity of male and female. The male-female polarity is striking illustrated in the *ardhanārīśvara* statues of Śiva-Pārvatī with the right side of the body male, the left side female. B. G. Gokhale in *Indian Thought Through the Ages: A Study of Dominant Concepts* says " . . . in the history of Indian thought there is always an interplay of two opposite trends running parallel to each other throughout the ages."[10] His examples are *dharma* and *artha*, *kāma* and *sannyāsa*, and war and non-violence. Frithjof Schuon contends that polar opposition is an ontological necessity in Vedānta: "The All-Possibility must by definition and on pain of contradiction include its own impossibility. It is in order not to be, that Being incarnates in the multitude of souls; it is in order not to be, that the ocean squanders itself in myriads of flecks of foam. . . . Nothing is external to absolute Reality; the world is therefore a kind of internal dimension of Brahman. But Brahman is without relativity; thus the world is a necessary aspect of the absolute necessity of Brahman. Put in another way, relativity is an aspect of the Absolute."[11]

The concept of dialectical polarity inherent in the fours of Hinduism may be a means for understanding and justifying the speculations of Aurobindo. When Aurobindo says "the evolution is still half-way on its journey,"[12] he means that man is only half-way on the evolutionary return to *Satchitānanda*, but the interpretation of Hinduism adumbrated in this paper is that evolution itself is only half of the journey of Brahman. Brahman both involutes (pluralizes) and evolutes (unifies) because each is meaningless without the other, or in Aurobindo's words, since "only what is involved can evolve," there must be "a descent from above, an ascent from below, a self-revelation of the Spirit, an evolution in Nature."[13] Spirit, though one, necessarily pluralizes; Matter, though many, necessarily integrates. The divine life is the harmonious opposition of the involution-evolution process. *Māyā* is not the activity of hiding, but the activity of revealing the implications inherent in Totality. This interpretation of Hinduism requires a fresh review of the Sāṁkhya philosophy, the philosophy which first called attention to the dualistic passages in the *Upaniṣads*. Probably philosophers have erred in regarding *Puruṣa* as spirit and *Prakṛti* as matter. *Puruṣa* denotes the integrative processes of the universe, and *Prakṛti* the pluralistic. *Sāṁkhya Kārikā* LIX, "As a dancer desists from dancing, having exhibited herself to the audience, so does *Prakṛti* desist, having exhibited herself to *Puruṣa*," seems to present a problem, the same sort of problem Aurobindo creates in passages which imply that the divine life is an escape in solitude to the Solitary. But "desist" here may not mean to vanish ontologically; it may mean to terminate a mode of operation. *Prakṛti's* cessation may be interpreted as a *parlaya*, a period of cosmic rest, a state of non-being alternating with a state of being.

These four theories to account for the movement from three into four in Hinduism—expanding, transcending, integrating, and polarizing—are related to each other in that strangely amorphous Hindu relationship which is often called "tolerance" but which deserves a more descriptive label—perhaps "harmonious opposition." Here, as so often happens in Hindu thought, we should reject the principle of this-rather-than-that in favor of the principle of this-as-well-as-that. Hence, each theory calls attention to part of the reason for the movement from three into four, and all four theories do not exhaust the possible explanations.

NOTES

1. Ernest Wood, *Yoga*. Baltimore: Penguin Books, 1959, p. 158.
2. *The Complete Works of C. G. Jung*, Vol. II. London: Routledge and Kegan Paul, 1958, pp. 102-200.
3. *Ibid.*, p. 168.
4. *Muṇḍaka Upaniṣad* 1. 2. 1. Robert Ernest Hume translation.
5. *Māṇḍūkya Upaniṣad* 12. Sarvepalli Radhakrishnan translation.
6. *Atharva Veda* 2. 1. 2. Franklin Edgerton translation.
7. Heinrich Zimmer, *Philosophies of India*. Cleveland and New York: World Publishing Co., 1956, Parts II and III.
8. See Troy Organ, *The Hindu Quest for the Perfection of Man*. Ch. IV "The Quest for Integration." Athens, Ohio: Ohio University Press, 1970.
9. Richard Lannoy, *The Speaking Tree*. London: Oxford University Press, 1971, pp. 173-174.
10. B.G. Gokhale, *Indian Thought Through the Ages*. Bombay: Asia Publishing House, 1961,p. 174.
11. Frithjof Schuon, *Language of the Self*. Translated by Marco Pallis and Macleod Matheson. Madras: Ganesh and Co., 1959, pp. 22-23.
12. Aurobindo, *The Life Divine*. New York: The Greystone Press, 1949, p. 736.
13. Aurobindo, *The Mind of Light*. New York: E. P. Dutton and Co., 1971, p. 81.

—20—

AŚOKA

The rock inscriptions of a third-century B.C. king of India reveal the mind and heart of one of ancient India's most interesting human beings. These inscriptions are not royal self-praise commemorating the acts of the king but "sermons in stone" intended as moral guidance for present and future generations of rulers and subjects. Many of the inscriptions were to be read aloud on festival days to remind citizens of their rights and duties. As working political instruments they were written in the common language of the people, i.e., in the Brahmi forms of the Prakrits, rather than in the Sanskrit of courts and scholars.

The first Westerner to identify one of the inscriptions was a Roman Catholic priest named Tieffenthaller. The date was 1756. The first deciphering was done by a scholar named Prinsep in 1837. The last inscription to be identified was in southern Afghanistan in 1958. This one is remarkable for another reason: it is in bilingual Greek-Aramaic. We do not know how many of these rock inscriptions there were originally, but forty-eight have been identified. These include ten standing pillars, the fragments of twenty other pillars, and eighteen rock walls. The total number of words is about five thousand.

Some historians have argued that this ancient king must have copied or adapted his pillars from Persian or Greek models, and a few have suggested he imported Persian workmen to erect the pillars. But Vedic Indians for generations had followed the custom of erecting tall poles with a fluttering pennant at the top to mark the site of a sacrificial altar. The king had them made of fine-grained sandstone. The stone comes from quarries not far from Banaras. The pillars vary from forty to fifty feet high, and each weighs about fifty tons. They rise abruptly from the ground without any pedestal. The shafts are perfectly plain and highly polished. Each pillar is a single piece of stone crowned by a lotus-petaled capital and a round slab which usually supports a carved animal—an elephant, horse, bull, or lion. The best known is the Lion Pillar at Sarnath with a capital composed of the forefronts of four lions, each lion facing a cardinal direction. This capital is about seven feet high. It is the official emblem of the modern nation of India.

Many of the pillars have in the centuries since their original erection been desecrated and ruined. For example, in Allahabad there is one which was dragged forty miles on Akbar's orders in the sixteenth century, and on this one the original inscription "The chiefest conquest is the law of piety" was half-obliterated by Samudra Gupta in the fourth century A.D. so he could inscribe a boast of his military conquests.

Perhaps the most remarkable fact about these rock inscriptions is that they are found in India, a land where historical records were usually not kept. René Grousset has described India as a "land without memory where men scorned temporal things and remembered only visions of eternity."[1] Aśoka Maurya, the king who left these inscriptions, has been praised as India's greatest ruler. B. G. Gokhale writes, "Ashoka stands towering far above the crowd of kings and princelings whose names and memories fill the Indian historical landscape."[2] A. L. Basham describes Aśoka as "the greatest and noblest ruler India has known, and indeed one of the great kings of the world."[3] Jerrold Schecter has recently given a different description of this Indian monarch: "Ashoka, like many present-day Buddhist political leaders, was an enigma. He was an ambivalent mixture of piety and cruelty; despite its Buddhist essentials, his style of rule also retained traditional forceful methods for retaining power. Despite the Buddhist reverence for all sentient beings, men were executed or cruelly tortured if they violated the law of the land; as a Buddhist, Ashoka gave them time to meditate on their ill deeds before the sentence was carried out. Some scholars have suggested that Ashoka was half monster and half idiot."[4] I wish Schecter had identified the scholars who say Aśoka was "half monster and half idiot." The rock inscriptions reveal the personality of Aśoka as one who had to make judicious compromises between ideals and realities and as one whose overriding concerns were the well-being and happiness of his subjects rather than personal gain or political power. Aśoka does not fit the Western image of the Buddhist as a passive, docile person who is quietly seeking *nirvāṇa*. Aśoka the activist helps us understand the Vietnamese monks who drenched their clothes with gasoline and burned themselves in the streets of Saigon as a form of political protest, the Vietnamese Buddhist youths who tossed tear-gas canisters back at government troups, and the aggressive political Buddhist sect in Japan known as Soka Gakkai. Today criticism of government leaders in Cambodia, Thailand, Burma, and Vietnam is most effective when it charges the leaders with being un-Buddhistic.

Aśoka came to his throne c. 274 B.C. and he died c. 233 B.C. To place him in proper perspective we must begin with the eastern expeditions of Alexander the Great. In 330 B.C. Alexander defeated Darius III, occupied the capital city of Persepolis, and set out to subjugate the eastern provinces of the Persian empire. The years 327-324 were spent in conquering northwest India, and thereby demonstrating the superiority of small well-trained armies over huge unwieldly armies. According to Greek sources a young Indian whom the Greeks called Sandrocottus advised Alexander to move down the Ganges River to attack Mahapadma Nanda, the king of the Magadha empire. Sandrocottus assured Alexander that the emperor was so unpopular that the people would rise in support of the invaders. Alexander was convinced and was ready to start down the Ganges, but his generals refused to go farther, and the Greek invasion of India came to an end.

This young man whom the Greeks called Sandrocottus was known by the Indians as Chandragupta Maurya. He became in time the founder of the Maurya empire and the grandfather of Aśoka. His beginnings were not promising. His father, a small chieftain connected in some manner with the royal house of Magadha, died before his birth. His mother appears to have been of the servant class. Shortly after his birth his mother gave him to a forest tribe. This would seem to indicate that the child was born out of wedlock. A few years after his birth scholars were invited to come from the entire empire to a conference at Pataliputra, the capital city. One of those who came was Kautalya, a pundit from Taxila in northwest India. Kautalya is believed to be the author of the *Arthaśāstra*, a guidebook for kings which is often compared with Machiavelli's *The Prince*. At the conference Kautalya was ridiculed, and he finally left Pataliputra in disgust. He went into nearby forests to think about what had happened to him. One day he came across a little boy in a clearing in the forest. He asked the boy what he was playing, and the boy answered, "Kings and courts." That boy was Chandragupta. Kautalya was so fascinated with the child that he bought him from the tribe, took him back to Taxila, and reared him as the instrument for avenging himself against the supporters of the Magadha emperor. Chandragupta's suggestion to Alexander, according to this legend, was part of Kautalya's plot of vengeance. When this plot was frustrated because of the revolt of Alexander's generals, Chandragupta began a people's rebellion against the Nanda line of emperors. The rebellion culminated with the storming of the capital at Pataliputra and the assassination of the last of the Nanda emperors. Thus Chandragupta Maurya rose from abandoned child to emperor. By 304 he had driven the Greeks out of India and had extended the empire from Bengal on the east to Kabul on the west, and from the Himalayas on the north to Mysore on the south. Pataliputra was rebuilt on magnificent lines as a city nine and one-half miles long and one and one-half miles wide. It was a walled city with sixty-four gates and five hundred and seventy towers from which it could be defended. The moat around the city was six hundred feet wide and sixty feet deep.

Chandragupta's life was in constant danger. He is said to have slept in a different room each night because of his fear of assassination. There is evidence that he become a Jain in his old age and finally fasted to death in accord with Jain custom.

He was succeeded by his son Bindusāra, a person about whom we know very little. The empire was expanded still more during his reign. Bindusāra maintained a regular correspondence with the

Seleucid kings of Syria, and in one letter he requested that Antiochus I send him "figs, wine, and a Sophist." To this Antiochus replied that the figs and wine were forthcoming, but that Greek philosophers were not for export. (Bindusāra may have remembered the Greek philosopher Megasthenes who had lived at his father's court.) Although Greek philosophers were not for export, Greek women were! There is a possibility that Aśoka's mother was one of the Greek women in the court of Bindusāra. This, if true, would mean that Alexander's dream of the mixing of Greeks and barbarians was realized in the person of Aśoka.

Upon the death of Bindusāra there may have been a power struggle among his sons. Aśoka was not the eldest of the sons. Singhalese records report that Aśoka put to death ninety-nine of his brothers. The fact that there was a delay of four years between the death of Bindusāra and the coronation of Aśoka may indicate a period of struggle among the claimants to the throne, but a more probable explanation is that inasmuch as Aśoka had ascended the throne at age twenty-one, he had to wait four years for the coronation since at that time no coronation was allowed until the prospective king was twenty-five years old. The ridiculous Buddhist chronicles of Ceylon portray young Aśoka as an extremely evil person in order to contrast his life before and after becoming a Buddhist. They refer to the pre-Buddhist Aśoka as "The Wicked One" and to the Buddhist Aśoka as "The Pious One."

The empire which Aśoka inherited had been organized and pacified for fifty years by his father and grandfather. It included most of modern Afghanistan, Pakistan, and India. The parts of India not included in the empire at the time of his coronation were the southern tip of India which was in the hands of the Cholas and the Pandyas, and the Kalinga country which corresponded roughly to the modern state of Orissa. The first eight years after his coronation were peaceful, but in the ninth year so much trouble had arisen on the border between his kingdom and the kingdom of Kalinga that he was forced to declare war. The result was a blood bath. Rock Edict XIII states, "The Kalinga country was conquered by King Priyadarśin, when he had been consecrated eight years. One hundred and fifty thousand persons were carried away as captives and one hundred thousand slain and many times that number died." "Priyadarśin" means Beloved of the Gods, but it is only a title like His Majesty, and I shall so translate it. Only once in the inscriptions does Aśoka refer to himself by name. Elsewhere it is always "His Majesty."

Not long after the Kalinga conquest Aśoka became a Buddhist. The Maurya family were a family of religious experimenters. Chandragupta became a Jain in his old age; Aśoka's mother was of the Ajivika sect; and his first wife (Devi) was a Buddhist. According to Buddhist accounts Aśoka had for three years previous to his conversion invited adherents of many sects to the court to expound their diverse doctrines. It may have been the contrast between the slaughter at Kalinga and the *ahiṁsā* (non-violence) principle of Buddhism which effected the change in Aśoka from some form of sacrificial Hinduism—probably a form of Śiva worship—to Buddhism. One legend is that a nephew converted him by reading to him from the *Dhammapada*; another is that a monk named Upagupta was responsible. The conversion was a moral conversion. Other portions of Rock Edict XIII record: "After that, the Kalingas being now secure, His Majesty is intensely devoted to the protection of righteousness, to action according to righteousness, and to offering instruction in righteousness. His Majesty, the conquerer of Kalinga, has remorse now, because of the thought that the conquest is no conquest, for there was killing, death or banishment of the people. This is keenly felt with profound sorrow and regret by His Majesty. . . . Now even the loss of a hundredth or even a thousandth part of all the lives that were killed or died or were carried away captive at the time when the Kalingas were conquered is considered deplorable by His Majesty. His Majesty considers that even he who wrongs him, is fit to be forgiven of wrongs that can be forgiven. . . . His Majesty desires that all beings should be left unhurt, should have self-determination, have impartial treatment and should lead happy lives." We must note that Aśoka gave up warfare as an imperial policy only after he became undisputed master of South Asia.

For some reason Aśoka decided after his conversion to Buddhism to record his conversion and his new patterns of living and ruling on rock surfaces throughout his kingdom. Most of what we know of him comes from these rock inscriptions. But the autobiographical passages are secondary to the stress on *dharma*. *Dharma* is the whole duty of man. *Dharma* denotes the social, moral, and religious obligations determined by one's position in society. The chief duties stressed in the inscriptions are respect for the sanctity of animal life and reverence to parents, superiors, and elders. A person's *dharma* is given no theological or metaphysical foundation in the inscriptions. *Dharma* is set forth as rules required for practical guidance for social living. These rules are propounded as self-evidently true and valuable. Aśoka's statements recorded in many of the inscriptions carry a simple sanction which belies the profundity of Buddhism: Do good so you will be rewarded here and hereafter. Aśoka of the edicts was primarily a man of action. He says in one of the edicts, "Whenever I see anything significant, I desire to translate it into action, and I begin it by proper means."[5] Aśoka the Buddhist was still Aśoka the King. Even in the edict repenting of his war in Kalinga he reminded the people that while he repented of having declared war on them, he had absolute power, and in spite of his compassion as a Buddhist he could turn on them again.

Yet the tone of the edicts is different. He has given up *daṇḍa* (royal authority based on force), and he has replaced it with *dharma* (dedication to righteous behavior). There will be no more appeal to force: "But now, on account of the practice of *dharma* by His Majesty, there is heard in place of the sound of war drums, the sound of proclamations of *dharma*."[6] He sees himself in a new role. No longer is he the potentate demanding the submission of his subjects; now he is father and benefactor to the people. Aśoka says in three places in his rock edicts, "All people are my children."[7] Scholars have interpreted this as a universalism, i.e., that he saw himself as teacher and promoter of righteousness to all people of all nations, races, and times. But I think this is much too sweeping an interpretation. It is sufficiently remarkable to find an oriental monarch who felt the obligation to be benevolent toward all the people of his empire: "All people are my children. Just as I desire on behalf of my own children that they should be fully provided with all kinds of comfort and enjoyment in this as well as in the other world, similarly, I desire the same happiness and enjoyment in this world and in the next on behalf of all people."[8] I cannot accept the *dharma* of the edicts as universalistic because of the limited understanding of Buddhism which Aśoka possessed. If Aśoka revealed a fuller understanding of Buddhism, this could be a possible interpretation. Siddhartha Gautama the Buddha presented a teaching for mankind, not a dogma for a sect. He was known as the *Sammā-saṁbuddha* (Universal Teacher).

Aśoka instructed his governors how to instruct the people: "Let them not be afraid of me. Let them be made to feel confident that they need expect only happiness from me and not misery."[9] Tell them, he says, "The King is like our father. He cares for our welfare, as much as he cares for himself. We are, to him, like his own children."[10] These were not merely high-sounding words and promises, for as he states in Rock Edict VI. 2, the King was on call at all times: "For a long time past, transactions of state were not attended to or reports received at all hours. Now this arrangement has been made by me that during all hours and in all places, whether I am dining or in the Lady's apartments, or in the inner apartments, or in the lavatory, or when riding, or in the garden, everywhere, the reporters should report to me the business of the people. I shall attend to it everywhere." Aśoka had no personal secretary to keep citizens away from his *sanctum sanctorum*. He gives up his hunting trips, and instead he now makes *Dharmayātras* (Tours of Piety) in which he visits ascetics and priests, calls on the elderly, distributes alms to the needy, visits the people in the rural sections, and discusses moral matters with commoners.[11] And yet he never feels that he has done all he should: "I am never completely satisfied with my work of wakefulness or dispatch of business. I consider that I must work for the welfare of all people; and the attainment of this is rooted in wakefulness and due dispatch of business. There is no other work for me more important than doing what is good for the well-being of all people."[12] But alas, good is so difficult and evil so easy: "It is very difficult to do a goodly act. He who does it, accomplishes a very difficult task. . . . it is easy to spread sin."[13]

Aśoka did not regard himself as a messiah who was going to redeem mankind single-handedly. He held no first mortgage on *dharma*. All people should unite to promote righteousness: "Let people unitedly devote themselves for the increase of *dharma* and not permit its decrease."[14] In the thirteenth year of his reign he established officials whom he called *Dharmamāhamātras* (Enforcers of *Dharma*). They were commissioned to move constantly among the people. Their duties according to Rock Edict V were:

1. To promote the welfare and *dharma* among followers of all religions.
2. To promote the welfare and happiness of the people on the borders.
3. To promote welfare and happiness among servants and masters, the protectorless and the aged.
4. To prevent unjust imprisonment and loss of life.
5. To give due consideration to persons with large families.

All officers, be they imperial or provincial or local, were required to visit every section of their districts once every five years. Aśoka seems to have been an ideal administrator in that he delegated authority: "My representatives . . . are commissioned by me to rule over several hundreds of thousands of people. The rewards or punishments meted out by them are left to their descretion. Why? In order that . . . [they] may confidently perform their duties unselfishly and fearlessly, bestow welfare and happiness on the people and the country, and act kindly towards them."[15]

His benevolence was made concrete in his ordering that wells be dug and trees be planted at convenient intervals along the highways. Hostels and rest houses were to be built for the convenience of travelers. He even established a form of public health care: "Two kinds of medical treatment were established by His Majesty, *viz.*, medical treatment for human beings and medical treatment for cattle. Medicinal herbs useful for human beings and cattle have been imported and grown, wherever they were not available. Similarly, roots and fruits have also been imported and caused to be grown, wherever they were not available hitherto."[16] Aśoka built hospitals for both human beings and animals. He has been credited with having started the profession of veterinary surgery. He urged the monks to raise the level of instruction in their schools, and he asked them to submit the Buddhist scriptures to what we today would call higher criticism. He championed education for women and provided funds for schools for girls.

One of the great changes in the life of Aśoka when he became a Buddhist was his adoption of vegetarianism: "formerly, several thousands of animals were slaughtered for the soups in the kitchen of His Majesty. But now, when this instruction on *dharma* is being inscribed, only three lives are being killed, i.e., two peacocks and one deer; even deer is not slaughtered regularly. In the future, even these three lives shall not be slaughtered."[17] All forms of cruelty to animals must be stopped.[18] He says he sees much evil in the sacrifices which accompanied religions. Aśoka was caught in his edicts on religious ceremonies between his desire to avoid killing of the sacrificial animals and his desire to be tolerant in religious matters. In Rock Edict IX he discusses the delicate matter of the Hindu ceremonies dealing with sickness, marriage, birth, and death, and, after saying that these ceremonies are "petty and meaningless," he adds, "Such auspicious rites have certainly to be performed. But they bear small fruit. The ceremonial of righteousness bears, however, great fruit."[19]

Rock Edict XII on tolerance in religion is perhaps the most arresting of all the edicts. It merits an extensive quoting: "His Majesty reverences persons of all religions, ascetics and householders, by gifts with various forms of reverence. But [he] does not value gifts or reverential offerings so much as that of an increase of the spiritual strength of the followers of all religions. This increase of spiritual strength is of many forms. But the one root is the guarding of one's speech so as to avoid the extolling of one's own religion to the decrying of the religion of another, or speaking lightly of it without occasion or relevance. As proper occasions arise, persons of other religions should also be honoured suitably. Acting in this manner, one certainly exalts one's own religion and also helps persons of other religions. Acting in a contrary manner, one injures one's own religion and does disservice to the religions of others. One who reverences one's own religion and disparages that of another from devotion to one's own religion and seeks to glorify it over all other religions does injure one's own religion more certainly."[20]

Aśoka was a monk for two years of his life. In the twentieth year of his reign he made the long and difficult pilgrimage to Lumbini, the birthplace of the Buddha nestled in the Himalayan foothills. He built many stupas and monasteries. His support of Buddhism has been compared to Constantine's support of Christianity. Two parallels are striking: (1) both called a conference of religious leaders in order to heal divisions which had appeared; (2) both had only superficial understanding of the religion they sponsored. Constantine called the Council of Nicaea; Aśoka called the Third Council of Buddhism. This Buddhist Council was important in that from it stemmed the final break between Theravāda and Mahāyāna. Aśoka is also the one responsible for turning Buddhism into a worldwide missionary religion. Vincent Smith in *Asoka, Buddhist Emperor of India*, calls him the St. Paul of Buddhism. Aśoka commissioned his friend, Moggaliputta Tissa, to carry the "Holy Flame" of Buddhism throughout the empire. His son, Mahinda, and his daughter, Saṅghamitra, are believed to be the first Buddhist missionaries to have been sent from India. They were sent to Ceylon. According to tradition the Bodhi-tree in the ancient capital of Anuradhapura grew from a branch brought from the original enlightenment tree by Saṅghamitra. Two monks named Sena and Uttara went to Burma to spread Buddhism to that country. These missionary efforts proved to be most fortunate, since when Buddhism ceased to be viable in India about A.D. 1200 it had already been well established outside India.

As for the understanding of the two religions—no one has ever claimed that Constantine had a profound grasp of Christianity; indeed, some historians argue that the Church began to fall from its pristine purity when it became affiliated with the Roman emperor. The pillar edits of Aśoka do not reveal a full understanding of Buddhism. One might even argue that Aśoka did not have an adequate understanding of Buddhism since no mention is made in his edicts of such fundamentals as the Four Noble Truths, the Eight-fold Way, dependent origination, and *nirvaṇa*. Much of what he called Buddhist *dharma* was the public morality which any emperor would encourage to preserve the stability of his kingdom. At one point Constantine and Aśoka were vastly different: Constantine started Rome in the direction of making Christianity the state religion, and Christianity entered that horrible period in its history when Christians tried their hands at persecution; but Aśoka did not make Buddhism a state religion. Despite his own devotion to Buddhism he did not insist that it be the official religion of the empire.

An important aspect of Aśoka's impact on Buddhism was his stress on the lay dimension. Buddhism, partly because of his efforts, became less a monkish retreat from life and more a set of practical moral rules for citizens. Aśoka may be credited with starting the tendency which resulted in Mahāyāna Buddhism in the displacement of the *arahat* (retiring monk) by the *bodhisattva* (outgoing savior). I should add that it is from the pillar edicts we note the stress on the laity; the legends of Ceylon insist that Aśoka's emphasis was on the order of monks.

Aśoka was an unusual emperor in that he was more interested in preserving righteousness than in preserving his kingdom. He says in one of the pillar edicts, "This rescript on *dharma* has been promulgated . . . that it [*dharma*] may endure as long as my sons and great-grandsons shall reign, as long as the sun and the moon endure."[21] But the Maurya empire collapsed a few generations after Aśoka. He was the last great ruler of the dynasty. We know very little about his successors. Some historians claim that Aśoka's pacificism was a factor which brought about the end of the empire. However, *dharma* remains a fundamental and all-embracing virtue in both Hindu and Buddhist cultures. I think Aśoka would be pleased. After all, it was *dharma*, not the Maurya empire, which he wanted to last "as long as the sun and the moon endure." In one edict he attempted to delineate the nature of *dharma*: "The father and mother must be served; so also the supreme value and sacredness of life should be firmly strengthened. Truth should be spoken. These virtuous qualities should be practised and spread. Similarly, the teacher must be reverenced by the pupil; and in families, fitting courtesy should be shown to relations. This is the nature of the ancient *dharma*."[22] In Judaism and Christianity the great prophets of righteousness are honored. But they were men out of power. Aśoka was a prophet of righteousness, and he was a man in a position of power. He demonstrated that power need not corrupt.

In ancient India there were three conceptions of the king. Two of these are presented in the *Mahābhārata*; the third is found in Buddhist literature. According to one theory the king is a divinely appointed ruler, appointed by Brahmā at the request of mankind. Manu, the first king, attained sovereignty through both human persuasion and divine appointment. According to the second theory the first king was Pṛthu, the son of Viṣṇu, and he was appointed because the gods requested that something be done to halt the decline in the world of men. But according to the third theory, the king is not in any way divine. He is selected by human beings to maintain moral law and social order, and he remains in office as long as he is the servant of the people. Aśoka vacillated in his thinking between the first and the third theory; that is, he regarded himself both as the Beloved of the Gods and as one whose responsibility was the promotion of the welfare of the people. If we look at Aśoka from the view of the West rather than from Indian conceptions perhaps we can say that he approximated the Platonic ideal of the union of wisdom and power: "Unless lovers of wisdom become kings in their countries or those who are now kings and rulers come to be sufficiently inspired with a genuine desire for wisdom; unless, that is to say, political power and the love of wisdom meet together . . . there can be no rest from troubles for states, nor for all mankind."[23] However Aśoka is evaluated, surely all will agree that he possessed some of the characteristics we need in our political leaders. Mankind always needs leaders who are concerned for the well-being of all people and who have the wisdom and ability to translate that concern into meaningful action.

NOTES

1. René Grousset, *In the Footsteps of the Buddha.* London: G. Routledge and Sons, 1973, p. 111.
2. B. G. Gokhale, *Ashoka Maurya.* New York: Twayne Publishers, 1966, p. 150.
3. A. L. Basham, *The Wonder That was India.* Bombay: Orient Longmans Ltd., 1963, p. 53.
4. Jerrold Schecter, *The New Face of the Buddha. Buddhism and Political Power in Southeast Asia.* New York: Coward McCann, 1967, pp. 29-30.
5. Kalinga Edict I. 2. EA, p. 53. All translations of the edicts are taken from G. Srinivasa Murti and A. N. Krishna Aiyangar, *Edicts of Aśoka.* Second Edition. Adyar, Madras: The Adyar Library, 1951. This volume is designated by EA.

6. Rock Edict IV. 2. EA, p. 9.
7. Kalinga Edict I. 2. EA, p. 53; Kalinga Edict II. 2. EA, p. 61.
8. Kalinga Edict I. 2. EA, pp. 53-54.
9. Kalinga Edict II. 3. EA, p. 63.
10. Kalinga Edict II. 4. EA, p. 65.
11. Rock Edict IX. 3-4. EA, p. 25.
12. Rock Edict VI. 4. EA, p. 19.
13. Rock Edict V. 2. EA, pp. 13, 15.
14. Rock Edict V. 6. EA, p. 13.
15. Pillar Edict IV. 1. EA, p. 97.
16. Rock Edict II. 1-3. EA, p. 5.
17. Rock Edict I. 3. EA, p. 3.
18. Rock Edict IV. 3. EA, p. 11.
19. Rock Edict IX. 3. EA, p. 27.
20. Rock Edict XII. 1-6. EA, pp. 33-37.
21. Pillar Edict VII. 10. EA, p. 123.
22. Brahmagiri Edict II. 3. EA, pp. 71-73.
23. Plato, *The Republic* 473E. My translation.

—21—

*INDIAN AESTHETICS: ITS TECHNIQUES AND ASSUMPTIONS**

The art of traditional Hindu India, i.e., India before the coming of the Muslims, is full of surprises, and none is more surprising than that authorities do not agree as to the role, or even the existence, of art in India. Heinrich Zimmer begins his book *The Art of Indian Asia* with this confident statement: "Indian art, besides documenting the history of a majestic civilization, opens a comparatively simple, delightful way into the timeless domain of the Hindu spirit; for it renders in eloquent visual forms the whole message that India holds in keep for mankind."[1] Two Indian scholars agree as to the centrality of art in Indian culture. Vasudeva A. Agrawala writes, "The spiritual and religious content of India's creative genius has found full and perfect expression in her aesthetic creations."[2] Radhakamal Mukerjee states, "Indian art has been through the centuries a sensitive organ of the Indian man's progressive apprehension of total Reality."[3] Yet the excellent four-volume work published by the Institute of Culture of the Ramakrishna Mission (Calcutta) entitled *The Cultural Heritage of India* contains essays on almost every religious and philosophical movement of the subcontinent but not one essay on art. Moreover there is no word for art in the Sanskrit language. The nearest equivalent is *śilpa*, a word

* This essay appears in *The Journal of Aesthetic Education*, Vol. 9, No. 1 (January, 1975), pp. 11-27. Reprinted by kind permission of the University of Illinois Press.

meaning diverse or variegated. This term was used originally to mean ornamentation, but in time it was used to denote skills in the broadest sense: painting, horsemanship, archery, cooking, etc. Ananda K. Coomaraswamy has warned, "'Art' in India and 'art' in the modern world mean two very different things. In India, it is the statement of a racial experience, and serves the purposes of life, like daily bread. Indian art has always been produced in response to a demand: that kind of idealism which would glorify the artist who pursues a personal ideal of beauty and strives to express himself, and suffers or perishes for lack of patronage, would appear to Indian thought far more ridiculous or pitiable than heroic."[4] V. S. Naravane, noting the estrangement of philosopher and artist in India, remarks, "The philosopher and artist seem to inhabit two different planets."[5] The conclusions we can draw are that there either is or is not an Indian art and that, if there is, it either is or is not integral with the religious-philosophical quest of India!

These divergent views of art in India grow out of an unresolved conflict within Hinduism regarding the reality and value of human life in the physical world. One of the most one-sided assessments of Hinduism has been that of Albert Schweitzer, who in his volume *Indian Thought and Its Development* argued that "Indian thought in its very nature is so entirely different from our own because of the great part which the idea of what is called world and life negation plays in it."[6] Schweitzer hinted at the source of his bias in the Preface when he observed that he first became acquainted with Indian thought through reading the works of Schopenhauer. Moreover, he admitted at the close of the book, "We Europeans have inherited from Schopenhauer and Deussen a tendency to give too little attention to the ideas of world and life affirmation which are found in the Upanishads."[7] He also recognized that both Rabindranath Tagore and Aurobindo Ghosh found world and life affirmation in the *Upanisads.*[8] Movements such as Chārvāka, dualistic Sāṁkhya, erotic Tantra, and integral *yoga* are embarrassments to those who think Hinduism ascetic, otherworldly, restrictive, and pessimistic. To keep a balance in thinking about Hinduism the student must remember that the culture which produced the great body of Vedic literature also produced delightful folk tales like the *Pañchatāntra*, Machiavellian works on kingship like the *Artha Śāstra*, and volumes on the techniques of sexual love like the *Kāma Sūtra*.

To put the matter flatly and without argument: there are two Hinduisms. One looks upon human life as a weary cycle of births and deaths from which the individual longs to escape but is unable until his *karma* has been exhausted. The other regards human existence as a state envied by the gods in which the individual has open before him the possibility of almost unlimited realization and fulfillment. The human ideal in the former is the *ātmansiddha*, the one who has paid his debts to the gods, his ancestors, his fellowmen, his family, and his own incarnations and who now awaits final absorption into the Absolute. The human ideal in the latter is the *nāgaraka*, the man of the world. He is handsome, healthy, rich, and above all accomplished in the sixty-four skills auxiliary to the goal of being a consummate lover. This form of Hinduism appears in the erotic sculptures on temples such as those at Khajuraho and in the thousands of tantric texts. The distance between the *nāgaraka* and the *ātmansiddha* may be indicated in that males aspiring to the former state were advised to pass semen every third day whereas those aspiring to the latter state were advised to pass semen only when a child is desired. Agehananda Bharati, a European who has adopted Hinduism, writing in 1964, said, "I have yet to meet an Indian-born scholar who stands squarely by the tantric tradition. . . . The official Indian culture, formulated by Vivekananda and his numerous admitted or unadmitted followers, by Gandhi and Radhakrishnan, keep tantrism well outside the ken of permissible interests."[9] One wonders why Bharati ignored Aurobindo, the poet-philosopher who in the first half of this century developed a system which attempts to cover both the *ātmansiddha* and *nāgaraka* ideals. Aurobindo has stated man's reason for existence as follows: "To find and embody the All-Delight in an intense summary of its manifoldness, to achieve a possibility of the infinite Existence which could not be achieved in other conditions, to create out of Matter a temple of the Divinity would seem to be the task imposed on the spirit born into the material universe."[10]

Indian art, like art in any culture, is associated with the world of the senses, the world of color, form, sound, touch, taste, and odor.

If that world is negated, then art has but a secondary role in human existence. In the framework of world-negation art may produce the artifacts of worship, the building to house the gods, and the forms of worship, but it does not enter into the clarification of the meaning of the gods and their relationship to mankind. Art is an ornament but not a necessity of the good life. But if the world of the senses is prized either for its own sake or for what it reveals about the reality it manifests, then art has a primary role in the life of man. Hindus have split on this issue for centuries—and the split remains. Vasudeva S. Agrawala, for example, writing in 1964 said, "The essential quality of Indian art is its preoccupation with things of the spirit."[11] But N. K. Devaraja wrote in 1967, "The claim . . . made by both the admirers and the detractors of Indian culture that the people here were highly religious, and therefore otherworldly, is both spurious and unreasonable. It cannot be substantiated by any kind of objective evidence. . . . All the varieties of fine arts, including dance and painting, formed an essential part of popular Hinduism."[12] With this divergence of opinion in mind we can examine the traditional education in India and then attempt to sketch a few assumptions of Indian aesthetics.

The Traditional Education

Hinduism is a total life style. Although the techniques of the quest for the good life are spelled out in meticulous detail in the sacred writings, very few Hindus have ever tried to observe them all. There are exact prayers to accompany most events of the day, e.g., the length of the *nim* stick one uses for brushing the teeth is prescribed according to one's *varṇa*, and the direction one faces while eating is recommended in accord with whether one at the time wishes wealth, fame, love, or wisdom.

The education of children was taken very seriously in traditional India. We can rely on the great works of Hindu law for a description of the techniques of education. Children from birth to ages four or five were pampered by doting parents and members of the joint family. There was almost no disciplining of children during these years. Breast feeding was the rule for the child until about age four, and there was no toilet training. Travelers since the earliest days have commented on the love Indians show their children. While the birth of boys was preferred, there are few records of female infanticide. During the infant years children were allowed and encouraged to explore the world of sound, color, touch, taste, and smell. Toys were simple homemade objects of wood, stone, pottery, ivory, bone, and cloth. Small carts, clay animals, drums, bows and arrows, balls, kites, tops, and marbles were made for them by members of the family. Dogs, goats, monkeys, birds, spiders, snakes, and mosquitoes were omnipresent. Sun and shade, grass and weeds, and dust and water were always part of their experience. Frequent baths in the village tank or nearby river were the chief means of keeping cool during the long hot summers. The children watched the sun, moon, and stars in their rotations and soon learned the signs of the seasons. If there was a universal aesthetic education in traditional India, it was this early non-programmed education of children.

At about five years of age the freedom of children abruptly ended. Girls joined the women of the joint family in the household tasks. They received no formal education but were trained to become wives and mothers. The sons of craftsmen and laborers were obliged to work with the men as apprentices in the family vocation, and finally to inherit often in a religious ceremony, the position and tools of their fathers. The sons of *Brahmins* and to a lesser extent the sons of *Kṣatriyas* and *Vaiṣyas* were given formal schooling. They began their education by attending a village school, a school associated with a temple, or a private school. After mastering the alphabet they progressed to the reading of simple selections from literature both sacred and secular. Much of the time in the school was spent in copying letters and words from models set by the teacher. Prayers and songs were memorized. Some arithmetic and sports rounded out the education. The boys remained in the school from three to seven years. The more promising pupils began Vedic study at age eight or eleven or twelve, depending upon whether they came from *Brahmin*, *Kṣatriya*, or *Vaiśya* families. This study was conducted by special teachers known as *gurus* in hermitages on the edge of a forest. An important sacrament known as *upanayana* (second birth) was administered, indicating spiritual birth and acceptance into the intellectual society. A sacred thread was given at this time as a reminder of the *dharmas* of the twice-born.

The *Brahmacārin* (student of sacred learning) lived with his *guru* for five or six months of each year in the austere conditions of the hermitage. The average length of this education was twelve years, but theoretically it could be as many as forty-eight. The student was obliged to secure wood for the fires and food for the table. He rose before his master each morning and went to bed after his master had retired. He tended the *guru's* herds of cattle and rendered every service asked for. He was expected to give absolute and unquestioning obedience. His diet was the simplest, his clothes were minimal, and his bed was only a pile of rushes. He was allowed no umbrella and no extra garments. During these years he was expected to become indifferent to heat, cold, dampness, and pain.

The *guru* was obliged to teach the *Vedas*, the ancient collections of poetic and ritualistic wisdom. Much of the teaching consisted in memorizing the stanzas in order that the oral tradition might be passed from generation to generation without modifications. Some masters insured perfect memorizing by demanding that the stanzas be memorized both forwards and backwards. There appears to have been a distinction between those who were trained as priests and those who were trained as teachers. The former memorized in order that no errors be made in the rituals, and the comprehension of the meaning of the *Vedas* was secondary; but the latter were particularly trained in the comprehension of the material. In addition the pupils were instructed in all phases of *dharma*, i.e., the obligations which befell one as a member of a family, a vocational group, and a *varṇa*. *Dharma* is a very special concept in Hinduism. Although the term is usually translated as duty, or responsibility, or obligation, it means the natural, proper, and expected way of doing things. *Dharma* is what one does to sustain one's self in his position in society. A *dharma*-trained person acts in an approved manner not because of the heavy hand of duty sanctioned by the consequences of aberrant behavior but because he has been so thoroughly conditioned that alternative ways of behaving are not even considered.

Other subjects taught in the forest schools were phonetics,

grammar, etymology, astronomy, and mathematics. The *Brahmin* boys were to concentrate on these. Usually they were forbidden to receive instruction in archery, swordsmanship, painting, sculpture, music, and dancing. These, which might be considered art education, were offered to the boys of the second and third *varṇas*. The *Brahmin* boys were expected to become priests and custodians of sacred lore; the *Kṣatriya* and *Vaiśya* boys entered public administration, the military, trade, and commerce.

It would be a mistake to assume that since art training was given solely to *Kṣatriya* and *Vaiśya* boys that the *Brahmins* received no aesthetic education. The most authentic aesthetic education was the direct experience of simple living close to nature. Each day the sun was adored in appropriate ceremonies at its rising and setting. Life in the hermitage was like an annual camping trip from July to January. By direct experience rather than by specific training the pupils identified with their natural environment. Thus Indian civilization became a rural rather than an urban culture. Indian culture to this day remains more a culture of villages, farms, forests, deserts, mountains, lakes, and rivers than a culture of cities, industries, corporations, museums, art galleries, concert halls, and theaters. This culture peaked in the life and leadership of Mahatma Gandhi, the simple-complex man who used the spinning wheel to symbolize his hope that India would become an independent nation of self-supporting villages. Today this ideal is being challenged, and the Indian people stand poised uncertainly between primitivism and the Atomic Age. Jawaharlal Nehru, fascinated by airplanes and wearing an omnipresent non-utilitarian red rose in his buttonhole, represented the urban ideal.

The Aesthetic Assumptions

It is possible to identify the aesthetic assumptions of traditional India provided one is not committed to the notion that the assumptions must be consistent. Great harm has been done in Indian studies by Western scholars who believed, or who acted as though they believed, that Indian life and thought must be uniform and coherent.[13] Either-or and nothing-but syndromes should be abrogated by both-and and something-more if the scholar is to understand the ways of the Hindus.

We have noted two forms of Hinduism, forms which have not yet been integrated: the world-affirming and the world-denying. The former exalts the man of the world; the latter exalts the man of retirement. Corresponding to the two Hinduisms are two theories of the function of art. One is the ornamentation theory. According to this theory the function of art is to decorate an otherwise plain object. Indians, having the *horror vacui*, lavishly decorate doors and wall panels, roofs of temples and temple gates, city arches, manuscript margins, taxi cabs, lorries, horns of bullocks, jewelry, etc. "The Indian idea is that only things covered with ornaments are beautiful," wrote Heinrich Zimmer.[14] Any Westerner who has attended a Hindu wedding is impressed by the bride's elaborate make-up and by the variety and quantity of her jewelry. More than seven hundred kinds of personal ornaments are named by Sanskrit writers. The other function of art may be called the sympathetic theory. According to this theory the purpose of art is to elicit a sympathetic response in the viewer or listener. This empathy varies from a fleeting feeling of harmony with the qualities of the object to the full absorption expressed in the Upaniṣadic *tat tvam asi* (that you are). While the skills of the artisan are taught to the young by elders in the home, or by a craftsman to whom a youth is apprenticed, or by his *guru*, aesthetic appreciations are acquired by natural exposure to the worlds of nature and art. Children are included in ceremonies familial, religious, and civic. Indians have not yet discovered the hired babysitter and the dubious value of excluding children from much of adult activity.

Seven attitudes may be distinguished toward art and aesthetic objects in traditional Indian culture. Two of these are variations of the ornamentation theory. They may be called the hedonic and the excess energy theories. Five attitudes are variations of the empathetic theory. They refer to the psychological states of power, will, emotion, thought, and integration. These seven are in some respects conflicting and overlapping—at least from the point of view of Western styles of thinking. Each will be indicated by a Sanskrit term.

TROY WILSON ORGAN

Art as kāma

The word *kāma* is translated desire, enjoyment, or pleasure. It refers especially to sexual pleasures. In Indian literature it is used in three ways: (1) as a cosmic force at the heart of creation; (2) as a principle for the perpetuation of the race; (3) as a weakness of human nature and an obstacle to liberation. According to *Ṛg Veda* 10. 129. 4 it was *kāma* which aroused "That One Thing" to the production of the cosmos. Kāma in mythology is an impish ever-young god armed with bow, arrow, hook, and noose. His weapons symbolize the four aspects of the art of love: confuse, submit, paralyze, and subdue. *Kāma*, according to the Hinduism which interprets *mokṣa* as escape, impedes the wayfarer on the road to salvation; but, according to the Hinduism which interprets *mokṣa* as realization, *kāma* is the zest which makes life worth living. According to this second evaluation *kāma* objects have the characteristic known as *chārutā* (pleasing). They promote *bhukti* (enjoyment). The paradigm is the *nāgaraka*, the town man, the man of the world. In the literature of Hinduism his life was thoroughly prescribed, e.g., he cleaned his teeth and scraped his tongue daily, anointed his body every other day, had coitus with his mistress every third day, shaved his beard every fourth day, cut his fingernails every fifth day, shaved his entire body every tenth day, had an enema every twelfth day, took a laxative every thirtieth day, and had a phlebotomy every six months. All these were done in order that hedonic satisfactions, especially those of sex, be intense. Lists of *kāma* skills enumerate as many as 528 subjects upon which *nāgarakas* were supposed to be proficient. The best-known of these lists is a group of sixty-four skills found in the *Kāma Sūtra* of Vātsyāyana. According to this fourth century A.D. writing both lover and beloved were expected to be dilettantes in performing and adepts in conversing about the sixty-four skills. It would be tedious to list them, but they can be classified into eleven groups: (1) The major fine and applied arts, e.g., dancing, drama, music, painting, architecture, medicine, and alchemy. (2) The philosophical arts, e.g., logic, systematic philosophy, and psychology. (3) The social arts, e.g., mathematics, economics, politics, history, weights and measures, and navigation. (4) The military arts, e.g., archery, tactics, and charioteering. (5) The literary arts, e.g., poetry, etymology, grammar, lexicography, rhetoric, and penmanship. (6) Handicrafts, e.g., goldsmithing, blacksmithing, carpentry, pottery, and weaving. (7) The agricultural arts, e.g., metallurgy, horticulture, animal breeding, and the training of animals. (8) The urbane arts. e.g., etiquette, field sports, parlor games, gambling, and festival celebrations. (9) The magical arts, e.g., juggling, legerdemain, casting of spells, argumentation, and divination. (10) The arts of personal adornment. (11) The arts that pertain to the bedchamber and sexual love. The sixty-four are not the skills of voluptuousness but rather they are the skills which emanate from the belief that love is too important to be left to chance. In the words of the *Kural*

> Love is more delicate than a flower;
> So few attain its perfect bliss.[15]

Art as līlā

The second function of art according to the ornamental theory is *līlā*. *Līlā* means sport which grows out of a sense of exuberance. It is an expression of high spirits, joyousness in existence, and a desire to express the manifold possibilities latent in reality. Divine cosmic creation is sometimes described in Hinduism as the Demiurge's whimsical desire to play. Śiva's cosmic dance is one of the mythological formulations of *līlā*. Aurobindo refers to a unity which can only be manifested in infinite multiplicity. He writes that "a real diversity brings out the real Unity, shows it as it were in its utmost capacity, reveals all that it can be and is in itself, delivers from its whiteness of hue the many tones of colour that are fused together there; Oneness finds itself infinitely in what seems to us to be a falling away from its oneness, but is really an inexhaustible diverse display of unity."[16] The theme of the necessary sportive multiplication of a one appears frequently in Hindu theology, e.g., "One . . . fire blazeth forth in various shapes."[17] Again, in the *Mahābhārata*, Agni, the fire god, celebrates his power to manifest himself in many ways: "Having, by ascetic power, multiplied myself, I am present in various forms."[18] Siva has one hundred divine names. Kṛṣṇa multiplied himself in the circle dance in the moonlight at Brindiban so that he was as many as the *gopis* (milk maids). According to the *Bhāgavata Purāna* Kṛṣṇa had 16,008 wives. The large numbers in the lore of Hinduism, e.g., the number of Vedic gods is said to be 330,000,000, the *Gheraṇḍa Saṁhitā* claims there are 8,400,000 *āsanas* (yogic postures), and in the *Rāmāyaṇa* Rāvaṇa is said to have 150,000,000 elephants and 300,000,000 horses in his army, are not to be regarded as the exaggeration of childish minds but as the workings of the minds of people who delighted in the plurality and diversity of things. Poverty has not always been India's lot.

In their architecture, sculpture, music and painting the ancients of India did not hold back in riches. There was no love of blank spaces. The roofs of *gopurams* (gateways) of South India are covered with a wealth of relief sculptures of animals, gods, and men. The temple at Chidambaram has a hall with 984 pillars and a gateway illustrating Lord Śiva in 108 classical dance poses.

The *līlā* of art production was so intense in traditional India that in order to increase their output artists specialized, e.g., in a painting one artist would sketch the outline of the figures, another painted only the landscapes, and a third did only the color work on human figures. To do art well was to imitate the productivity of the gods.

Art as māyā

Art as *māyā* is related to art as *līlā*. Both are forms of manifestation. But whereas *līlā*-production is the free, spontaneous, purposeless, playful manifestation of a creative matrix, *māyā*-production is seriously designed creation. *Māyā* has teleological connotations. The term comes from *mā* which means to measure, to shape, and to display. It is sparingly used in the *Upaniṣads*, but the idea is found frequently in these ancient writings. For example, in *Bṛhad-Āraṇyaka Upaniṣad* 2. 4. 12 the seer says that the real self is like a lump of salt cast into water. The salt is no longer real "as it were," yet when one tastes the water one experiences the salt. The expression "as it were" is the translation of the Sanskrit term *iva* which is the germ of the idea of *māya*. *Iva* calls attention here to a being which has shifted its ontological structure from an overt reality to a covert manifestation, from noumenon to phenomenon. Real beings are like that, says the seer. They appear to vanish, but in fact they have only changed their ontological mode.

The early Hindus concluded that if anything has power to change its appearance, then it has magical powers. *Māyā* came to mean the power to conceal, to hide, to create illusory effects. It was *māyā* in this sense which was developed by the great philosopher Śaṅkara in the ninth century A.D., and the argument continues as to whether *māyā* means an illusion which is false or a perspective which gives less than the whole. Part of the resolution may proceed by pointing out that Śaṅkara had a purist notion of reality. For him reality meant complete, absolute reality. He designated this by *Sat* (Being), and he contended that only Nirguṇa Brahman was *Sat*. At the other end of the ontological spectrum was *asat*. *Asat* was complete, absolute unreality. *Sat* is that which cannot not be; *asat* is that which cannot be. *Asat* is a peculiar sort of "reality"—the reality of unreality. The classic example is the son of a barren woman. The term *māyā* was used by Śaṅkara to denote and connote all that lies between *Sat* and *asat*. *Māyā*, then, is the reality of things which neither absolutely exist nor absolutely non-exist. The world of contingent realities is *māyā*. *Māyā* objects are illusions only to the person who does not understand that they are *māyā*.

Māyā with reference to art and aesthetics has three aspects. Just as the philosophical notion of *māyā* may have grown out of magic as a form of production so *māyā* with reference to art meant a way of making things happen. According to an ancient story a singer was reputed to have the power to create fire by his singing. A king commanded that he give a demonstration. The singer protested but finally obeyed the king. He did produce fire, but the fuel was his own body and he perished even though he jumped into a river to put out the flames.

A second feature of the *māyā* theory of art is that although art is a form of production what it produces is inferior. This Platonic view is still held in India by many intellectuals. The artist is a misrepresenter of reality. He calls attention from the One to the many, from the Brahman to the world, and from the Self to the selves.

A third view of art as *māyā* is now attaining respectability in India. This to a large extent is the work of Aurobindo. He offered an evolutionary interpretation of the Vedic literature in which he insisted that the manifested pluralities are not an illusory or deceptive manifestation but a necessary manifestation of the One. *Māyā* is the divine art which expresses the Real in indefinitely varied modes. Frithjof Schuon has stated this position as follows: "The All-Possibility must by definition and on pain of contradiction include its own impossibility. It is in order not to be, that Being incarnates in the multitude of souls; it is in order not to be, that the ocean squanders itself in myriads of flecks of foam. . . . Nothing is external to absolute Reality; the world is therefore a kind of internal dimension of Brahman. But Brahman is without relativity; thus the world is a necessary aspect of the absolute necessity of Brahman."[19] The artist is not the concealer; he is a revealer, an instrument of Brahman's necessary pluralization.

Art as yoga

Yoga is an ancient mental and physical discipline which tends to overtones of occultism and sorcery. The term is derived from *yuj* meaning to yoke or join. This may refer either to the yoking of the body and mind or to the identifying of the human self and the universal Self. Above all, *yoga* denotes the control of the physical and the mental within definite limits for the realization of desired ends. The assumption is that latent powers within the body can be brought into action by willed measures.

Art as *yoga* may be regarded either as the discipline of the Hindu carried over into the realm of artistic productions or as the development of the disciplines in handicrafts and skills with the expectation that such attitudes and actions will carry over into the pursuit of ultimate concerns. Perhaps the best example of aesthetic discipline is the classical music of India. Music is also an excellent subject from which to distinguish discipline in the West and in India. Western music is played from set compositions. Its discipline is a fixed following of specific notes in sequences indicated by the composer. But the discipline of Indian music is a melody type (*rāga*), i.e., a series of fixed notes within the octave, and a time measure (*tāla*), i.e., a series of unstressed beats. Within the framework of the rigidity of *rāga* and *tāla* the Indian musician extemporizes. Whereas the Westerner thinks of freedom as the absence of restraints the Indian finds freedom in functioning well within the set limits of rules and laws. The master musician is the one who functions freely within *rāga* and *tāla*. The Hindu discovers existentially that the freedoms he enjoys as an infant are not abrogated by the *dharmas*. Freedom in the profoundest and final sense is possible only within the confines of *dharmas*.

The *yoga* or discipline of art is illustrated by the *ganya-māna* (reckoned measurement) which applies to architecture and sculpture. According to Indian sculpture the unit of measurement is the length of the face. The correct height for women is seven times the length of the face, eight for men, nine for goddesses, ten for minor gods, and eleven for major gods. There are additional canons of proportion for the various parts of the anatomy. While this resulted in a stylized sculpture, it also cut the sculptor loose to do what he wished within the language of the form of his art, i.e., to say something about the types of gods or humans so depicted. In architecture there were rules governing the ratio of height and breadth of a building in terms of the psychological state the building was intended to foster. If the intent was to produce a peaceful effect with calm gracefulness and contentment, height and breadth should be equal. If a feeling of stability and assurance was sought, the height should be one and one-fourth times the breadth. If joy and pleasantness was the desired emotional response, the height should be one and one-half times the breadth. An impression of strength and affluence was assured by making the height one and three-fourths the breadth, and a feeling of majesty and loftiness was created by making the building twice as high as its breadth.

The rules and canons of art turned artists into artisans. They formed craft guilds. Arts tended to become vocations rather than forms of self-expression. Even today an Indian youth may be warned that since six years are required to develop the neck muscles for the Manipuri dance and twelve years to play the vina, he ought not to study an art unless he wishes to make it his vocation.

Another feature of the *yoga* aspect of art is that it has encouraged imitation and discouraged innovation. The Indian imitation of the Greeks can easily be seen by examining the statues of the Buddha. The Aśoka pillars were perhaps adapted from the Greeks. The emperor Jahangir is said to have amazed a European when he displayed an original and five copies of a European painting and challenged him to select the original. To this day the art schools require their students to spend a great deal of time copying designs.

Art as anubhāva

The key concept in Indian art theory is *anubhāva*, a term which can best be translated as emotional empathy. It is not a term of aesthetics in the broadest sense since it refers to an ingredient in a work of art, not to an aspect of beings in the natural world. The object of *anubhāva* is always a work of art. One may empathize with a tree in a painting but not with a tree which grows in the yard. Religious values are found in rivers, mountains, sunsets and sunrises, clouds, and stars, but there is no *anubhāva* with respect to these objects. We can only guess why Indians since Vedic times have not had a love affair with nature. Perhaps the best guess is that they suffered too much from droughts, floods, heat, cold, dust, and insects to empathize with nature. At least half of the year the weather of India can be described as uncomfortable. *Anubhāva*, then, is a term of art theory which holds that all works of art are intended to create in the viewer or listener responsive emotional states. The quality and the quantity of the response is determined by the relationship between the *guṇas* (properties) of the object and the *dosas* (humors) of the person. Since *anubhāva* denotes the response of a person to an art object, it is not surprising to discover that there is one term to designate the property of the object and another to designate the kindred response of the subject. These two are *rasa* and *bhāva*.

Rasa is an ancient term meaning the quality of the juice, sap, or pith of an eatable object. In the *Ṛg Veda* it is used for the juice of the soma plant,[20] for water and milk,[21] and for flavor itself.[22] In the *Upaniṣads rasa* is used for the flavor of things tasted,[23] but it is also used more abstractly for "the essence of existence."[24] Although *rasa* is often translated "taste," it does not imply any ethical evaluation; there is no good or bad taste. *Rasa* is that in the art object which causes it to be relished, appreciated, and enjoyed. Again the term *rasa* does not necessarily mean that which gives pain or pleasure, for the emotional response determined by an art object is inadequately described as pleasant or painful. "Arousing" or "stimulating" are better terms. If an object does not produce an identifiable emotional response in a prepared recipient, it cannot be an art object. Thus a "poem" which brings forth no emotional response in the qualified reader may be said to have no *rasa*, and therefore to be no poem.

Rasa is also a term in Indian classical medicine. Here it refers to properties of things which produce six distinct tastes: sweet, salty, bitter, sour, pungent, and astringent. The language of art theory has lifted the term from both the Vedic philosophical tradition and Ayurvedic medicine to indicate the mood, emotional tone, sentiment, keynote, temper, etc. of a work of art. The *rasas* are applied to painting, music, dance—in fact, to any art. *Rasa* in literary criticism is sometimes described as the soul of a poem, a short story, or an essay. The *rasas* are eight in number: erotic, furious, comic, heroic, wonderful, pathetic, disgusting, and terrifying. But to these eight a ninth is often added—the peaceful—and according to some it is the supreme *rasa* or the name for the *rasas* considered collectively. Ananda K. Coomaraswamy, for example, refers to the *rasas* as "no more than the various coloring of one experience."[25] Thus *rasa* in the broadest sense seems equivalent to the term *saundarya* (beauty), but specifically a *rasa* is the property which elicts a *bhāva*.

The *bhāvas* are the empathetic responses to the *rasas*. The nine *bhāvas* correspond to the nine *rasas*: love, anger, high-spiritedness, laughter, astonishment, sorrow, disgust, fear, and tranquillity. The *bhāva* experience is not to be confused with intellectual understanding. It is possible for one to study art during his entire life and never to have experienced *bhāva*. This may account for the already noted tension and misunderstanding between philosophers and artists in India which makes it possible for philosophers to write volumes on Indian culture with no reference to Indian art.

Art as pramāna

Indian culture is a philosophical culture. Knowledge in its many forms is said to be the means of salvation. To know one's self as the Absolute is the goal of the principal *Upaniṣads*. Hajime Nakamura calls attention to the Indian stress on universals as the key to their philosophical nature: "Indian people are inclined to consider the universal seriously in expressing their ideas of things. This can be easily seen in the fact of their verbal usage in which they have so great an inclination to use abstract nouns."[26] Art becomes a mental activity (*chitta-saññā*). Artistic creation depends upon the sort of mental concentration associated with *yoga*, and artistic appreciation depends upon universalizing. Indian art depicts the generic rather than the specific. The Indian artist draws what he means, not what he sees. He seeks to express the essential rather than to copy the model. In fact, the classical sculptors and painters did not work from models. Hence the monotony of the paintings of Rādhā and Kṛṣṇa and of the sculptures of gods and heroes. Coomarswamy says that "the mere representation of nature is never the aim of Indian art. . . . Possibly no Hindu artist of the old school ever drew from nature at all. His store of memory pictures, his power of visualisation, and his imagination were for his purpose finer means; for he desired to suggest the Idea behind sensuous appearance, not to give the detail of the seeming reality, that was in truth but *māyā*, illusion."[27] One of the ideals of Indian art is *sādṛśya* (similitude), but it is a resemblance of the art object and the species, not of the art object and the natural object. The Indian artist painted the idea, not the shape.

Art as sādhana

No people have pursued salvation with greater dedication than the traditional Hindus. Everything they touched was transformed into a means to attain *mokṣa*. Benjamin Rowland may express this too simply when he writes that "art is religion in India, and religion art. . . . In India all art, like all life, is given over to religion. Indian art is life, as interpreted by religion and philosophy."[28] But he is correct in giving art in India the widest possible dimension. The difficulty in statements like this is that the terms "religion" and "philosophy" are so differently conceived in the West and in India that to say art is religion may obfuscate. The meaning is that Indian art in final analysis is a *sādhana*, a disciplining of human endeavors for the realization of ideal goals. The Hindus see no conflict between the pursuit of aesthetic pleasure and the cultivation of moral virtues. Art does not cease to be art when it is integrated with the pursuit of *mokṣa*. The integration is frequently unstable. For example, Indian dancers and singers are advised to forget the external world in their performances and to avoid all temptation to please the audience. These admonitions are difficult to follow. I witnessed a corruption of religious art in a recent trip to India. The Baul singers of Beŋgal are contemporary troubadours who wander over the countryside singing and dancing their love for God. When I first witnessed the Bauls in 1958 they mysteriously appeared in villages to sing, dance, and play the ektara in a simple extemporaneous manner. But when I saw and heard them again ten years later their performances were productions with advanced publicity, a special tent, and a public address system. This, unfortunately, is what will probably happen increasingly in India. The art forms which were once merely life lived aesthetically may in time become exhibitions to be seen in museums, art galleries, theaters, and concert halls. Indian art will then perhaps be better understood by Westerners. But will it be Indian art?

NOTES

1. Heinrich Zimmer, *The Art of Indian Asia*, Vol. I. New York: Bollingen Foundation, 1960, p. 3.
2. Vasudeva A. Agrawala, *The Heritage of Indian Art*. New Delhi: Ministry of Information and Broadcasting, Government of India, 1964, p. 7.
3. Radhakamal Mukerjee, *The Flowering of Indian Art*. New York: Asia Publishing House, 1964, p. 12.
4. Ananda K. Coomaraswamy, *Introduction to Indian Art*. Delhi: Munshiram Manoharlal, 1966, Introduction.
5. V. S. Naravane, *The Elephant and the Lotus*. Bombay: Asia Publishing House, 1965, p. 210.
6. Albert Schweitzer, *Indian Thought and Its Development*. Translated by Mrs. Charles E. B. Russell. Boston: The Beacon Press, 1936, p. 1.
7. *Ibid.*, p. 242.
8. *Ibid.*, pp. 242, 249.

9. Agehananda Bharati, *The Tantric Tradition*. London: Rider and Co., 1965, p. 11.
10. Aurobindo, *The Life Divine*. New York: The Greystone Press, 1949, p. 527.
11. Agrawala, *op. cit.*, p. 7.
12. N. K. Devaraja, *The Mind and Spirit of India*. Delhi: Motilal Banarsidass, 1967, pp. 2-3.
13. William Jones in his essay "On the Gods of Greece, Italy, and India" warned that "nothing is less favourable to inquiries about truth than a systematical spirit." See *The British Discovery of Hinduism in the Eighteenth Century*. Edited by P. J. Marshall. Cambridge: Cambridge University Press, 1970, p. 198.
14. Zimmer, *op. cit.*, p. 236.
15. *Kural* 129. 9. *The Sacred Kural*. Translated by H. A. Popley. Calcutta: Y.M.C.A. Publishing House, 1958, p. 87.
16. Aurobindo, *op. cit.*, p. 308.
17. *Mahābhārata, Vana Parva*, Section 134. *The Mahabharata*, Vol. III. P. C. Roy edition. Calcutta: Oriental Publishing Co., no date, p. 285.
18. *Adi Parva*, Section 7. *Ibid.*, Vol. I, p. 53.
19. Frithjof Schuon, *Language of the Self*. Translated by Marco Pallis and Macleon Matheson. Madras: Ganesh and Co., 1959, pp. 22-23.
20. *Ṛg Veda* 9. 63. 13; 9. 65. 15.
21. *Ṛg Veda* 8. 72. 13.
22. *Ṛg Veda* 5. 44. 13.
23. *Bṛhad-Āraṇyaka Upaniṣad* 3. 2. 4; *Praśna Upaniṣad* 4. 2.
24. *Taittirīya Upaniṣad* 2. 7. 1. Sarvepalli Radhakrishnan translation.
25. Ananda K. Coomarswamy, *The Dance of Shiva*. New York: The Noonday Press, 1957, p. 37.
26. Hajime Nakamura, *The Ways of Thinking of Eastern Peoples: India, China, Tibet, Japan*. Honolulu: East-West Center Press, 1964, p. 44.
27. Ananda K. Coomarswamy, *Essays in National Idealism*. Madras: Natesan, 1909, p. 32.
28. Benjamin Rowland, *The Art and Architecture of India*. Harmondsworth: Penguin Books, 1953, pp. 2, 7.

Index

INDEX

Īśvarakṛṣṇa, 16.
iva, 146, 266, 267.

Jahangir, 270.
Jaimini, 234.
Jainism, 71, 120, 245.
James, William, 34, 98, 160, 162.
jāti, 100.
Jefferson, Thomas, 54, 58, 95, 128.
Jesus, 156-157.
jīva, 45, 51, 59, 71, 80, 182.
jīvanmukta, 25, 78, 79.
jīvanmukti, 79, 80, 83.
jīvātman, 59.
jñāna, 17.
jñāna mārga, 89, 145, 146, 236.
Joad, C. E. M., 19.
Jones, William, 274.
Judaism, 6, 50, 123, 136, 253.
Jung, C. G., 27, 233, 234.

kali, 234.
Kālidāsa, 64.
Kali Yuga, 100, 140, 234.
kalpa, 25.
kalyāna, 78.
kāma, 236, 237, 240, 264-265.
Kāma, 264.
kamalasila, 202.
Kāma Sūtra, 258, 264.
Kane, P. V., 105.
Kant, Immanuel, 33, 41, 135, 155, 175, 187.
kāraṇa, 200, 221.
kārikā, 24.
karma, 46, 78, 166, 183, 185, 187, 202, 258.
karma mārga, 89, 236.
kārya, 200, 201.
kārya-kartva, 199, 268.
Kaṭha Upaniṣad, 46.
Kātyāyana Brāhmaṇa, 235.
Kauravas, 81.
kausala, 89.
Kautalya, 245.
Keith, A. B., 184, 186, 188, 189.
Kevaddha, 195.
Kevaddha Sutta, 190.
Khemā, 193.
Kierkegaard, Soren, 58.
koan, 157, 168, 171, 173.
Koller, John M., 16.
kriyā, 78.
Kṛṣṇa, 77, 81, 82, 137, 147, 265, 266, 272.
kṛta, 234.
Kṛta Yuga, 234.
kṣanikavāda, 202.
Kṣatriya, 101, 236, 260, 262.
Kumārila, 190.
Kural, 265.

Langer, Susanne K., 141.
Laṅkāvatāra Sūtra, 162.
Lannoy, Richard, 23, 25, 239.
Laski, Harold, 96.
Lātyāyana Brāhmaṇa, 235.
Leuba, J. H., 160.
Leucippus, 210-211.
Li, 146.
līlā, 218, 238, 265-266.
Lincoln, Abraham, 93.
Logic, 24-26.
Lovejoy, A. O., 66.

Machiavelli, 245.
Macmurray, John, 44.
Mahadevan, T. M. P., 74.
Mādhyamika, 146, 187.
mahābandha, 233.
Mahābhārata, 72, 81, 83, 85, 235, 253, 265.
mahākalpa, 25.
Mahāvagga, 192.
mahāvedha, 233.
Mahinda, 252.
Majjhima Nikāya, 182, 194.
Malinowski, Bronislaw, 142.
Malkani, G. R., 13, 74.
Māluñkyāputta, 182, 194.
Māṇḍūkya Upaniṣad, 235.
mantra, 16, 77, 235.
Manu (the lawgiver), 234.
Marco Polo, 9.
mārga, 83, 88, 89, 236.
mārgayāta, 90.
Marx, Karl, 133, 140.
mata, 18.
Matilal, Bimal K., 19, 74.

Ramakrishna, 77.
Rāmānuja, 79.
Rāmāyaṇa, 81, 85, 266.
Rank, Otto, 47.
rasa, 270, 271.
Rāvaṇa, 266.
Renou, Louis, 27, 73.
Ṛg Veda, 16, 46, 77, 106, 234, 235, 236, 264, 270.
Robinson, N. H. G., 138.
Rowland, Benjamin, 272.
Roy, Ram Mohun, 10.
ṛṣi, 77, 100, 142.
Ṛta, 146, 205, 238, 239.
Rubenstein, Richard, 6.
Russell, Bertrand, 13.

sādhana, 18, 21, 40, 74, 75, 76, 77, 81, 82, 85, 88, 90, 91, 203, 272-273.
sādhu, 142.
sādṛśya, 272.
Saguṇa Brahman, 145.
sākṣin, 46.
sakti, 115.
Sāmañña Phala Sutta, 183.
Sāma Veda, 234, 235.
saṁhitā, 235.
Sāṁkhya, 17, 65, 66, 211-217, 240, 257.
Sāṁkhya Kārikā, 16, 212.
Sammā-saṁbuddha, 249.
saṃsāra, 131.
saṃskṛta, 203.
saṁtāna, 202.
Samudra Gupta, 243.
Saṁyutta Nikāya, 185, 190, 195.
sanātana dharma, 115, 140.
Saṅghamitrā, 252.
Śaṅkara, 22, 41, 55, 80, 131, 145, 146, 169, 170, 172, 217, 218.
sankhāra, 203.
Sannyāsa, 236, 237, 240.
Santayana, George, 10.
Sāriputta, 186.
Sartre, Jean-Paul, 14, 32, 41, 47, 51.
sarvajña, 190.
sarvākārajñatva, 190.
sarvamukti, 69, 72, 102.
sat, 61, 146, 147, 169, 185, 201, 218, 238, 239, 267.
satchitānanda, 66, 89, 148, 151, 221, 238, 240.
satkāraṇavāda, 201, 217-222.
satkāryavāda, 201, 211-217.
satori, 48, 157.
satyāgraha, 77.
saundarya, 271.
Schecter, Jerrold, 243.
Schlick, Moritz, 32.
Schopenhauer, Arthur, 10.
Schuon, Frithjof, 240, 268.
Schweitzer, Albert, 5, 6, 60, 83, 257.
Self-knowledge, 30-53.
Sen, Keshub Chunder, 84.
Sena, 252.
Sextus, Empiricus, 211.
Siddhartha Gautama. See Buddha.
Sīha, 192.
śilpa, 256.
Sircar, Mahendranath, 79.
Sītā, 81.
Śiva, 22, 72, 126, 235, 240, 265, 266.
Smith, Huston, 13, 14.
Smith, John E., 177.
Smith, Ronald Gregor, 156.
Smith, Vincent, 252.
smṛti, 100.
Socialism, 102-103.
Socrates, 31, 32, 41, 117, 140, 220, 221.
soma, 77.
Sorokin, Pitirim, 5.
Spencer, Herbert, 5, 187.
Spengler, Oswald, 4, 5.
sṛṣṭi, 239.
śruti, 140, 210.
Stace, W. T., 162, 163, 164, 165, 166, 168, 169, 173.
sthitiprajñā, 77.
St. John of the Cross, 162.
Stoicism, 41.
Śūdra, 101, 125, 236.
Suhrarwardy, Shaheed, 120.
śūnya, 24.
sūtra, 24.
Śūnyata, 68, 146.
Suvarna Prabhā Sūtra, 188.
Suzuki, D. T., 168, 197, 198.
Śvetāśvatara Upaniṣad, 20, 46.
swāmi, 26, 69, 74, 146, 258.
swaraj, 115.